Another Prodigal Son

another homecoming

by

Stephen McDonald

Dedication

To Rhonda, thank you for your infinite patience, understanding, encouragement, editing and love, which made this book possible.

♥

Stephen

Acknowledgements

The following chapters are my subjective memories. I take full responsibility for any errors, fully aware that

"some recollections may vary."

I apologise to the following people I pestered with questions and emails to help me construct coherent and accurate accounts of particular times and events.

Drew Gibson, Graham Connor, Eddie Spence, Anita McNair, Ottilia Selmeczi, Susan McDermott, Rachael Davison, Nicola Elwood, Rhonda McDonald, Rebekah Barr.

The above people have only read chapters which they contributed to.

None of them have read or added their endorsement to the complete book.

Chapter: Old Soldiers Never Die

Participants disagree on the chronological order of some events. However, this doesn't change the significance or impact these incidents had on everyone involved.

Chapter: Northern Telecom

Ref: Hanif Lalani OBE revoked. The Telegraph 22nd Sept 2020

Chapter: If God Builds It.

Ref: Britannica. Charles Martel / Ottoman Empire

Chapter: Campbell College

To anyone offended by my recollections, tough!

There were witnesses.

Chapter: The Gnome Office

Some names have been changed to protect the guilty.

Contents

Prologue

The Moral Side of Murder

Oh no! You're behind the wheel of a vehicle on which all the brakes have failed. You're hurtling down a steep incline and gathering speed every second. What can you do? Panic! You're approaching a fork in the road. Which one should you take? On the road to the left three people are crossing, unaware of the approaching danger. On the road to the right, one person is in the middle of the road, totally oblivious to impending doom.

You have a choice to make. Steer left and kill three or steer right and kill one? What shall it be?

I didn't make this dilemma up. It was presented to students at Harvard University by Professor Michael Sandel in a Philosophy lecture he delivered entitled "The Moral Side of Murder."

Ponder this for a moment and ask, what would you do?

Maybe, you decide to kill one. Surely, that's preferential to killing three and more morally correct.

Afterwards, you discover the three people crossing the road had robbed a bank and the person you killed was an undercover policeman going to challenge them.

Let's rewind and try again. This time, you choose to kill the group of three people instead.

Oh no! The three victims were volunteers collecting donations for Cancer Research and the person you let live was about to rob them.

How can you ever make the right choice? I have a simple answer. This dilemma isn't a Philosophical one, it's a Theological one.

Referring to our lives, we are never behind the wheel. We were never designed to be our own drivers.

Carrie Underwood puts this beautifully in a song called "Jesus, Take the Wheel."

Pull over for a while. Take your hands off the wheel and read on.

Beginnings

This is my story: Maybe, someday you will share your story too. This memoir is in response to how blessed I have been on my journey through life. My journey and destination would be completely different without the people I recall on the following pages.

Many have passed away but, when we read their names, they live on in our memories, as I hope I do in yours. This is a testament to how blessed I was to have known them. Each of them was a thread that, stitched together, helped weave the tapestry of my life.

I pray these pages are a legacy to all my family, near and far. I thank Rhonda for her encouragement to finally commit to printing what I talked about for so long. Without Rhonda's love and support, this story would never have been written. My motivation was to share my faith and conviction the Bible is infallible when it says, "And we know that in all things God works for the good of those who love him." Romans 8:28.

Thank you to my daughters Claire, Lorna and Rebekah for your unconditional love. You'll know best when to share my story with Ethan, Noah, Eva and Micah. I trust Phillip and Louise will share it with Eliza and William when they too are old enough to take an interest in their family. I know the following pages will have a special significance for Frances. I trust they'll convince her she made correct decisions in the past and let her put painful memories to rest.

I love every one of you. I trust this will encourage you to discover God has a plan for you too and trust Him as your Saviour. Jeremiah 29:11. I regret I never had the opportunity to tell you all this in person because a hostile world will try to mould you to its paradigm, just as it did me.

This legacy has no monetary value; life has taught me money can't buy everything. What I have is priceless. I am wealthier than Midas with even greater riches stored up for eternity. If your story imitates mine, those riches will be yours as well.

One of my favourite quotations comes from Michael Parkinson. "You meet a nicer class of person down Memory Lane."

Richard Littlejohn, my favourite columnist is my contemporary. He likened entering his eighth decade to a toilet roll. "You pull and pull and it doesn't appear any thinner. Then, one day you pull, and all you're left with is the cardboard tube." This old tube is delighted to write this for posterity.

God willing, you too will be a tube one day. I pray this helps you keep a healthy perspective on life as your role in it rolls out just like mine.

Mark Twain said, "The two most important days of your life are: The day you were born and the day you find out why."

The biggest regret of my life is not finding out, "Why?" sooner.

This is my journey to answer Why? Come with me, you might agree it's a miracle I made it this far.

Soudan Street

The 26th January 1953 was an auspicious day at 14 Soudan Street, Belfast.

On that Monday at six am, I was born in an upstairs bedroom of this neat, little terraced house off the Donegall Road in South Belfast, much to the relief of my parents William & Hazel McDonald, especially my Mum. I joined my sister Elizabeth, born in 1949, to complete our family.

I was born eight years after World War II. Sweet rationing wouldn't end until February 1953 and I continued to thrive thanks to the benefits of National Dried Milk.

I was a lump of a lad and tipped the scales at over ten pounds when I joined the Baby Boomer generation five days before the sinking of the Princess Victoria, as it sailed from Stranraer to Larne, with the loss of 133 souls. On 29th May 1953, Hillary and Sherpa mountaineer Tenzing Norgay became the first climbers to reach the summit of Mount Everest. The coronation of Elizabeth II as Queen of the United Kingdom and Commonwealth took place on 2nd June 1953 at Westminster Abbey in London. She acceded to the throne at the age of 25 after the death of her father, George VI.

I was named after my father's brother, Stephen, and baptised in Townsend Street Presbyterian Church by the Rev. WFD Marshall. My Baptismal Hymn was By Cool Siloam's Shady Rill. This was sung at the baptism of every child in Townsend Street. The words are still poignant today as God continues to draw me to Him.

By cool Siloam's shady rill
How fair the lily grows!
How sweet the breath,
beneath the hill,
Of Sharon's dewy rose!

O Thou, whose infant feet were found
Within Thy Father's shrine,
Whose years with changeless virtue crowned,
Were all alike divine.

Lo! such the child whose early feet
The paths of peace have trod,
Whose secret heart, with influence sweet,
Is upward drawn to God.

Dependant on Thy bounteous breath,
We seek Thy grace alone,
In childhood, manhood, age, and death
To keep us still Thine own.

Dad completed a seven-year apprenticeship as a Bookbinder after turning down an offer to play football for Linfield. When he finished his apprenticeship in 1953 someone "invented" filing cabinets and the need for skilled Bookbinders diminished. However, Elizabeth and I had the best-covered books in school.

We lived in Soudan Street until I was three years old. My earliest memories are playing in the street and on the waste ground behind the terraced houses. There's a photo somewhere of me walking our garden wall holding onto the attached fence. I remember the smell of its peeling brown paint. Across the street lived the Sloans who were great friends with my parents. One of their sons Noel, was fascinated by the Red Army and I sat with him when he played his collection of The Red Army Ensemble records. Noel went on to be a Russian Translator.

Next door to them lived the Garrett family. From overheard conversations and what Elizabeth told our parents, I learned from an early age all families weren't as caring and loving as our own. Joan Garrett became Elizabeth's lifelong friend. I realise now what a caring heart Elizabeth always possessed because Joan confided in her she was beaten regularly by her father. Eventually, the beatings resulted in Joan requiring brain surgery which left her with slurred speech. Joan was a beautiful woman, wife, and mother who died when she was only fifty.

Just across the street was Gibson's Bakery. While playing on the waste ground beside it, I decided the windows were dirty and needed washing. I filled a bucket with water and started wiping away decades of dirt and grime from the glass. A window opened slightly. I thought I was going to be scolded. No one appeared. Just a mysterious hand that deposited an assortment of buns on the windowsill. I never found out who that kind person was but the two of us let a little sunshine into our lives that day.

I was older before I realised our next-door neighbour wasn't really my Aunt Min. This dear lady always sat in her front room wearing a long brown coat and a beret. Min babysat Elizabeth and me to enable our parents to go to work. Elizabeth attended primary school while we lived in Soudan Street, but I didn't start school until we moved to Woodvale Street in 1956. Another "virtual" aunt was Katie Welch. Katie and her brother Jim lived in Eia Street and were friends of Mum and Dad. "Aunt Katie" took us on outings to Helen's Bay and Bellevue Zoo where there were rides on swing chairs and a little train which I enjoyed more than looking at animals. The last trip I remember with

Katie was when she took Mum, Elizabeth, and myself to an Army Open Day at Palace Barracks in the early '60s. I was to return there again in the late 80s for completely different reasons. Katie was a spinster all her life and eventually moved to Moira Park in Bangor to escape "The Troubles" in Belfast.

Our local GP was Dr Rollock. He was from the West Indies and practised Homoeopathy. His surgery was upstairs in a first-floor room, in a row of houses on Donegall Road, just over the railway bridge, before the corner to Donegall Avenue. Every illness I had was treated with tablets that resembled small ball bearings. He was married to Janette and they had three sons, Hartley, Ivan, and James. Like everyone else my Mum and Dad spoke to, the Rollock family became friends and we visited them occasionally in their Balmoral home. My Mum reminded me of the first time I met the Rollocks and asked her why they had such deep sun tans.

Tragedy struck one evening when James was knocked down and killed when he went to buy sweets at the local filling station which stood where the Eurospar stands today, adjacent to the King's Hall. James was only six years old when his life was cut short. I wasn't much older when I witnessed the grief and heartbreak of the Rollock family. That memory has stayed with me for a lifetime.

Woodvale Street

We moved to 23 Woodvale Street off Woodvale Road in 1956. My father's parents and his brother Stevie lived "down the road" at 103 Westmoreland Street and my mother's parents lived around the corner from them at 54 Dover Street along with their disabled daughter, my Aunt May. I joke that this **is** when we became snobs because I could stand at our front door and see grass. The grass in Woodvale Park. It was a two-up two-down with an outside toilet and no bathroom. Hot water came from a gas geezer mounted over our Belfast Sink. The next sixteen years proved to be among the happiest and most carefree years of my life.

This story nearly didn't get any further because, at the age of four, I set our house on fire. Early, one Saturday morning, I put a match to the newspapers my father kept in the cubby hole under the stairs for lighting our coal fire. My little cousin Edna Orr was staying with us that weekend. I crept back to bed, pulled the covers over my head, and pretended nothing was happening. I heard Mum shout, "Get up Bill, I smell smoke." Fortunately, the stairs hadn't caught fire, and Dad put the flames out with two buckets of water. The moral is, "Don't let children play with matches." There could have been tragic consequences, and I learnt my lesson. Don't play with fire. Well.... not for a while anyway.

Why do mothers always find a way to embarrass their children? Mum had seen a young 10 year old Prince Charles on television and was very impressed by his hairstyle. She liked the way his hair was cut straight across the back. She was so taken with it, that she gave me 2s 6d (15½p) and dispatched me with instructions to Bobby Weir's Men's Barbers' Shop on Woodvale Road opposite St. Matthew's Church. It was a Saturday morning and the shop was full of customers. Most of them were smoking and the air was thick with cigarette and pipe smoke. The constant chatter between customers and barbers added to the buzz of a busy saloon.

"Who's next?" Shouted Bobby. He was in his fifties and wore a white coat. His face bore a good resemblance to a seeded potato. It was well-worn, wrinkled and craggy. What hair he had left was slapped flat on his head with lashings of Brylcreem which gave it a deep shining gloss. I stepped forward and Bobby placed a plank across the arms of his barber's chair to lift me to the correct height so he didn't strain his back cutting a child's hair. "What way do you want it today young man?" He asked. "Can I have a Prince Charles haircut, please?" Bobby bent over holding his sides in laughter much to the amusement of everyone in the shop. They all stared at him in anticipation of discovering what caused the hilarity. After he caught his breath Bobby announced to everyone, "This gentleman has just asked me for a Prince Charles haircut." You can imagine the comedy that caused in Bobby Weir's that infamous Saturday morning. However, I returned home with my hair cut straight across the back. Good old Bobby! Happy days!

Bobby Stewart's Barber's shop was on Peters Hill. Mum only risked letting him try cutting my hair once. He placed youngsters on a rocking horse to keep them amused while he practised his skills. Fortunately, she didn't ask him for a "straight across the back." It might have resulted in a straight across the throat. But it was good fun.

Some years later, after my previous experience with fire, I procured a bundle of 2d bangers. These were serious explosives in a young man's careless hands possessed with a too vivid imagination about what to do with them. I was playing with my collection of Airfix toy soldiers in our outdoor coal bunker adjacent to the outside toilet in our backyard. I had strategically placed my soldiers amongst a quarter ton of the best Welsh coal and was determined to blow them out of their positions. To do this, I lit different lengths of wax string. When I blew the flame out the end smouldered away, the glowing point gradually burning its way along the string. Depending on the length, times could be adjusted accordingly. I had just inserted my "fuses" into the bangers and lit them, blew out the flames, and I was watching my devilish plan unfold when my father appeared in the yard with a Belfast Telegraph under his arm and ordered me into the house. There was serene silence inside the house, only the noise of Mum peeling potatoes in the kitchen, then......BHAM, BHAM, BHAM, Dad screamed and lumps of coal bounced off our yard's whitewashed walls.

"Where is he, Hazel?" Shouted Dad staggering up the yard, trying to pull up his trousers. He burst through the door to the yard as I legged it out the kitchen door and bolted for the stairs. I made it halfway up when Dad grabbed one ankle and pulled me back down to him. Fearing the worst, I braced myself for a good skelp across my legs. Instead, my dear father collapsed in fits of laughter. We recalled that incident many times over the years and I was never allowed to forget I had set the house on fire.

Halloween was more fun before we copied Tricking & Treating nonsense from America. Although maybe not so much fun for our neighbours. A string tied to a knocker kept us amused. Retire to a safe distance, pull the string, wait for someone to answer the door and look confused when they look up and down the street for their mystery caller. More 2d bangers. This time in milk bottles. BHAM, WOW! What an explosion! Broken glass flew everywhere and not a pair of safety goggles in sight. I thought it would be good fun to place one beside a dog. BHAM, the dog jumped up and sank its teeth into my backside. Just right too! Clever dog!

You have never seen people scatter so quickly as when a lit Jumpin' Jinny is thrown into a crowd watching a bonfire. I remember the stink of candles burning inside hollowed-out turnips and youngsters setting fire to piles of fallen leaves with sparklers. The best fireworks display I ever witnessed occurred one night in 1964. I wondered why the footpath was glowing green. When I looked up at the sky there was the most glorious display of the Aurora Borealis. I haven't seen it since.

My favourite time of year was Christmas. The excitement began a fortnight before the big day when Dad put up our decorations. One was an old cardboard star wrapped around our living room light bulb. Miraculously, it never caught fire. He hung chains of coloured paper diagonally across our ceiling, and tinsel was evident everywhere. We blew up balloons, and rubbed them vigorously on our jumpers, the static electricity held them onto the wall. We owned one artificial tree our entire time in Woodvale Street. We decorated it with the same baubles and lights every year. It was always placed in our parlour so the neighbours could admire it. There was a smell of Christmas in the air.

Christmas Eve buzzed with activity as final preparations were made for the next day. I'd ask Dad for a Ten Shilling note (50p) and walk to the city centre, packed with people. I usually went to Robb's Department Store on High Street and bought Dad a box of Hamlet cigars and a pen for Mum. Shopping done for another year. There was usually a busker outside Robinson & Cleavers, playing Christmas Carols on a saw. He played it by flexing the saw while drawing a bow across the edge. Eerie and beautiful.

I thought I'd never sleep after I hung up my pillowcase, but exhaustion always prevailed. Two hours later, "YHEW!" I'd dash out of bed to see what Mum and Dad bought me for Christmas. Elizabeth was four years older than me. She told me Santa Claus wasn't real when I was six. My first dose of reality. Ouch!

Mum was a great cook and skilled baker. Christmas dinner was always a great treat, although I never ate potatoes until I was sixteen. How she prepared dinner for seven people in a small scullery on a gas stove is a credit to her abilities. There was Granny Kirk (Day), Aunt May, Uncle Stevie, Elizabeth, Mum, Dad, and me. Six squeezed around our small, drop-leaf dining table while May sat on the settee with a tray on her knees.

One Christmas, a mystery occurred that no one could explain. Mum liked to remind us about it occasionally. We had a cat called Bubbles. Mum cooked the turkey on Christmas Eve and left it in the oven overnight. When she stepped into the scullery on Christmas morning, Bubbles was gnawing on the remains of a turkey leg, but the oven door was closed. How did a cat open and close the oven door? Was Bubbles a Master Cat Burglar? Another "pet moment" occurred when our budgie Peter died, Elizabeth buried him in a shoe box with a sausage on each side of him to keep him warm.

Woodvale Street epitomized what it meant to grow up in a caring neighbourhood. Everyone knew all their neighbours and youngsters thronged the street playing long-forgotten games like Kerby, Marbles, Skipping, and Hopscotch. There were well-off neighbours and some less well-off, but most were employed one way or another. The Cunninghams, Ena & David, liked to flaunt their good fortune. Think Hyacinth Bucket. David was a glazier and the inside of their home resembled the house of mirrors. They had two sons David & Samuel. David, the elder of the two, was "slower" than his contemporaries but had a kind, gentle and innocent nature.

David made a habit of getting into trouble, either by his own efforts or through the encouragement of others who took advantage of his naivety. On one such occasion, we were mucking around their house when Samuel removed the bulb from a table lamp, thrust his hand through the top of the shade, and pretended to place his fingers on top of the bare pins. "Thhhhaaaat's lolololooooovely," he stuttered as he shook vigorously with an ecstatic grin on his face. "Let me have a go," said David pushing Samuel out of the way and shoving his fingers onto the pins. BHAM!! David landed in a heap across the other side of the room.

At BB camp in Saltcoats, the police gave him a lift back to camp when they discovered him on the railway line. Why not put a sixpence on a railway track and allow a train to turn it into a shilling? I couldn't help liking David whereas, Samuel tried to emulate his parents too much which I found irritating.

17

David lived in Castlereagh Parade, and I met him occasionally when I lived in Ardgowan Street. However, I didn't see him for thirty years after moving to Irwin Drive in 1993. In October 2023, I received a phone call from Rev. Jack Lamb. He was a former minister of Townsend Street Presbyterian Church. David's brother Samuel had asked him to contact me to invite me to David's graveside funeral in Roselawn Cemetery. David had passed away on 10th October 2023 after a long illness. I was blessed to know this dear man. Different? Yes, in the best possible way. Slow, but always on time.

The Cunninghams' cousins Robert & David Ashe lived directly opposite them. The Ashes were more down to earth although I don't recall ever being in their house. There was an older cousin Raymond Ashe who was a quiet, gentle soul and had a crush on Elizabeth. I often wonder how things might have been different for Elizabeth if Raymond had asked her out. Mrs Ashe was very house-proud and was the first person in our street to have fitted carpet in her living room. When I left Woodvale Street in 1972, it was still covered with cellophane after twelve years.

There were two shops in Woodvale Street. Downey's, on the corner of Disraeli Street, was a general merchant store selling groceries and an assortment of hardware. The Downeys' daughter,

Margaret was one of Elizabeth's friends. They attended Glencairn Secondary School together. A few doors below 23 was a shop run by the two Hill sisters. The shop was in their front room with a counter covered in linoleum in front of shelves packed with sweets. They were two little spinsters, in their 70s then. They always wore blue gingham smocks and kept their hair up in nets.

I could never tell one from the other, perhaps they were twins. Their shop always had a sharp clean smell and was always spotless. Generally, neither was behind the counter when I entered to buy 2d Chews and Sherbet Dabs. I'd have to rap the counter with a penny and shout, "Miss Hill." Eventually, one of the sisters would appear through the door from their kitchen and slowly make her way behind the counter. I can't remember a cash register or anything resembling one in the shop. I dearly wish I knew more about them. I'm sure they had stories to tell if only someone had asked them.

Two doors below the Hills lived the Simpsons. Next door to the Simpsons lived Jean Patterson and her mother. Jean tried valiantly to teach me piano, and I made it through Grade 2 before I exhausted her patience and my abilities as a musician. Mum insisted I try again with Peter Harris, the organist at Townsend Street church. Peter lived at the top of Squires Hill. When I got off the bus at Silverstream bus terminus and walked up to his house, I was too exhausted to concentrate on crotchets and minims. When I offered Peter my regrets about being unable to continue classes, I'm sure he was secretly relieved but too polite to say so. However, I still loved piano music. This love would have a significant impact later in my life.

The annals of Woodvale Street would not be complete without mentioning the Hoys. Samuel and Ena lived in twenty-seven next door to the Youngs. They had six children, George, Murray, Samuel, Lorraine, Doris, and Dale. Samuel, the father was a gentle soul who enjoyed his drink. His second home was The Mountainview Tavern on the corner of Cambrai Street & Woodvale Road. The story goes that, during the Troubles, the Mountainview was bombed three times and Sammy survived all three attacks. I imagine Sammy dusting himself off and ordering another pint.

One evening, I was standing with the Ashes and Cunninghams outside Downey's shop, when an army jeep appeared and proceeded to trundle down the street towards us. This was the first time we had seen British soldiers on our streets after they arrived in N. Ireland. The jeep was open at the back and six soldiers sat three facing one another in the rear. When they passed us, Sammy appeared further down the street, just out of the Mountainview. He proceeded to berate the soldiers at the top of his voice, "Why don't you get yourselves up the Falls Road and catch some real terrorists?" He shouted.

The jeep stopped and a sergeant hopped over the rear of the jeep, walked over to Sammy and began talking to him. BANG! The door of twenty-seven hit the wall and Ena stormed up the street swinging her handbag around her head like a bolas. When she reached her husband and the soldier, she started beating Sammy with her handbag shouting, "You're not taking my Sammy." The sergeant reached down, grabbed Sammy under his elbows, and lifted him into the back of the jeep. "You'll be safer with us Sammy," he said. We followed behind and watched as they dropped Sammy off at the dart club on Olive Street just around the corner. The sergeant followed him in and bought him a pint.

The Hoys didn't have much as Mr Hoy probably drank his wages, but the girls and boys managed to go to school and eventually make lives for themselves. I met Lorraine later in life when I lived in East Belfast and surprised Ena one evening when she was babysitting for Lorraine and her husband at their home in Tildarg Street off Cregagh Road. I rang the front doorbell and when she answered she asked me who I was. "Guess," I said. She looked at me momentarily, then screamed "STEPHEN MCDONALD," before throwing her arms around me. That was the last time I ever met Ena, a beautiful rough diamond of a woman.

Later in my life, her son Murray lived nearby on Ardgowan Street. I called to visit Murray one day and his wife informed me he had died from Alcoholic poisoning. Another life destroyed. Rhonda came to know and work with Dale Hoy on the Shankill Road. From another friend, I learned "wee" Samuel was running a Shebeen off Glenvale Street before the police put him out of business. George Hoy emigrated to Australia, and I hope Doris did well for herself. They all had a tough start in life, and it didn't end well for Murray or his father. Ena was away for a few days visiting relatives and when she returned, she found Sam lying dead in their backyard. Alcohol had caught up with Sam as well.

Back then, my best friend was Jim Leckey who lived with his parents and sisters Marie, Eleanor, and Jean at 3 Olive Street. Marie brought us in to listen to her latest 45rpm record she bought on her Dansette Record Player. It was The Platters' version of Red Sails in the Sunset. Dad bought Elizabeth a Decca record player and her first 45 rpm record. The A-side was The Student Prince by

Mario Lanza. The B side was The Band of the Royal Marines playing The Last Post. Dad certainly knew how to pick good records considering Elizabeth was a Beatles and Rolling Stones fan.

Jim always had an interest in food and cooking which nearly had disastrous consequences one day. We climbed over the wall of St Matthew's Church and ate a load of red berries off a tree growing in the grounds. They gave me cramps but Jim had to have his stomach pumped out. Jim's food fad appeared unusual back then; he persevered and, when I met his parents years later, they told me he managed the catering at Earls Court in London. We were never in touch again.

The Leckey family was one of the few families that owned a car. Their car was a black Morris Minor 1000cc split front windscreen Saloon. Mr Leckey was driving that car when we arrived in Woodvale Street in 1956; he was still driving it when we departed in 1972. Incidentally, the Morris Minor was launched at The British Motor Show in Earls Court in 1948. Our family only "had" a car during the Twelfth fortnight holidays when Dad and Stevie hired one for two weeks from Kelly Brothers (Cowboys and Engines) on Shankill Road.

We didn't realise how much we endangered our lives in some of those cars. A hand brake came off when applied. The bonnet of another hired car flew up and smashed the windscreen on our way to Newry. A VW Beetle didn't have a petrol gauge. Instead, it had a reserve tank but it was empty. We broke down on Bradshaw's Brae on the way out of Newtownards. Stevie made a brew on his Primus stove at the side of the road and waited for my Dad to return with a jerry can of petrol.

Despite all the risks, we made it around Ireland. We travelled to Connemara, Killarney, Cork, Dublin, and Waterford on different adventures each year. Granny Kirk came with us once and we slept overnight in our car outside the Kennedy Homestead in New Ross, County Wexford. That was the furthest "Day" ever travelled in her life. We stopped in Moll's Gap to photograph a donkey stood at the side of the road with a little dog sitting on its back. Strangely, when I returned in 1999, the donkey and dog were still there, surrounded by American tourists taking pictures. They were either body doubles or stuffed. The donkey & dog I mean.

One morning, I was playing in our street when Aunt Violet and Uncle Tommy arrived in a hired Mini. My two excited cousins Edward & George sat in the back with only swimming trunks on. They'd called to see Mum & Dad before driving to Portstewart for a day trip. After the obligatory cup of tea, they left for their day out. I was disappointed to miss out but pleasantly surprised when they reappeared five minutes later and asked me if I would like to join them. I needed no encouragement, grabbed my trunks and a towel, and bailed into the back of the car with the other two ruffians. I experienced a real sense of dread this was all too good to be true.

My premonition materialised in the shape of a petrol tanker that pulled out in front of our car at a junction outside Antrim town centre. Our Mini was only prevented from going directly under the lorry by the side guards fitted to protect drivers in such a predicament. We stopped with a bang. There were no seatbelts in cars then and I was thrown into the front, landing upside down in the passenger footwell. No one was seriously injured but that was the closest we ever came to Portstewart. The police arrived and arrested the tanker driver on suspicion of drink driving. Uncle Tommy was able to drive back to Coulters Car Hire on Cliftonville Road to report the accident and fill out the relevant paperwork. The three miscreants spent the time in Belfast Waterworks. At least we were close to water.

I did make it to the seaside on another occasion. George Hoy had borrowed a bicycle and encouraged me to, "Steal Elizabeth's bike," and join him on his seaside adventure. Elizabeth's bicycle had been left to her by the district nurse who helped care for Granny McDonald until she passed away. The problem was her bicycle was too big; I couldn't sit on the saddle and reach the pedals. So, I stood on them, and cycled from Woodvale Street to Holywood and back again. I was exhausted when we made it home. Mum was too relieved to see me to give me a good slap for worrying her so much. I never owned a bicycle of my own but I bought a motorbike when I started work. More about that later.

During school holidays we played outdoors all day long. One of our more challenging sports involved placing a hardback book, usually a Beano or Topper on top of a skate, leaning back, holding our legs straight out in front, and steering around obstacles by gripping the book tightly and twisting our bodies into the bends. Our Luge course ran from the top of Woodvale Street down Woodvale Road, praying we made it around the tight bend, opposite the gates to Woodvale Park, at maximum speed. There were no fatalities but lots of cuts and skinned knuckles.

Woodvale Park wouldn't pass today's Health and Safety regulations. The nearest nod to rules was a uniformed warden who shouted at people, "Stay off the grass." The playground was built on concrete and every apparatus could cause serious injuries if not treated with respect. The Horse would be banned today. When we polished the slide with the wrapping of an O'Hara's plain loaf, it guaranteed enough downward speed to ensure the slider landed three feet clear at the bottom. The craziest thing I witnessed was a lad standing on a swing and gaining enough momentum to loop the loop. He took the swing right over the top of the bar. The roundabout was called the Three D Bit. It could be spun fast enough to induce nausea and catapult anyone who wasn't holding tight enough into the surrounding scenery.

We played "Who Falls the Best" on steep grass banks surrounding the bowling green. Our imaginations were fired by reading dozens of Commando comics and the latest war films like The Longest Day. My friend, Gordon Bleakley, had a great collection of these comics which he let me borrow. I hope I gave them back. Gordon was the fastest person I've ever known. He could run like the wind and might have been a professional athlete if he had wished. He was slightly built and not your stereotypical rugby player. Ernie Davies, the Vice-Principal picked him to play for the Boys' Model. Once he caught the ball, WOOSH! No one could catch him.

At home, Mum administered discipline in the form of corporal punishment to Elizabeth & me. Her preferred method was a leather belt, kept in the third drawer of the sideboard. Two or three smacks around the legs made us reappraise how we had incurred her wrath. I only remember Dad admonishing me twice. Once, when he was kneeling to light the fire, I pushed him over. He sprang up and pushed me so hard I flew backwards, broke through the door of the cupboard under the stairs, and ended up slumped over our mangle. Of course, Dad rushed over to help me and asked, "Are you OK son?" The only time Dad seriously smacked me was when the neighbour from number forty-seven told him I was rude after he scolded me for kicking a football against his gable wall. When Dad opened our front door, he landed an almighty slap across my face before he closed the front door. I heard my friends say, "Did you see that?" Tough love but a lesson learnt.

I witnessed a lesson being administered one evening. I was getting off a number 73 Bus at Woodvale Park when a lad smacked the bottom of the rubbish bin attached to the bus stop. All the litter in the bin popped out and scattered over the footpath. "STOP!" shouted a police officer who appeared out of nowhere. The boy took off as fast as he could, ran across Woodvale Road, and headed down Woodvale Street. The policeman, wearing his helmet, calf-length heavy overcoat, and boots gave chase. They ran down the full length of our street, turned left into Olive Street, left again, and proceeded up the back entry to the houses. I was watching from the top end of the entry where it met Disraeli Street when the long arm of the law caught up with the litter lout outside the back door of our house. The officer duly pointed out to his captive the error of his ways. He gave the lad an almighty kick in the backside to reinforce his point before letting him go. Instant justice. I doubt that lad ever dropped as much as a sweetie paper again. I like to think he ended up working for the Belfast Cleansing Department.

If setting fire to our house was the stupidest thing I ever did, the craziest thing I ever did occurred at the same bus stop outside Woodvale Park. I was returning from BB one Monday evening on the bus, standing on the rear platform waiting for the bus to stop when my mind went blank. As soon as the bus halted, I leapt off the platform and ran blindly around the back. Without looking left or right, I dashed headlong across the road. Nothing was coming on my right side but, after crossing the middle of the road, there was a loud screeching of brakes and blast of a car horn. The edge of a car's bumper brushed the back of my legs as the car skidded to a halt behind me. When I reached the footpath, I looked back. The car was a blue Ford Corsair and the driver stared at me in shock and disbelief. Thank God for his reactions and good brakes. That was a moment of total, nonsensical madness that could have ended in my death or paralysis. Surely, that was a miracle of deliverance.

Our move from Woodvale Street in 1972 was prompted by Dad losing most of his right hand in an accident caused by a faulty machine in the Newsletter where he was working at the time. Medical advice was that he would make a better recovery living somewhere "away from the troubles" which began in earnest on 18th August 1969. We gave any useful household furnishings to Matt Young and his wife Yvonne at number twenty-nine. If the Hoy family didn't have much, the Youngs had even less. Matt invited me into his home one evening to show me the 9mm "personal weapon" he'd been licensed to hold because he was a member of the Ulster Defence Regiment. Well! There's not much point in owning a gun unless you're sure it works. So, Matt lifted a floorboard in front of his fireplace and fired the weapon into the foundations of the house. Yep! That works. Tested and approved. That was the last time I ever saw Matt and his wife. But not the last time I thought of them. I sincerely hope life improved for them.

My life was about change in ways I never imagined.

Westmoreland Street

As I mentioned before, 103 Westmoreland Street was the McDonalds' family home, where I spent a considerable part of my childhood. It was around the corner from 54 Dover Street, and I was continually backwards and forwards between both sets of grandparents. Dad and Stevie's Aunt Ena was a spinster who lived with her brother Jimmy in 107. Elizabeth and I knew them as Aunt Ena and Uncle Jimmy. They were unassuming people who led simple lives and were content with life.

Granda McDonald died in 1957 followed by his wife Agnes in 1960. They are both buried in Plot X444 at Belfast City Cemetery. Granny McDonald suffered greatly from cancer before she passed away. She never went to hospital. Mum moved her and me into Westmoreland Street and nursed her Mother-in-law for six months day and night.

I was seven years old then and didn't understand what was happening. I went into Granny's bedroom each morning to say, "Hello." Miraculously, she had a threepenny piece to hand me every morning to buy a Wagon Wheel on my way to school.

Outside, the street was filled with kids playing football and swinging from ropes tied to the gas lamp posts. Others were skipping, playing Hopscotch and Cowboys and Indians. Friends and I played soldiers and ran after one another with cardboard rifles and cap guns. A customer came out of The Gluepot, a pub at the corner of Argyle Street and Westmoreland Street. He asked what we were doing, and I explained we were playing soldiers. He replied, "Step this way" and we followed him into the bar.

Inside, opposite the bar, a fully occupied long bench seat ran the length of one wall. We could just make it out through the haze of cigarette and pipe smoke. Our "friend" explained what we were playing and asked everyone to stand up. They all complied. They opened the lid of the bench seat they had been sitting on. To our amazement, the men reached into the storage space and handed a Lee Enfield .303 rifle to each of us; we carried on with our game. Thank goodness they didn't give us bullets.

The 11th July in Westmoreland Street was an opportunity for a big street party which was hugely exciting for me and other youngsters. It appeared everyone in the street was taking part. Our "friends" from the Glue Pot entertained everyone by "rolling the barrels." Empty wooden beer barrels were borrowed from the pub and brought onto the road. Several customers stood on the barrels and competed to find who could "roll" one furthest by turning it under their feet before falling off. That took some skill, especially after a few pints. The party activities culminated in the lighting of the bonfire. It was a late night for everyone.

The next morning there was only the smouldering remains of the previous night's fire in the middle of the street to show there had been a party. On 12th July, the 29th BB Old Boys' Pipe Band assembled in Northumberland Street to begin its march down Westmoreland Street to the city centre. Pipe Major Jim Murdoch led the band which set off six abreast, with pipes and drums playing. Everyone looked immaculate in their tartan kilts and bearskins. All the bandsmen appeared over six feet tall. Everything went well until the band reached the remains of the bonfire. The band leader and following musicians duly parted ranks to circumnavigate the red-hot ashes but no one warned the bloke on the bass drum who couldn't see where he was going. He marched straight into the smouldering remains of the bonfire. He lost the beat and let out a yell as sparks flew up his kilt, much to the amusement of his fellow band members and spectators.

After Granny McDonald died, our parents took Elizabeth and I out of school during the term to travel to Edinburgh together with Mum's friend "Aunt Katie" for a week. We stayed in a neat, little hotel behind Princes Street. Breakfast, each morning, was in the basement around one big table with other guests. Mum needed rest and relaxation after all she had been through.

Dad only spent a few days with us as he had to return to work. We returned to Stranraer via Glasgow where we went to the cinema to see The Nun's Story with Audrey Hepburn and Peter Finch. It was blowing a gale when we left the cinema, and my last memory of our holiday is Mum and Katie chasing Katie's hat up the street. They caught the hat and I caught the cold.

The 29th Boys' Brigade

The mission of the Boys' Brigade is "The advancement of Christ's Kingdom among Boys and the promotion of habits of Obedience, Reverence, Discipline, Self-Respect and all that tends towards a true Christian Manliness."

The motto of the Boys' Brigade is "Sure & Steadfast."

I didn't truly understand or appreciate the significance of these words when I was a teenager. Neither did I appreciate the time, dedication, and sacrifice the leaders gave and the effort they made to shape young boys' lives. Thank you to Jack Storey, Roy Kennedy, and Jim Moore for having patience and not giving up on me. Subliminally, I acknowledge their touch on my life through some of my habits. I still like to polish my shoes.

I've learned over the years first impressions are important. People invariably look at a person's shoes and fingernails. Dirty shoes or chewed fingernails don't give a good first impression. I've proven them a good indicator of a person's character. I dislike people who slouch when they are standing to worship in church. The BB taught me to stand straight and keep my hands out of my pockets. This shows respect for where you are and the people around you. Nowadays, most people lean on the pew in front as if they'd fall over if they weren't holding on.

In Bloomfield church, BB captains have all been men of faith and dedication. The 24th BB Company has been led by Lendrick McMaster, Harry Downey, Trevor Wilson, Tom Reid, Billy Manson and Alan Galbraith. The object and motto of the BB are still the same, but the work and challenges have changed greatly over the years. Mention "Drill" to young boys and it's doubtful they'd turn up every week. Hence, the boys slouch or stand with their hands in their pockets at their annual Enrolment Service. Nevertheless, some young men have progressed through the ranks better than I ever did and taken on leadership roles.

I was never a dedicated member of the 29th Boys' Brigade Company, unlike Dad and Stevie. I enjoyed the discipline, polishing and whitening my uniform; I looked forward to Drill lessons and summer camps; I even completed my Wayfarer's Badge which, apart from the Queen's Badge, was recognised as one of the most difficult awards to attain. I aimed to avoid responsibility. I never wanted to be in a position where I had to give orders or be responsible for other people. I succeeded in my ambition. I joined the BB as a Private at age eleven and left the company seven years later still a Private. I never even earned a stripe.

Sometimes, I "beaked off" the odd Monday evening. I left home for BB but called to Jim Leckey's in Olive Street or walked to Ivan McStea's in Leopold Street and played with his Scalextric. I was never allowed to stray for too long before Captain Jim Moore visited Dad and asked him, "Where is he, Bill?" I was invited to explain why I wasn't attending BB. There were never accusations or angry words, just gentle encouragement to come along because, "We miss you." I did go back, and Jim's daughter taught me to swim. I earned my Life Savers badge at the Grove Baths on Shore Road.

Jim Moore took over the Captaincy from Roy Kennedy who had served the company as leader for many years. Parents saved money with the company throughout the year to pay for our annual camps which were always "across the water." One year we set off, via Stranraer, to travel to Edinburgh and set up camp at Craigentinny Primary School on the city's outskirts. When we disembarked at Stranraer, there was no transport to meet us. Roy found a public call box and rang the bus company to enquire about the delay.

Shortly afterwards, our coach arrived, and we set off for our destination.

An hour or so into our trip, I noticed Roy in a huddle with the officers before he approached the driver and leaned in to whisper to him. The driver stopped the bus, turned it around and drove us back to Stranraer. I found out later what happened. When Roy had called the bus company, he left his briefcase in the phone box. The briefcase contained everyone's pocket money for the ten-day holiday. I imagine he was sick with worry on that journey back to Stranraer. On arrival in Stranraer, he went to the phone box he used earlier. Of course, the briefcase was gone. He called into the local police station to report what had happened. To his surprise and delight, his briefcase had been handed in and all the money accounted for. Perhaps, that was when he decided a younger man should take over as Captain.

I was 14 at the time of our camp in Craigentinny. We played in the streets with residents our age and two caught my attention. Their names were Cora D'Angelo and Afion Brodiemends. The former was a beautiful teenager originally from Italy and Afion was a beautiful Black teenager whose parents were from Nigeria. Before I could muster the courage to ask Cora for a date another suitor pre-empted me. I asked Afion if she would go to the cinema with me and was relieved when she accepted. The four of us went to watch Winnie The Pooh in Edinburgh city centre. I hope my memory is wrong and Afion didn't pay her way in......and they say romance is dead. Few 14-year-old boys from the Shankill can say their first-ever date was with an African teenager.

Inevitably, amongst a large group of boys, a few thought they were a little grander than the rest. Admittedly, their homes in Dhu Varren and Lyndhurst had indoor bathrooms but that's no excuse for acting like prigs towards boys from humbler backgrounds. I did pick up some social graces in their company. When asking for a cup of tea to be refilled, hand the saucer and cup to the person with the teapot and never, ever dip the knife you used to butter your toast into the jar of marmalade afterwards. It's bad form to sleep with your socks on and, if someone is kind enough to lend you their coat, give it back without cigarette burn holes in the sleeves. Yes, Robert Hamilton, Stephen Cairns and Jim Fleming, it's you I'm writing about.

Robert Hamilton went to Belfast Institute. He was the first person I knew who went abroad with his school. He and other fifth-formers visited Paris for a week. He said he paid 2s 6d for a Mars bar in "la confiserie". That's 12.5p. Extortionate! A Mars bar was threepence at home (1½p). Little did I know, that 38 years later, I would also visit Paris on a school trip. I would have the dubious pleasure of sharing my 50th birthday in Disneyland Paris with 30 sixth-formers from Campbell College, Pinocchio and his father Geppetto.

However, affluence and ego can give a person a false sense of entitlement because they think they are a little smarter than their contemporaries. This can prove especially useful and I used it to my advantage on a weekend camp to Guysmere Centre, Castlerock in 1967.

Myself, Robert and our church organist Mr Lilley were obliged to share a bedroom for the weekend. There was one bunk bed and a fold-out camp bed in the room. Because of his age, we all agreed Mr Lilley should have the bottom bunk for the weekend; the top bunk would be shared between Robert and myself, with me taking it for the first evening leaving Robert the camp bed. Getting out of bed the next morning, I made groaning noises commenting the lumpy mattress had hurt my back, and I hadn't slept well. Our film on Saturday night was The Wooden Horse. Afterwards, when we retired to our room, Robert piped up to say it was too late to change our sleeping arrangements. I reluctantly agreed of course. I put my head on the pillow with a smile on my face.......and slept very well. Thank you, Robert. You weren't that smart.

One of the proudest days of my life was when Dad discovered his son had been awarded eight Northern Ireland GCEs. However, this paled in comparison to Dad laying the wreath in church on Remembrance Sunday each year. An occasion I never missed. In those days, at those moments, Bill's wee son was bigger, taller, richer and prouder than any idiots who had illusions of grandeur.

I never wanted to lead but was happy to volunteer and muck in as best I could. David Crawford was completing a Wayfarer's challenge by walking from Belfast to Maze via Black Mountain and Divis as part of his Duke of Edinburgh Award. I volunteered to accompany him. We set off from the Glen on Ballygomartin Road and made it as far as the BBC transmitter on Divis before thick fog made it unwise to walk further. We decided to pitch our tent for the night. Always check twice, then check again what you think you need and what you are taking with you. The BB company owned two André Jamet tents, one with pegs and one without. We had packed the latter. We found an abandoned outhouse with an old wooden door lying on the floor. We laid our sleeping bags on top to keep us dry. Not the best night's sleep I ever had, and I felt sick the next morning when we set off to complete our 26-mile walk to Maze where Sergeant Stephen Shields and the rest of the BB Company had pitched camp and were waiting to greet us.

We arrived on a glorious sunny Saturday afternoon in a field full of mown hay. Exhausted, I shrugged my arms out of the straps of my heavy rucksack and let it drop to the ground. Oh dear! Something on the rucksack caught the top of my anorak and ripped it from top to bottom. I turned around and looked down; the stuffing from inside the anorak was lying at my feet. The problem was the anorak wasn't mine. Elizabeth let me borrow her new coat when she knew I was helping David with his Duke of Edinburgh's Award. I dreaded telling her but she only laughed when I told her what happened.

The last time our BB Old Boys gathered was at the 29th Boys' Brigade Company's 100th Anniversary Celebration Dinner in 1996. It was held in the Lecture Hall at Townsend Street Presbyterian Church. Dad was with me. It was a pleasure to meet old acquaintances and share memories of the "29th" over the years. Eventually, we were asked to take our seats because dinner was about to be served. There were five tables on each side of the hall and a top table for the current officers and clergy. We waited in anticipation. We didn't know the dining arrangements had been outsourced to a catering company that didn't get the memo the dinner was in a church for a Christian organisation hosted by the great and good of the Presbyterian Church in Ireland.

The doors from the adjoining room opened and the catering staff walked in wearing Guinness t-shirts and carried plates of food on Guinness trays to our tables. One server's t-shirt stood out. She had a well-endowed bosom which drew the attention of every man in the room who had a pulse, including Dad & me. The wording on the material that strained across her ample chest read, "If you think I'm a bitch." As she passed by, every head turned to read what was on her back, "You should meet my mother." My father looked at me and we dissolved into laughter. I never found out what the Reverend Jack Lamb made of the display. Jack had a strange name for a vegetarian.

In 2007, when I worked in the Identity and Passport Service in High Street Belfast, I met a Team Manager named Alison Skillen. I asked her if she was related to Victor Skillen an officer during my time in the 29th BB. I was surprised to learn Victor was Alison's father and suffered from Dementia. She also informed me my old BB Captain, Jim Moore and his wife Iris, now in their 80s, sold their house in Orby Drive and moved to an apartment on Holywood Road, around the corner from where I lived in Irwin Drive.

I bought flowers and called in with them at their new home. They remembered the times Jim visited us to ask me back to BB. I'm glad I took the opportunity to tell him his efforts weren't in vain. Jim cried when I described how I came to faith in Christ and that he and the Boys' Brigade were important steps along the way.

Jim's anchor held for another year. Iris suffered a fall and died a brief time afterwards.

The 29th BB Vesper Hymn was:

The day Thou gavest, Lord, is ended.

I would like that sung at my funeral.

The Men From UNCLE

I had four uncles, Stevie, my father's brother. Jackie and Eddie were my mother's brothers and Tommy was my uncle by marriage to Mum's sister Violet.

None of my uncles starred in one of my favourite TV programmes in the 60s, The Man from the United Nations Counterespionage and Law Enforcement Agency. I don't believe they would have passed the relevant entrance examinations. However, they were no less interesting characters.

Jackie died from lung cancer when I was young. His daughter Margaret married Jackie Swann and emigrated to Canada. His other daughter Hazel married John Welch and still lives in Belfast. Mum's nieces kept in touch with her and May all their lives. Thank you for your unwavering love through all the years. Mum treasured the regular cards she received from Margaret's son Gary. Gary is the Airport Manager for Avis at Winnipeg International Airport. Good to know!

I knew Uncle Edward better because, in 1966 our family moved into his flat on top of the War Memorial building in Waring Street. "Eddie" struggled with his health and Dad volunteered to cover his duties as caretaker while he took a leave of absence to seek more treatment. This was typical of my parents when anyone asked them for help. Eddie would have lost his job if Dad hadn't covered his work. Dad didn't have an easy job in Bairds where he worked on a printing press all day; then he had to clean the War Memorial building in the evenings and make any necessary preparations for the following day's events.

It's too late to apologise to the member of The Corps of Commissioners on duty when I dropped a water bomb on him from our 5th-floor balcony.

Eddie eventually recovered. He gave up his job at the War Memorial to become a porter at Purdysburn Hospital. He moved to nearby Belvoir Park where he, his wife Dolly and daughter Jean made their home. Day and May moved to Belvoir Park from Dover Street in the mid-70s and lived in Kirkistown Walk, a short walk from Eddie. Sometimes, when I visited Day and May, Eddie called in while walking his dog. Lucy was a black, Miniature Poodle and one of the cleverest dogs I've ever known. Lucy seemed to know everything Eddie said to her. He asked her where his house keys were and Lucy trotted into the kitchen, jumped on a stool, and retrieved his keys off the kitchen table.

Eddie enjoyed his work in the hospital and became a valued and respected staff member. Nothing was too much bother if it was to help others. When Eddie's health relapsed, he was treated in Purdysburn Hospital by doctors and nurses who knew him and cared greatly for him. Mum and Dad took me to visit Eddie one Sunday afternoon. We all realised Eddie's condition was terminal and my parents were concerned about going on holiday to Tenerife. Eddie told them, "Go and enjoy yourselves, I'll wait until you come back."

Eddie did wait, much to my parents' relief. When we visited again. I innocently asked Uncle Eddie how he managed to get such a good tan. I didn't realise he was jaundiced because his liver had failed. He passed away several days later. Dolly died several years later, and Jean emigrated to Toronto.

If Jackie and Eddie were quiet, Uncle Tommy was the opposite. Tommy had a "presence." He was loud and opinionated but not in an ignorant way. I enjoyed his company and loved listening to his stories about work and travelling. He did quite a bit of both because, every time he visited and mentioned work, it appeared he had changed jobs yet again. Tommy was always "Management" in firms such as Bobritch, Goblin and Setright, to name a few. Mum worked in Bobritch under his management at one time. Wednesday was her day off each week and I always looked forward to coming home from school to find out what she had baked. Tommy Smith cottoned on to this and walked home with me on Wednesdays. This always pleased Mum and she sent Tom away with a share of what she'd baked.

At one time, Uncle Tommy and his family lived in New Barnsley before they were forced to move at the beginning of the troubles. This was when housing estates became polarised according to residents' religion. His sister-in-law Betty lived nearby and was a regular pillion passenger on Tommy's BSA 250cc motorcycle because they worked in the same factory. I stayed overnight with my cousins and watched Betty sit on the bike the next morning and wave goodbye to her sister Violet. Unfortunately, Betty was too busy waving to hold on and, when Tommy drove off, she tumbled off backwards onto the road. Thankfully, she wasn't hurt, and both departed safely on their second attempt to go to work.

Later in the 1960s, Tommy was Personnel Manager at Setright, based on Donegall Road. Setright made Pay-on-entry ticket machines that replaced conductors on public transport. Modernisation was replacing jobs again. Coincidentally, I later became friends with John Maxwell, who drove the first conductor-less bus in Belfast fitted with a Setright ticket machine.

Like most firms then, Setright closed for the Twelfth fortnight. After the holidays, Tommy noticed one of the employees hadn't returned. The employee didn't show up until August and Tommy invited him into his office to explain why he was late returning to work. Tommy regaled us with this story over tea and homemade cake.

"Well Mr Philips, I apologise for my late return but let me explain. My wife and I decided to take our children and my mother-in-law on a camping holiday to Spain. We had a safe journey and were in the middle of nowhere in Spain when my mother-in-law died in our car. You can imagine how shocked and upset we were, especially our children at this unexpected turn of events. The temperature was in the 90s and we couldn't keep Granny's body beside our children in the car. I decided the best thing to do was wrap her in a tent and load it onto the roof rack before driving to the nearest British Consulate in Barcelona.

We spent a considerable time in the consulate explaining what happened and arranging the repatriation of Granny's remains. All that was stressful enough until we returned to where we had parked and discovered our car stolen. It took time for the Spanish authorities to find our car with its contents and allow us to return home. Granny came back on her own later."

Imagine the conversation the thieves must have had. "Si Pablo, nice one. Stupid British driver leave zee car unattended with all zee goodies inside and on zee roof. Let's check out zee big tent on zee roof rack. Maybe I use it for my holidays hah, hah. Let me give you a hand to unroll it. AAAAH! LEG IT QUICK PABLO!"

Aunt Violet died from cancer in the Mater Hospital on 11th of January 1985. Uncle Tommy retired before moving to live on Belfast Road in Bangor close to his daughter Lilian and sons Edward and George. Tommy passed away on 31st of December 2006. Tragically, the younger of their sons, George, died from cancer on 24th of June 2018 and is buried with his parents. Lilian, Edward and George had another brother named Thomas. He was Tommy and Violet's firstborn and died in hospital when he was less than a year old.

This brings me to Uncle Stevie. Stephen McDonald, the man I'm named after. Stevie McDonald deserves a book all to himself. His love, kindness, and patience with a brat of a nephew were priceless and gifted me with many treasured memories of a good, decent, honest, and tight man. He was a simple man who enjoyed the little pleasures in life.

Stevie was Dad's younger brother. He was born in 1921 and lived in Westmoreland Street until 1976. Stevie lived with his father and mother until they died in 1957 & 1960, respectively. Stevie took me with him regularly to tend to his parents' grave. I always enjoyed Stevie's company when we did this.

Stevie didn't own a car. However, he would turn up often to take us out in "the car." He borrowed cars from his friend, Dickey Gilchrist. Dickey would be with him on occasion. There was plenty of room. I rode with Stevie in a Morris Oxford and a Morris Cambridge.

Full bench seats front and back, full ashtrays and no seat belts. It was like sharing a sofa on wheels. I remember the smells, leather, petrol and cigarette smoke. It was a wonderful, heady combination that I associate with adventure. I never knew what Stevie had planned or where we were going but, it was always great craic.

One evening, Stevie drove Mum, Dad, Elizabeth & myself to Nutts Corner. This was Belfast's airport before it moved to Aldergrove. We parked, climbed over a gate and walked into a field to get a better view of the planes taking off and landing.

Then, "What's that noise?" The thunder of hooves as we spotted a bull charging towards us at full tilt. We all cleared the gate at Olympic High Jump record-breaking speed. To settle our nerves, we needed tea. Stevie always carried a Primus stove in the boot. I loved the smells of Paraffin and Methylated spirits as he pumped away on the piston to get a good flame and boil the kettle for teas all round.

Another great adventure happened in 1962. Stevie arrived in another borrowed car and invited us to come and see the new road called a "Motorway." Mum made a picnic, Stevie checked his Primus was in the boot, and we drove from Donegall Road to Lisburn, along the newly opened M1 motorway. Then, it was laid in concrete slabs and vibrations from the road made it a rather noisy journey. Whoa!!!! No traffic lights.

Very exciting! We must have reached 60 mph. After all that excitement, we pulled over on Saintfield Road in Lisburn for a brew-up and sandwiches before heading back on the M1 to Belfast. A journey that has stayed in my mind. Leather, petrol, cigarette smoke, the sound of Friday Night is Music Night and a beautiful sunset. Happy, happy memories. Every time I travel home on the M1 from visiting Rebekah, Tim and Micah in Lisburn, I think of that evening.

I'm reliably informed that, as a young man, Stevie possessed a full head of red hair. He was his mother's favourite son as he did what he was told. My Dad was too independent for Granny McDonald's liking. Dad had found love and told his Mum to like it or lump it. Stevie was a homebird and never strayed too far from Westmoreland Street. Both Stevie and Dad were members of the 29th Boys' Brigade Company. The company had a Pipe Band in addition to the traditional Bugle Band. Stevie was the musician in the family and, one year was BB Champion Piper. Somewhere, I hope you find it, there's a photograph of Stevie in his Piper's uniform taken at Balmoral Showgrounds in 1936. Musically, Dad's only claim to fame was playing "Dummy Bugler" in the 29th BB Bugle Band.

The only pet I remember Stevie owning was a black and white cat named Fluff. Fluff could sit on the bench seat of the outside toilet and do his business in the bowl. How's that for house training? I'm sure Stevie was annoyed but didn't show it when I used his faux leather sofa as a target for my homemade bow and arrow resulting in half a dozen punctures in the fabric. Stevie was the first in the family with a three-channel TV. BBC1, BBC2 and UTV. The first program I watched on BBC2 was The Awesome Universe, in black & white. Awesome!

Despite my annoying behaviour, Stevie took a great interest in my hobbies and how I was progressing at school. He gave me an interest in mechanics by demonstrating how engines worked and gave me my first driving lesson. That was on the indoor track at Barrys in Portrush and cost 2 shillings. 10p to you. Stevie tried to interest me in playing the Bagpipes by taking me to the 29th Old Boys' Pipe Band practices in the Minor Hall at Townsend Street Presbyterian Church. To Stevie's disappointment, I never took an interest in the pipes. However, I supported the band by accompanying Stevie, my Dad and their best friend, Billy Leonard to the annual, National Pipe Band Competition, in Dunoon, Scotland.

On our last trip, in 1964, we boarded an old steamer in Belfast which docked where the Belfast weir is today, for the overnight sailing to Dunoon. We were booked into a dormitory at the rear of the boat. The bunk beds followed the curve of the stern and there were no port holes. Billy, "The Bull," Leonard was a unique character who hailed from Twaddell Avenue off Ballygomartin Road. Billy was single, still lived with his parents and literally, couldn't boil an egg for himself. He couldn't speak a word of German but his impersonation of Hitler giving a speech, accompanied by hand actions, would get him arrested today for inciting a sense of humour.

Billy was meticulous in his ablutions; he washed and shaved before climbing into a top bunk. I saw my Dad and Stevie whispering and knew they were up to some mischief. They gave Billy 15 minutes before Stevie shook him and said we had docked in Dunoon. Billy got up, stretched, and commented, "I've never slept better, in my life." He returned to the communal sink, washed, shaved, dressed and said he was going up on deck for a look around. Stevie and Dad waited for Billy's return. When they saw the, "I've been suckered," look on Billy's face the four of us laughed. Good Craic!

Another great trip occurred in 1965 when Stevie asked cousin Edward and me, "Would we like to travel around Scotland with him?" Three of us, with camping gear and the ubiquitous Primus stove, piled into Stevie's green Morris 1000 Sation Wagon for the sailing from Belfast to Stranraer. We innocently waved goodbye to our parents on the quayside not knowing what Stevie McDonald had in store for us. As soon as the ship set sail, Stevie said, "I don't know about you lads but, I'm going to the bar." The licensing laws might have been less strict then, but I still don't think a couple of 13-year-olds had any chance of ordering a beer in the bar.

With no plan, we left Stranraer and headed in the general direction of Edinburgh. The M8 was still under construction and the journey along winding and hilly roads proved very educational. Long before "Green" became fashionable for the Liberal Intelligentsia, Stevie pioneered saving the planet from burning fossil fuels. His actions weren't so much Just Stop Oil as Just Stop Engine. At the top of a hill, Stevie would switch off the ignition and freewheel down the other side to save petrol. Don't try this as modern cars have steering locks.

Another skill Stevie taught us was how to drive without using hands. Maybe, he was a pioneer for Tesla. This skill is essential when you have a box of cigarettes in one pocket and a lighter in another. Riding in the front passenger seat I witnessed how Stevie was able to press his knees up tight to the steering wheel. By alternating pressure between his left and right knees, he steered the car. This freed his hands to explore his pockets and find his cigarettes and lighter. Maybe, I'm the nervous type but, it was always a relief when Stevie managed to light a cigarette and put both hands on the steering wheel again.

By the time we neared the outskirts of Edinburgh, it was pitch black. There was no way "the budget" was extending to a B & B so Stevie decided to park and sleep in the car. Park somewhere we did, sleep we didn't. Eddie and I decided to pitch our tent and leave Stevie to snore alone. My main memory of that night in the tent is Eddie spraying insects with a tin of shoe polish which stuck them to the canvas. We found out at daybreak the reason there were so many flies in our tent. We had camped on the edge of a municipal rubbish dump.

We eventually made it as far as Oban, exhausted, dirty and hungry. Even Stevie admitted we needed warm beds and access to hot running water. We all shared the same bedroom with three single beds. Stevie announced he was going to a Pipe Band competition and left Eddie and me reading our comics. There were no TVs in Oban at that time. Oban is situated between high mountains and there was no local television transmitter until the 1970s. All was quiet and Eddie and I were content to switch off the lights and catch a good night's sleep. Our sleep was interrupted when Stevie tried to sneak into our room around 11 pm. He didn't turn on the lights, placed one foot in the wastepaper basket, lost his balance and cartwheeled onto his bed. Eddie and I reckoned the "Pipe Band competition" was held in a local pub and Stevie's imagination. Somehow, we all made it home safely.

The last "foreign" holiday I shared with Stevie didn't get off to a good start. The bus taking us from Glengall Street to Aldergrove Airport broke down on Grosvenor Road outside the Royal Victoria Hospital. Somehow, the replacement bus delivered us in time for our flight on a Vickers Viscount to the Isle of Man. Then, the Isle of Man was a popular holiday destination before cheap airfares lured people to warmer climes. However, the summer season only lasted until September. We arrived in late October 1967 and basically, Douglas and the rest of the Isle of Man were closed. As soon as we entered our room, Stevie had a serious asthma attack. It was frightening to watch him fight for breath and struggle to take his inhaler. There was absolutely nothing I could do. It was a huge relief when the colour returned to his face and I realised he would be ok. Stevie "found" a car somewhere and we managed to tour the island. Someone took a photo of us together outside the Laxey Wheel. It's in a box somewhere.

In 1977, I returned to the IOM with Jennifer, two years after we were married. Douglas town was in decline after the Summerland Complex had been destroyed by fire in 1973 with the loss of 50 lives. My lasting memory of that trip is skipping the island without paying a parking fine. I parked in the town centre and my ticket slipped off the car window but was visible on the driver's seat. I decided to stick it to Mr Jobsworth. I panicked while driving onto the Seacat in case car registrations were checked for security reasons and outstanding violations. I received a letter from Douglas Council some weeks after we arrived home requesting payment which I decided to ignore. I'm sure the Statute of Limitations has expired by now.

Stevie continued to be a faithful member of Townsend Street church and, at 55, became engaged to the church's organist Ethel Shields, the aunt of my old 29th BB officer Stephen Shields. They subsequently married on 19th November 1977 in the same church where they met and enjoyed 25 years of happy marriage. Their home was in Dunkeld Gardens off Oldpark Road. Ethel was a gentle lady with a zest for travel and took Stevie to America, Canada, and Europe. Occasionally, Mum and Dad would travel with them and return with souvenirs that we kindly accepted but didn't display anywhere. They were dreadful ornaments but brought smiles when we came across them occasionally. I was happy for Stevie. He had found the love and contentment he deserved with the woman he loved dearly.

Eventually, as years took their toll, Stevie and Ethel sold their house and moved to sheltered accommodation in Lowry Court off Ormeau Road where they spent the remainder of their lives together. Ethel gently faded away and died peacefully in 2000. Stevie was content in his remaining years as a widower, passing the time indulging his passion for completing the Belfast Telegraph Cryptic Crossword and spending time with neighbours in Lowry Court who loved him for his gentle ways.

In the first week of July 2002, Rhonda, Rebekah and I were with a team from Bloomfield Presbyterian Church helping a community children's outreach team in Fermoy, Co. Cork. It was a glorious week of weather and companionship. The event drew about 100 young people from the town to play, make crafts and hear the Gospel. The teenagers had never heard Bible stories before and were a keen audience. The last evening ended in a worship service which included all the young people and volunteers who had participated throughout the week. It was a wonderful event, and we were sorry to say goodbye. I mentioned to Rhonda on the way back to our accommodation that I couldn't wait to tell Stevie what happened that evening. Rather than call him, I decided to wait and tell him in person.

As soon as we crossed into Northern Ireland on Saturday afternoon, my mobile rang. It was Frances who told me the Warden in Lowry Court had found Stevie dead in his bed that morning. It struck Rhonda and me like a hammer blow and we pulled to the side of the road to take in the news and gather our thoughts. We'll never forget the 6th July 2002.

I scattered Stevie's ashes on the coast of Belfast Lough near Cultra in sight of the shipyard where he enjoyed his working life. I pray I did the right thing for him. He'll let me know in God's good time.

Stevie's and Dad's friend Billy Leonard died in 2022. I'm still aggrieved I wasn't at his funeral. I knew he was frail and in care. I had asked Jack Lamb, the minister of Townsend Street, to let me know when Billy died so I could represent our family at his funeral. I met Jack at a Men's Breakfast in Bloomfield one Saturday morning and asked him about Billy. Jack put a hand on my shoulder and said he was sorry to tell me Billy had died the previous month. I had to leave the room I was so annoyed and disappointed. I have never felt more let down, and angry.

Recently, Alex, one of the nurses from Carnalea Care Home who was devoted to Mum and Aunt May, texted me to enquire about the whereabouts of my parents' grave. She said she had a day off and wanted to visit Mum's grave.

While looking for the grave papers, I found a sympathy card from Stevie's neighbour in Lowry Court. It reads:

A Message of Deepest Sympathy

Stevie,
I'm sure God is smiling on you as you so generously smiled on your friends.
Bon voyage old friend

Desi

May words of deepest sympathy help somehow to convey the warmth and understanding in thoughts of you today.
In humble and grateful remembrance of a kind, thoughtful, humorous and genuinely gentle wee man. Your being my neighbour these past seven years was made so easy by your consideration of everyone.

Thank you, Desi, for your beautiful tribute to Uncle Stevie. It sums him up perfectly. 22 years later, by God's grace, I trust you are neighbours again.

Regrets? Yes. I wish I spent more time with Stevie, especially when he was alone. I was too busy with my own life and interests to understand what I would regret in later years.

Take good advice and spend time now with the people you know and love. Don't say, "I'll go tomorrow." Tomorrow mightn't come for you or them.

There's always Divine Intervention to contend with. I still miss Stevie.

Hobbies

I loved my electric Hornby train set even though the train only went around a three-foot diameter circle of track. The smell of ozone permeated our parlour when the 00-gauge engine rattled around the track. I considered myself a bit of an artist and enjoyed sketching and painting. The real artist in our family was Elizabeth. Elizabeth had a gift for copying Rowel Friers's cartoons from the Belfast Telegraph which were hilarious insights into "Norn Ireland" culture and humour. Example: Two women were overheard on an East Belfast bus discussing a mixed marriage. One lady said to the other, "She's one of them and he walks."

I loved Spirograph and Lego which arrived in Britain in 1960. My favourite toy of all time was my Meccano Set. This was real engineering, and I spent many happy days constructing cranes, engines and bridges following the beautiful, detailed plans in the instruction handbook. Meccano Sets began at No.1. They increased in complexity and cost, up to the ultimate No.10. I could only afford a No.6 and only dreamt of owning a No.10. Then a No.10 cost £49. I recently searched for one on the Internet and wasn't surprised to find I could buy one for the princely sum of £7,500.

As I grew into my teens, I took an interest in electronics. Transistors were gradually replacing valves and I enjoyed making transistor radios as small as possible. Eventually, I was able to fit a shortwave radio into a matchbox. However, the aerial consisted of 100 feet of wire wrapped around my bedroom ceiling a few times. Not exactly portable. One of my larger radios used valves and was powered by a 90-volt Ever Ready battery about the size and weight of a brick. After reading Amateur Radio along with Amateur Electronics and choosing a project to build, the challenge was to source the parts.

This was long before catalogue shopping and the Internet. There were "Spares" shops that catered for amateur enthusiasts like me. Probably, the most unusual place to shop for specialist parts, such as variable capacitors, was a little stall run by "Tommy" in Smithfield Market. Tommy was illiterate, wore a suit that looked like it had been sprayed on and topped his ensemble off with a greasy-looking Trilby. What Tommy didn't know about electronics wasn't worth knowing. He couldn't sign his name but could work out alternative components to use, in place of parts that were impossible to find. If your project didn't work, let Tommy look at your circuit diagram; he could suggest a solution and find you the parts required.

At the corner of Montgomery & May Street stands Ross's Auction House. Beside the entrance to the auction house is the door to Ross's Cafe. In the 60s, this was the entrance to one of my favourite places in all Belfast. Through that entrance, down a short flight of stairs and to the right was Granny Smith's Electronics Emporium. This was an Alladin's Cave to me. I was fascinated by the size, shape and variety of electronic components Granny Smith had on display. I wish I knew more about this lady, and I've searched in vain for information on who she was. I suspect she was ex-military because of her depth of knowledge of all things electrical, especially radios and their workings. Then, I guess she was in her sixties. She wore a blue overall and always gave me a warm welcome. After enquiring what I was building, she would offer her help and advice.

These were the type of people I would invite to dinner. Real, genuine, kind, hardworking entrepreneurs who lived lives I would love to have known more about. When we are young, we seldom or never take the time to ask an older person their story and miss out so much when they pass away. Who cares about celebrities and

Celebrity Culture? I was quite chuffed when Rebekah said to me once, "Dad, my definition of a celebrity is someone you don't know." Maybe, in God's will, I will meet those I've mentioned again. In the meantime, this is my nod of appreciation to each of them, for what they meant to me and the opportunity to thank them for wonderful memories.

Eventually, I progressed to mounting a valve Long Distance (DX) radio onto a metal chassis. The chassis was built in Harland and Wolff from a piece of stainless steel which, I suspect, belonged to the Canberra. The craftsman in question was my dear Uncle Stevie, an Iron Turner by profession. A weird sense of humour has passed on genetically through the male McDonald line. Stevie made a drawing of a device he invented for carrying dogs onto ships as hand baggage. Perhaps, to have avoided the attention of the NSPCA, it's better it never saw the light of day. Imagine a bracket with a handle attached. mounted on one end of the bracket is a leather nose cone. At the other end of the bracket is a threaded ball cock with a handle. Turning the handle clockwise pushed the ball cock towards the nose cone: turning the handle anti-clockwise retracted the ball cock away from the nose cone.

Now, imagine you want to carry little Daisy on board the Stena Line to Stranraer because you don't want to leave her in the car. Good job you remembered to bring your Patented McDonald Dog Carrier. So, you place Daisy's nozzle into the leather nose cone and, holding her gently but steadily, turn the handle clockwise until the ball cock reaches her backside. Pause, time to rub a little Vaseline around the ball cock then....one more quick turn and, pop, the ball cock is in place. Voila! You and Daisy are good to go. Daisy is supported by her snout in the nose cone and the ball cock in her rear. Mind your step, you don't want to let go of that handle. Just imagine the opportunities your hand luggage will give you to engage in conversation with fellow passengers over your Frappé in Stena's Travellers' Lounge. A great start to your holidays. Bon voyage!

Back to the story of the radio. When I completed putting everything together, it didn't work. Everywhere was closed for the Christmas holidays and the only person I could think of who might be able to help was Uncle Tommy. My cousins lived at 103 West Circular Crescent a 30-minute walk from Woodvale Street. When Uncle Tommy had a look at it, he suggested several dry joints needed re-soldered. He didn't have a soldering iron and mine was at home. "Here, take Edward's bicycle," he said. I pedalled home as fast as I could, collected my soldering iron and pedalled as quickly back again. Uphill all the way. I arrived back and walked into the kitchen where Aunt Violet was cooking dinner, then everything went black. I came round when Uncle Tommy helped me drink sweet tea. I stood in a daze and watched Aunt Violet fry eggs perfectly. Slow, over a low heat, spooning oil over the yoke. Every time I fry an egg now, I see Aunt Violet. And, SURPRISE, SURPRISE! We managed to get the radio to work.

I called another day when Edward and George were just home from school. Both were sitting on the stairs because Aunt Violet had a visitor in the living room. So, I joined them in the hall. They were both chewing gum and I asked them for a piece. "No," was the answer. "Give me a piece and I'll tell you a dirty word," I said. Always eager to broaden their knowledge and develop their language skills, they agreed; George handed me a strip of Wrigley's Spearmint. "So, what's the word?" They asked. "Bollocks," I replied. Later the same day, Uncle Tommy arrived home from work. I don't recall what Edward did to displease him but SMACK! right across Eddie's legs. "BOLLOCKS," shouted Eddie at his father and incurred another smack for his troubles. "Where did you learn that word?" Shouted Uncle Tommy. This was one of those defining moments when you discover who you can depend on in life. Even after another scolding, Edward never confessed who taught him how to swear. I'm glad Tommy didn't smack George. There might have been a different result.

The only sport I ever showed any talent for was running. I discovered this at the Boys' Model when I turned up for a rugby trial, got my gutties dirty and decided rugby wasn't for me. I joined the cross-country team instead, under the leadership of my art teacher Spud Murphy. I found I enjoyed the sport and represented the school in the event. I would have won the cross-country race against Orangefield School if I hadn't been so far in front and taken the wrong turn. I only realised my mistake when I heard Spud shouting, "Come back, McDonald."

In 1986, when Rhonda and I lived in Ardgowan Street, she accompanied me on her bicycle as I went for a run. When we returned home, it took me some time to catch my breath and my pulse to return to normal. I called with my GP and explained what had happened along with the fact I had lost my sense of smell. I guess the young GP wasn't good at mathematics. He asked me what year I was born, wrote down 1986 with 1953 underneath and subtracted them. Quelle surprise! He deduced I was 33 and asked me, "What do you expect at your age?" I'm certain this is where a diagnosis of asthma was missed and, untreated, developed into Chronic Obstructive Pulmonary Disease.

In later years, my hobbies are reading and listening to classical music. I enjoy books by C J Box, Marc Cameron and Michael Connelly, nothing too serious. My classical "Go-to list" is the works of Rachmaninov. His piano concertos are sublime. If only I had practised harder...........

School Days Were Happy Days

My scholastic journey began in September 1958. Mum dragged me screaming and shouting into Woodvale Primary School off Cambrai Street. The Headmistress was Mrs McCandless and my teachers included Miss Love, my first crush, Miss Tomb and Miss Holmes. I eventually settled down to school life. Mum worked in the Bobritch factory in Cambrai Street making electric blankets. With both parents at work, I walked home at lunchtime, pushed my hand through our letterbox and retrieved the front door key tied to a string hanging inside. Mum left me lunch on our dining table. Egg in a cup and bread springs to mind.

One day, I rushed back to school after lunch and ran across Olive Street. Halfway across I was hit by a cyclist and sent crashing into the road. My cheek was so badly swollen by the time I arrived at school my left eye had closed. The lesson that afternoon was on road safety delivered by an RUC constable. No wonder he kept giving me funny looks. One bright morning Mum was talking to our next-door neighbour Mrs Boyd. They both waved me off to school. I was too busy looking back at them with both hands in my pockets when I tripped over the kerb and fell face-first into the pavement. My forehead split open, and I couldn't see because there was blood in my eyes. My mother screamed but it was Mrs Boyd who took me by bus to the Royal Victoria Hospital. I can still smell the rubber sheet they placed on me while cleaning and stitching my forehead.

I enjoyed all my lessons and was keen to learn. I was happy to help hand out our free, daily, third-pint milk bottles and other classroom duties but never made it to Prefect. Well, if you can't join them, beat them. I punched a Prefect on his nose when he scolded me in the playground. I can't remember the reason; a psychologist might have noted an early indication that Stephen McDonald would have a bad attitude towards authority throughout his life.

I proudly attribute this chink in my character to my genes. Dad landed on Juno Beach on D-Day, 6th June 1944 driving an amphibious vehicle called a DUKW. DUKW is a manufacturer's code based on D indicating the model year, 1942; U referring to the body style, utility (amphibious); K for all-wheel drive; and W for dual rear axles. The vehicle was shaped like a boat. He was a Private in the Royal Army Service Corps under the overall command of the 3rd Canadian Division. This story might not have been written, only Dad failed his medical for the Royal Ulster Rifles due to an accident in childhood. His Mum accidentally spilt boiling water over him, scarring his left leg. A work of grace that possibly saved Dad's life. Even the bad things in life can turn out to be blessings. I certainly attest to that. The Rifles were involved in tough battles across Northern France after they landed at Sword Beach on D-Day and suffered many casualties.

On landing, Dad disobeyed orders and drove out to sea again to retrieve bodies of soldiers from the waves. My treasured possession was a St. Christopher "Medal" given to Dad by a Roman Catholic friend before he left for France. The medal was more like a credit card. It had been badly water-damaged during Dad's exertions. I presented this to my nephew Philip on his wedding day. Philip is a police officer and I told him to treasure the keepsake and remember that sometimes breaking rules is the right thing to do. How many times has that been proven true in this era of "'Elf and Safety?"

Good job Dad wasn't superstitious. His DUKW was No.13. Dad had come to faith when he was a member of the 29th Boys' Brigade Company and believed he was in God's hands no matter what happened. Dad had a quiet faith. He never forced his beliefs on anyone. He showed by example what it was to be a Christian husband, father and all the other titles God had blessed him with. Dad's faith never wavered and on his deathbed in 2006 he whispered to me, "No fear here son." I trust and pray I can say the same when my time comes.

When he found time, he wrote a note to Mum to let her know he was safe. He used the back of the letter from General Eisenhower issued to all the troops before they embarked for France; it was his only writing paper and he signed it "Monsieur Bill." This letter is framed but we no longer display it to protect it from sunlight. Somewhere near Hamburg, Dad fell into a well that had been shelled flat. A captured German doctor treated his injuries. He did a good job because I have a photograph of Dad in the football team that won the Antwerp Cup in 1945.

The evidence suggested the problem with authority ran on the Kirk side of the family as well. My Grandfather, Edward Kirk punched a British officer unconscious when he referred to his platoon as, "A shower of Irish Bastards." Thankfully, this didn't happen on the battlefield or there might have been a different ending. He was duly detained in Carrickfergus Castle until my father arranged with the relevant authorities to have him released. I'm sorry all the details are lost in the mist of time.

Edward served in the First World War as well. He fought on The Somme twice. Wounded the first time, patched up and returned the second time to be captured and spend the rest of the war in a German salt mine. Sadly, we have lost his medals and POW papers.

Back to school.

An ignominious corporate incident happened in P3. There were 30 pupils in the room and Miss Love was late arriving to take our class. It invited mischief to leave so many seven-year-olds to arrange their antidote to boredom. I suspect this was when I first heard the "F word." Some scoundrel began shouting the word out loud. It had a ripple effect as more of the class joined in. Eventually, we were all chanting the word at the top of our voices. The noise must have reverberated around the school because suddenly, the classroom door burst open, and in charged Mrs McCandless, the Headmistress with Miss Love. Our version of a team-building event resulted in the class receiving a severe reprimand, followed by Miss Love smacking everyone several times with her ruler. A good lesson learned the hard way. I never swore again for the remainder of my school days.

Woodvale PS only taught up to P5. For P5 & P6 we transferred to Glenwood Primary School in Upper Riga Street, Belfast. I must hold the record for the most corporal punishments in one day. Mr Clarke, my P6 teacher didn't approve of talking during class so he administered "two of the best" to me for breaking his prohibition. He used his two-foot ruler. Ouch! I couldn't help telling my friend beside me how much my hand hurt so I was called out to the front again. Smack. Two more of the best. When I sat down this time, I turned to those behind and told them how much my hands hurt. Some people are slow learners. "McDonald," shouted Mr Clarke, "Out to the front." Two more of the best. Maybe I earned a little respect from him because I never cried.

I enjoyed P7 taught by Mr Love although I became a suspect in an unrequited love affair. Elaine Simpson, who lived in Woodvale Street was a real stunner to us 11-year-old boys. She looked very mature for her age and someone had taken quite a shine to her, to the extent of sending her love letters. Her father didn't take too kindly to the attention his daughter was receiving and reported the matter to the Headmaster and Mr Love. We all had to write out Elaine Simpson ten times. Our scholarly judges subsequently checked our efforts. The poor lovelorn couldn't spell Simpson correctly.

He spelt it "Simson." Well, so did I and a few others so I don't know if that case was ever resolved satisfactorily. Maybe, the case will be reopened, and I'll be asked for a DNA sample. Keep watching True Crime. My favourite time was when Mr Love read us chapters from Tom's Midnight Garden by Philippa Pearce. This is when my fascination with books and literature began. Good teachers are inspirational and priceless.

At the end of P7, I failed my Eleven Plus.

Sometimes it's not what you know but who you know. My Dad was the Property Convenor in Townsend Street Presbyterian Church. A fellow Elder was David Caruthers, a teacher with connections in the teaching establishment whose wife taught Mathematics at the Boys' Model School on Ballysillan Road. After David had my Eleven Plus results investigated, I was invited to sit an entrance examination for the Boys' Model.

The Boys' Model, under Principal Norman McNeilly and Vice-Principal Ernie Davies, was the first school in the UK to split its curriculum into grammar and technical streams. After my entrance examination, I was deemed capable of joining the grammar stream for which I am eternally grateful.

Lessons were hard, discipline was tough, and homework abounded, but I enjoyed almost every minute. I earned the nickname "Mysteron" after the baddies in Joe 90. Why? Probably, because I didn't curse and swear like some other boys. I was never bullied because I was best friends with Tommy Smith from Ottawa Street. Tommy was big for his age, and I was protected by his reputation for enjoying a good punch-up. His reputation must have been based on his looks because I never witnessed him deliberately hurt anyone.

Teachers left their marks on me. George Clingan slapped me across the face every time I answered an English grammar question incorrectly. At the end of the class, he had the decency to ask me, "Are you alright McDonald?"

I trust you appreciate the care I've taken with my spelling, grammar and pronunciation marks. This is all down to George and the appreciation he taught me for the English language. I was awarded Northern Ireland O Levels in English Grammar and English Literature. Northern Ireland O Levels were tough examinations before they were replaced by the London-based GCSE system. All in the interest of bringing N. Ireland examination standards into line with the rest of the United Kingdom. "Dumbing Down" had begun.

Cecil King was our Geography teacher. Another disciplinarian but a fantastic teacher who gave me great interest in the subject. While we were studying The Black Country and the Welsh and Scottish coal mines, Mr King worked on writing his very own Geography textbook. No typewriter or word processor and computers were in the distant future. He wrote it all using stencils. Carefully, adding each word by rubbing a pencil over the desired letters. He also took us for Religious Education. We had to sing hymns and learn Bible verses.

I discovered Mr King was a Seventh Day Adventist and drove a huge, blue Cadillac. He took us through Daniel's prophecies to predict when Christ would return to the exact day and hour. As it turned out, the Bible is correct when it says, "No one knows about that day or hour." Matthew 24:36. Even Mr King. He believed the 1967 Six-Day War in Israel pre-empted Christ's return. A strange thing happened one day. Mr McNeilly appeared and asked Mr King to step out into the corridor. That was the last time Mr King was ever seen in the school. He didn't even come back for his belongings. I've often wondered what could have happened and wished it had been the last we saw of Mr McNeilly instead.

Joe Cowan, our French teacher, all mean five feet of him, caned Tommy Smith and myself because I copied a French homework from Tommy. I should have known better. Tommy lived in Ottawa Street; he made English sound difficult, never mind French and I copied his mistakes. Even "tough" Tommy admitted Joe hurt him that day. I called with Tommy one Sunday at lunchtime to check another homework; I'm a slow learner, and he invited me in. Sunday dinner that day for Tommy, his two brothers, sister, mother and father was a bowl of porridge. It made me appreciate what my parents were able to provide for our family. I get annoyed when someone says, "I'm starving." No, you're not. You've never starved and, hopefully never will. You are just a selfish idiot who thinks the world revolves around you and your needs. Sorry, rant over.

Joe was on the receiving end one afternoon. "The Colonel" was absent that day and Joe was sent to take his class of 4G. Let me explain. Year 4 consisted of two grammar classes O1A and O1B. They were followed by the technical classes 4A, 4B, 4C, 4D, 4E, 4F and 4G in descending order of intellectual capabilities and respect for authority. Comparing 4G to Neanderthals would be unfair to our ancestors. Joe didn't grasp he wasn't dealing with "nice" grammar stream pupils and decided to apply his usual method of class control. He called two lads to the front for insubordination and gave each of them six of the proverbial best with his three-foot cane. The two boys looked at one another, looked at Joe, then proceeded to give him a beating; they were ably supported by other members of the class who felt obliged to avenge their friends.

Joe should have considered himself fortunate to survive with only a few cuts and a bruised ego. One of the pupils was Lenny Murphy later renowned as a member of a murder gang called The Shankill Butchers. Lenny met his end in 1982 when he was murdered by the IRA. After his beating, "Wee Joe" decided he didn't want to teach anymore and joined the ranks of The Northern Ireland Civil Service. I last met him at Argyle Business Centre on Shankill Road. He came out of the Making Belfast Work office where Rhonda worked. I greeted him, "Bonjour Monsieur Cowan." He mumbled, "Hello," and kept on walking. Wee Joe confirmed he was a particularly unpleasant person and no great loss to the Education Authority or the Civil Service when he resigned from it as well. Bon débarras Monsieur Cowan.

Robert Dinsmore, a Physics teacher, could put the fear of God into anyone who displeased him. Norvel McClurg wasn't paying attention one day. Nowadays, Norvel would probably be labelled with ADHD and allowed to sit and do nothing. No such thing existed in the Boys' Model. Dinsmore crept round behind Norvel, put his mouth to Norvel's ear and screamed, "McClurg." Norvel jumped so hard his knees cracked the underside of the bench and the poor lad turned bright crimson with shock and embarrassment. Norvel was awarded a Northern Ireland, O Level in Physics. Well done Norvel and Mr Dinsmore. Norvel went on to run his own printing company.

Some teachers applied other forms of corporal punishment. "Blinkers" Cassidy taught Mathematics and ripped a sleeve off a miscreant's blazer in a fit of temper, much to our amusement. In modern parlance, Mr Cassidy was a few French Fries short of a Happy Meal. Perhaps this was when the Gilet was invented. Trevor Hazlett, another English teacher and ex-basketball player liked to use "The Slipper." My backside was on the receiving end one day. Haslett was six feet six inches tall. Imagine the height the slipper came down from. When it connected with my backside, everything went blank. He didn't need to hit me twice. A big thank you to Joe Boylan, our Chemistry teacher who gave me a fascination for the subject. "Ma Caruthers" taught me Pure Maths which I'm still interested in today. I didn't do well in Additional Maths; I could never understand Sets and Indices. It was the only O Level I failed.

The Boys' Model has been rebuilt. One of the new buildings is named after my old Principal, Norman McNeilly. This wee man, all five feet of him put the fear of God into everyone, pupils and teachers alike. Everyone dreaded the "click, click, click" of his steel-tipped heels as he walked down the corridors. We would all hold our breath until we heard him pass our classroom and disappear down the corridor. One day, it was our turn. Mr Smith, another Physics teacher, was taking the class when the clicking stopped outside our door and Norman entered. Everyone stood to attention and waited to be told, "Sit." Bearing in mind this was a Physics class, Norman wanted to check our grasp of the subtleties of the English Language for some reason. "YOU," he shouted, pointing at me. I felt my sphincter twitch. "Which football match were you at on Saturday?" He enquired. Unlike Dad, I had no interest in football and had never been to a football match. This is easy I thought. "I wasn't at a football match on Saturday," I replied. SLAP, right across my face. "I'll ask you again boy, which football match were you at on Saturday?" I was beginning to wonder if I had been to a football match and suffering from early-stage Dementia. "I wasn't at a football match on Saturday," I reiterated. SLAP, the other cheek this time. "I didn't ask you if you weren't at a football match, I asked you which football match you were at." I think the whole class, including Mr Smith, was baffled at this stage and I was completely embarrassed. Just in case you are confused as well, the answer I should have given was, "I was at no football match on Saturday, sir."

Who needed school bullies when teachers did the bullying?

Another injustice occurred when someone threw their lunch out a window. It landed on the roof of a Portacabin, scattering egg and onion sandwiches across the roof. No one owned up when questioned so Mr McNeilly caned everyone in the room, including myself. Not that I was paranoid, but he did pick on me again one morning. The Special Bus that departed every morning from Twaddell Avenue was delayed and around 50 pupils arrived late in assembly. Why that was my fault I'll never know. Mr McNeilly picked me out of all the latecomers and caned me in front of the school. That was the only time I told my parents I had been punished in school. Dad wrote a letter to the Principal and sealed it in an envelope. I never opened it and Dad never told me what he'd written. I delivered it to Mr McNeilly. That was the last time he ever bothered me. Maybe Dad mentioned that hatchet he kept under the stairs and what he would do with it. I never asked him. I can take criticism and punishment if I have done wrong. It would be an understatement to say I become annoyed if I am accused in the wrong.

This was the catalyst that ignited my genetic bias toward authority that would cause me so much grief in life.

One of the proudest days of my life was when Dad walked me to the public telephone at The McCallum Hall on Woodvale Road to call the school and ask for my O Level results. No one had telephones in their homes. Out of nine examinations I sat, I passed eight with credits. As mentioned, I failed Additional Mathematics. Dad was jubilant and proud of his son. Mum was ecstatic and took the opportunity to visit school and speak with my form teachers to ask what they advised for my future.

Mr Smith told Mum, "Stephen is university material," and advised her I should return at the beginning of term and begin A Levels. Considering university education was free then, big decisions had to be made. However, I decided to leave school at sixteen. Rash? Yes. It was one of the best decisions I ever made.

A short time later, something happened, that meant I couldn't have completed any degree course I had begun. Back then, I never realised God is always in control. I'm proud of the fact I went to the Boys' Model School which took boys from working-class families, with holes in their pants and turned them into Doctors & Scientists, with a few idiots along the way. In my case, the school turned out someone who wasn't quite sure what to do. However, God knew. He had a plan for me.

In 1986, I passed my HNC with Endorsements in Telecommunications after I resat the examination due to medical reasons. Someone advised me all qualifications have a "shelf-life." In other words, my 1986 HNC wouldn't hold much value if I applied for a position in a different telecom company five or ten years later, simply because technology is always evolving, and my technical knowledge would be past its sell-by date. The best way to future-proof a qualification is to become a member of a professional body and take letters after your name. In other words, play the game.

I applied to join the Institute of Electrical and Electronic Incorporated Engineers. I was accepted as a full member after an interview with the institute's representatives at the University of Ulster, Jordanstown. I was also accepted into the Institution of Engineering and Technology. Membership in both enhanced my earning potential and career prospects regardless of when I obtained my qualification. For five years, I had letters after my name. I could write Stephen

McDonald MIEEIE IEng. However, yearly subscriptions to each institute became too big a financial burden when I was rebuilding my life after Jennifer and I separated. However, I still have two letters after my name. I received my BA in 1992. It didn't cost me a penny. Someone else paid the full price. "Born Again."

"For I know the plans I have for you," Declares the Lord, "plans to prosper you and not to harm you, plans to give you hope and a future." Jeremiah 29:11.

Trouble Brewing

I believe I never met a Roman Catholic until I started work when I was sixteen years old in 1969. I never realised until then what it meant to have been brought up in the Protestant community of the Shankill and Woodvale Roads. There was never a mention of Catholics at home, and we were certainly never taught to treat anyone else differently. However, that didn't mean others weren't taught to hate based on faith and religion; that became apparent to me from the age of five.

Granny and Granda Kirk lived at 54 Dover Street. This was a large attic house on the corner of Upper Cargill Street which ran down to cross over Boundary Street before it joined Townsend Street. In 1959 I was a member of the 29th Life Boy Company in Townsend Street Presbyterian Church, equivalent of today's Anchor Boys. However, in those days we wore a blue uniform with a lanyard attached to our badge and a sailor's hat bearing the name of our company. On a Monday evening in spring, I said my goodbyes and left for church at 6:30 pm. I was crossing Boundary Street when a stranger ran up and threw pepper in my eyes. I screamed in pain until I made it back to Dover

Street and my grandparents bathed my eyes. Who taught that person to hate someone or something so badly they would try and blind a five-year-old boy?

In 1966, on my 13th birthday, I was at Falls Road Baths with the 29th BB Company learning how to swim. I left to walk home and went into Dunville Park to use the toilet. I felt a tap on my shoulder. When I turned around, I was punched in the face and called, "a Protestant bastard," because I was wearing a BB Buttonhole badge. When I arrived home, my face had swollen, and my left eye was closed. No one realised my nose was broken and the damage wasn't properly repaired until 50 years later when I had surgery to remove nasal polyps and the surgeon realigned my nostrils with the nasal cavities in my skull. How's that for a long waiting time? My birthday party proceeded that evening. Mum baked a cake and Dad gave me a watch with my name engraved on back. I couldn't see properly when Mum handed me the cake and I dropped it on the floor. Hugh and Martha Boyd joked for years afterwards, "Have you any hairy cake, Hazel?" When they called for a cup of tea.

In 1969, I left school and was looking for work. My old school friend Ivan McStea invited me to his home in Wheatfield Crescent at the top of Crumlin Road. We played with his Scalextric Set and played records until 10 pm when I told him I had to go home. He lent me several LPs including two by John Fahey and Louden Wainwright. It was raining as I walked home, and I placed the albums under my Parka to keep them dry.

I got as far as Ardoyne Fire Station when I was stopped by someone who asked if I could say the Hail Mary. I didn't reply and pushed the lad out of my way. Survivor instinct kicked in and I ran as fast as possible towards Woodvale Road. I was a good runner and might have made it to safety only I was trying to protect Ivan's records. I made it as far as Holy Cross Church when I was tripped and fell to the pavement. I was kicked around the head and saw bright flashes as my head split open and blood pooled around me. I only heard footsteps running away as I couldn't see anything. Cars drove past but no one stopped to help.

 Two young lads found me and helped me to my feet. They walked me the rest of the way home, each supporting me with an arm under each of mine. By the time we reached Woodvale Street, I looked a real mess with my face and clothes covered in blood. I never saw Dad as angry as he was that night when he saw the state of his son. He thanked the Good Samaritans, went to our cubby hole, dug out the hatchet he used for chopping firewood and told my mother he was heading to Ardoyne to wreak revenge.

By then the word was out in the street what had happened and neighbours began calling to see what they could do to help. The first thing that helped was taking the hatchet off my Dad and hiding it. Mr Bell from across the street owned a car and volunteered to drive me to casualty at the RVH. After a wash and twenty stitches, I nearly looked human again.

Ena Hoy was Woodvale Street's version of Dot Cotton. She ran the launderette on the corner of Glenvale Street and Woodvale Road. Ena asked Mum for my bloodied clothes and took them away in a plastic bag. A few days later, Ena returned my clothes, washed and ironed; she refused to take any payment from Mum.

This was when a choice would make a huge difference in my life. After my beating, I was a prime candidate to join one of the paramilitary groups forming at the start of "The Troubles." I certainly didn't consider myself a Christian, but something nagged my conscience about seeking revenge. I had been attending church and going to BB all rather reluctantly. Perhaps, somewhere in my subconscious, I had stored "It is mine to avenge, I will repay" Hebrews: 10 v 30. I decided more violence wasn't the answer, but I needed to do something to help prevent what happened to me from happening to others.

On reflection, I was fortunate this beating occurred in 1969, before the official beginning of "The Troubles." A year or two later, those lads might have been armed and I could have been shot or stabbed to death. Innocent people were murdered daily, simply for being from a different denomination, in the wrong place at the wrong time. Very dangerous days.

My friend Tommy Smith had a similar epiphany. Tommy was already involved in violence, taking part in riots between "Prods and Taigs" occurring daily in Flax Street off Crumlin Road near Ardoyne. This was a flashpoint between the Catholic and Protestant communities. What were once mixed neighbourhoods were becoming polarised with one side trying to force the other out of their homes and the RUC trying to keep the factions apart. Tommy stuffed newspapers into his Donkey Jacket to soften potential blows from bricks and bottles thrown in his direction. Tommy and his "comrades" broke through the police line one evening aiming to cause as much mayhem and damage as possible. The police gave chase and one shrewd officer caught up with Tommy. He didn't hit Tommy anywhere he was expecting. The officer brought his baton down sharply on Tommy's right kneecap. Tough, Tommy Smith was sick with pain and limped home, never to partake in another riot. Lesson learned. Violence hurts both ways.

Like me, he joined the Ulster Defence Regiment in 1972. He didn't exactly have a distinguished service record. Tommy was guarding the gate into BLUE 5, the call sign for the water pumping station off Westland Road where our platoon was on duty when shots were heard from nearby Oldpark Road. We cocked our SLRs and tried to establish if we were under attack. Eventually, all clear was given and we lined up to "clear" our weapons into a pit surrounded by sandbags. Tommy forgot he had loaded a round into the breech of his rifle and the safety was off. BANG!!! His rifle wasn't even pointed at the sandbags. The 7.62mm round went through the wall of the guardhouse, through an electrical conjugate and blew all the lights. In his panic, Tommy forgot what the "SL" stands for in SLR. "SELF LOADING." Fortunately, he was pointing his rifle at the sandbags when it discharged again, and no one was injured. He was fined £100 for two accidental discharges. That was a huge amount of money then and Tommy volunteered for extra duties to pay it off. He realised he got off lightly considering what could've happened.

That cracked kneecap probably saved Tommy from jail or worse. Tommy married his childhood sweetheart Violet when they were both 18. He ran his own security and satellite TV installation company. Tommy's final job was with Belfast City Council in charge of retail security in Belfast City Centre before ill health forced him to retire. They lived in Spain until Violet's death in February 2024. They had been happily married for 53 years.

Service Please

After recovering from my beating at Ardoyne in July 1969, I said to myself, "I don't want this to happen to anyone else." A fine ambition but how could I put my words into action? So, I put the matter to the back of my mind and got on with looking for work while Belfast and the rest of N. Ireland were about to be transformed by unfolding events.

The Troubles in Northern Ireland began with a banned Civil Rights march in Londonderry on October 5th, 1968. The march led to clashes between police and protesters, which sparked widespread disorder and rioting across Northern Ireland. For many, this is when 30 years of violent conflict known as "The Troubles" began. The Civil Rights Movement that formed in Belfast in January 1967 drew inspiration from the campaign for equal rights in the United States led by Martin Luther King. The Northern Ireland Civil Rights Association (NICRA) called for wide-ranging reforms, including equal voting rights in Local Government elections, a fairer system for the allocation of public housing, an end to 'Gerrymandering' which was the manipulation of electoral boundaries to give one community an electoral advantage, an end to discrimination in employment, the disbandment of the 'B-Specials' which was an all-Protestant auxiliary police force, and the repeal of the Special Powers Act which allowed for internment of suspects without trial.

In the wake of riots, the Hunt Report, which provided advice on policing in Northern Ireland, recommended a locally recruited 4,000-man part-time non-sectarian force to take over military duties from the RUC and replace the B Specials. The Ulster Defence Regiment was formed by an Act of Parliament in 1970. And so, the opportunity to counteract violence presented itself to me and I joined the UDR in early 1972. I belonged to 10th Battalion D Company 4th Platoon, based in Girdwood Barracks, Belfast.

Our training was basic and consisted mainly of how to handle firearms. Our main weapons were the Belgium FL SLR 7.62mm and Browning 9mm SMG. Incredibly, in the early days of hostilities, some recruits didn't have weapons. One Friday morning, our platoon was sent to relieve another stationed at Fairmount off the Antrim Road. When we arrived, two sentries were guarding the entrance with baseball bats. That was a scene straight from Dad's Army. Later, I was washing potatoes for our platoon's evening meal when I heard a series of explosions, one after another. It was 21st of July 1972. At least twenty bombs exploded across the city in the space of 80 minutes, most within a half-hour period. Nine people were killed, six civilians, two British soldiers, a Royal Ulster Constabulary reservist and 130 were injured. Six of the fatalities took place in Oxford Street Bus Station. That is my memory of Bloody Friday, peeling potatoes while innocent people were being murdered.

In 1972, I was working for Post Office Telecommunications set up as a division of the Post Office in October 1969. Working full time, I volunteered in the evenings and reported to my Platoon Commander, Major Drewitt, at Girdwood Barracks in Cliftonpark Avenue. After kitting up and putting on flak jackets we reported to the armoury and signed for our weapons before leaving on our allocated patrols. Some of the patrol sites were preferable to others. Blue Five was the Waterworks off Oldpark Road, where Tommy Smith had his accidental discharges. Red Nine was the dole office in Corporation Street. I never figured out why Army intelligence thought the IRA would attack the office where "their heroes" collected their benefits every week. My least favourite posting was Black One. It was aptly named. This was the Gasworks on Ormeau Road, now an industrial park and location of the

Gasworks Hotel. It stank of coal gas and the barracks was dirty. It was grim work patrolling the site and quite dangerous. In adjacent Eliza Street, was a dividing wall between the Gasometers and Inglis's bakery creating a 50 yard alleyway. On two occasions, when terrorists heard patrols' footsteps in the alleyway, they lobbed nail bombs over the wall. We learned to tiptoe in our army boots.

Part of our military service was to attend a week-long camp at Ballykinler Army Barracks, outside Newcastle, Co. Down. To qualify for our "Bounty payment" of £30 we had to hit a target 14 times with 30 shots from 600 yards. I'm unsure who I inherited my skill set from, but I excelled on the rifle range and hit my target 16 times. Quite good when you consider the target was barely visible and wind direction together with "drop" had to be factored in. Accuracy is not as simple as aiming straight at a target. I might have been a Company Marksman, only for another member of our Platoon, named Chancellor Cuttie. As his name might suggest, Chancellor was a chancer and as blind as a bat. He circumnavigated the part eyesight had to play in obtaining his bounty by arranging for his co-conspirator and friend, Bobby Orr, to man the Butts beside Chancellor's target. I'm reliably informed Chancellor didn't hit his target once, but Bobby stuck black tape over the "pretend" holes in Chancellor's target while calling out the results to the sergeant keeping marks of hits on the targets. Chancellor managed 18 hits "on target" and was awarded "Company Marksman." Hilarious.

To celebrate, Sergeant McIlwaine and Corporal Cosgrove took our platoon to Sands Home for the evening to enjoy some beers. Then, Sands Home was outside the perimeter of Ballykinler Barracks, and we had to show our passes to the sentries before we were allowed to re-enter the camp. Oh dear! I had forgotten mine and ordered to report to the kitchens at 5 am the following morning. I expected to be on breakfast duty; instead, I was shown how to peel the skin off chickens and prepare them for boiling in huge vats for that evening's meal. Aaaaagh! After breakfast, a sergeant appeared and shouted he was looking for volunteers to travel to Belfast. I shot my hand up......anything to get out of that kitchen. I packed my gear and climbed into a waiting Land Rover. As we exited the gates, the same sentry who had checked me the night before was on duty. I shouted at him and gave him the universal two-finger salute. Little did I know that I had volunteered for Operation Motorman.

Operation Motorman was carried out on 31st of July 1972 by 27 battalions of the British Army. It aimed to break down Catholic "No-Go" barricades in West Belfast, along with the Bogside and Creggan in Londonderry. This is when I completed my six weeks of continuous duty which qualified me for the Northern Ireland Service Medal. I wear it with Dad's medals each year on Remembrance Sunday. Long hours and long patrols. One such patrol was at 6 am through Cornmarket in Belfast City Centre. Just as we crossed the road, a newspaper lorry appeared, and the driver began throwing bundles of Sunday papers off the back of his lorry. We were shocked to see our platoon's group photograph on the front page of the Irish Times with the title, "Proof of Collusion in the North."

During our week's camp in Ballykinler, we had posed for a group photograph outside our barracks. Five of us were in the back row. Along with those in the middle, we weren't aware the group kneeling at the front had unfurled a Vanguard Flag. The Ulster Vanguard movement was originally a political pressure group within the UUP. It was formed on 9th of February 1972 and was led by William Craig. The photograph was taken by Sergeant, Ivor McMaster, who naively left his film into the Co-op in York Street to have it developed. Ivor was disciplined and demoted for committing a serious security breach and public relations disaster for the UDR.

I risked my life on patrol with some decent, brave soldiers but I also rubbed shoulders with some scoundrels who eventually brought their uniform into disrepute. I met some members of my platoon when they were manning UVF and UDA barricades. Some, I had been on duty with the previous night. It made it difficult to know who I could trust if we were attacked. Those traitors earned the biggest regiment in the British Army a reputation as a sectarian organisation. This sullied the memory of those members murdered by the IRA. Over 190 UDR soldiers were killed on active service, the vast majority by Republican paramilitaries. Another 61 were killed after leaving the regiment.

I knew more members of the regiment who shot themselves through accidental discharges than were shot by terrorists. A sergeant who shot himself in the hand was discharged from the regiment. I know another self-inflicted casualty very well. Cousin Edward and friend left Girdwood after a night's patrol and drove along the Sydenham bypass towards Holywood. The car in front suffered a blowout and swerved across their path. Thinking the worst, that they were about to be attacked, Edward reached into the glove department and pulled out his friend's "personal weapon," a Browning 9mm automatic. This is when testosterone, adrenaline and inexperience make a lethal cocktail. Edward had never handled this weapon before. When they realised it was all a false alarm, Edward tried to make the gun safe and shot himself in the left leg.

The bullet went through his shin and into the chassis of the car. To stop the bleeding, Edward inserted his right index finger into the entry wound and his left index finger into the exit wound. Fortune shone on Edward that day. When they reached the junction where Knocknagoney Tesco is today, there was a police roadblock The RUC officers administered First Aid and called an ambulance. The ambulance duly arrived with a nurse and paramedic onboard. Edward was helped into the ambulance and the nurse put her arms around him and held tight to keep him from going into shock. Edward told me, "The nurse was beautiful. If my leg hadn't hurt so much, I would have enjoyed myself." I visited Edward in hospital where he spent 14 weeks recovering from his wound. Amazingly, the patient in the next bed was up and walking on crutches before Edward could get out of bed. He was a young Roman Catholic targeted by the UVF simply because of his religion, shot 14 times and dumped at waste ground on

Springfield Road. I guess he wasn't shot with a Browning 9mm.

I was nineteen when I served in the UDR. I was growing up quickly in a violent world where my beliefs and values were being challenged daily through my experiences with other people. I had joined the University of Life. One Sunday morning, we were ordered to accompany a platoon of Paratroopers to familiarise them with the New Lodge Road area of Belfast. Then as now, it is staunchly Republican. I didn't bother to speak to my six-foot, black Paratrooper companion.

As far as Paratroopers were concerned, we were "crap hats" and didn't deserve their attention. I stood beside this man from dawn to dusk without a word between us. As it grew dark, our sergeant appeared with a tube of camouflage cream and ordered me to rub some of the cream over my face and cap badge. He jokingly remarked to my "chum," "Well, you don't need any," and moved on to the rest of our platoon. A little boy of around six appeared and walked over to where I was crouching beside the Paratrooper. He took one look at me, stared at my companion then moved in for a closer look. I can say for certain, in Belfast in 1972, on the New Lodge Road, this was the first black man this child had ever seen. He was fascinated. Up to then, Mr Paratrooper hadn't noticed the boy or had chosen to ignore him.

The boy plucked up his courage, reached up and pulled the Paratrooper's flak jacket. The soldier stared down at him and said, "Yeah?" The boy asked, "Are you a Catholic or a Protestant?" Verbatim, our friendly soldier replied, "F??k off kid, it's bad enough being a Ni?er." On further occasions, we discovered Paratroopers considered themselves a law unto themselves. In hindsight, everyone would admit the Parachute Regiment should never have been sent to Northern Ireland. They exacerbated the violence; they became the IRA's greatest recruitment tool; they disgraced themselves and the British Army.

Mr Strowger

You probably have never heard of the man to whom I owed my livelihood and 31 of the best working years of my life.

Almon Brown Strowger was an American inventor who gave his name to the Strowger switch, an electromechanical telephone exchange. He was born on 11th of February 1839, in Penfield, New York, and died on 26th of May 1902, in St. Petersburg, Florida. Strowger's invention was motivated by his undertaking business, which was losing clients to a competitor. Someone manning the switchboard was directing callers looking for the services of an undertaker to one of Strowger's competitors. He invented the first automatic telephone exchange in 1889. The Strowger Automatic Telephone Exchange Company was formed with the help of his nephew William. The company installed and opened the first commercial exchange in La Porte, Indiana, on 3rd of November 1892, with about 75 subscribers. The first automatic telephone exchange in Britain opened in Epsom, Surrey in 1912.

In 1969, to the disappointment of Mr Smith, my Physics teacher, I decided not to return to school and continue with A Levels. I felt I should contribute more at home and began looking for employment. With eight N. Ireland O Levels, I was confident I could have my pick of jobs. Shipbuilding, Sirocco Works, Mackies, Grundig, Michelin, Phillips, Berkshire, Courtaulds, British Enkalon, Setright, ICI, carpet factories and textile manufacturing provided decent jobs and wages for the working class of Belfast. Most of these companies are gone now. They didn't go out of business. They were moved from the Northern Hemisphere to the Southern Hemisphere in a deliberate redistribution of wealth that occurred during the 70s and 80s. Why? That's for another book. Then as now, as the Post Office Scandal has demonstrated so well "little people" didn't count. To investigate how we've all been lied to about climate change, I recommend reading Maurice Strong's obituary in the Daily Telegraph entitled, "Farewell to the man who invented 'Climate Change'" by Christopher Booker dated 5th December 2015. It can still be sourced on the internet.

Because chemistry had been my favourite and strongest subject at school, I set my mind on a scientific career and applied for Chemical Assistant posts in Imperial Chemical Industries and Gallaher's Tobacco. Somewhere, along the way, I applied for a post as a Post Office Telephone Trainee Technician Apprentice. I received replies from ICI and Gallaher's, both invited me to interview. At my interview for Gallaher's, I was asked if I had any moral reservations about working with tobacco. I had never thought about it before because practically everyone I knew smoked. However, It gave me pause for thought and I decided not to pursue this line of work. I passed the interview for ICI and was sent for a medical examination at Whiteabbey Hospital. While waiting on the results, I received an invitation to a job interview for the Post Office at Churchill House in Belfast.

I reported on time and was interviewed by a gentleman called John McAnee. He seemed impressed with my O Level results, produced a bunch of wires and asked me if I could identify the colours. I proved I wasn't colour-blind and received my acceptance letters from ICI and the Post Office simultaneously. My heart was still set on a career involving chemistry, but I had to consider how to get to the ICI plant in Kilroot at 8 am each day. Bad enough if I could drive but I had to make the journey by public transport. I checked the UTA timetables in Winetavern Street depot and realised it would be impossible. So, I reluctantly became a telephone engineer. The Post Office letter advised me to report for duty to its depot in Stewart Street, in the Markets area of Belfast on 18th August 1969 at 8 am. On my first day of school, I was accompanied by my mother. On my first day of work, I was accompanied by my father. There had been serious riots overnight in Belfast. Dad heard on the news that the Albert Bridge was littered with burnt-out buses and cars. He travelled with me to ensure I made it to work without incident.

I didn't realise when I started work, that some of my fellow apprentices would become lifelong friends and remain in touch to this day. My lasting friendships with Alan McKinstry & Greer Sloan began on my first day at work. After completing the requisite paperwork and forms, a staff member explained what we had signed up for and how our training would progress. We were now officially TTAs. Trainee Technician Apprentices. In the next three years, our training would cover all the disciplines that made the telephone network work. We would work externally with gangs on pole erection and overhead duties; we would work on underground cables and distribution networks with "Jointers;" we would work on Internal construction teams building telephone exchanges; we would work on exchange maintenance and subscribers' maintenance before we would be allocated a particular field to begin our careers on the rank of Technician 2A.

Let the fun begin.

In the beginning, everything to do with work and my new colleagues was a culture shock. I didn't realise how sheltered my life had been until I started work. I never swore at school, nor did many of my friends. Here, the air was blue with men who couldn't string sentences together without expletives. I discovered many were ex-servicemen who had joined the GPO after the war through preferential recruitment for ex-servicemen. "You helped your country, now it'll help you," basis. Help your country now, it'll try to forget about you. As well as my sensitivities taking a battering, I also had my cultural shortcomings to address. Until 18th of August 1969, I had never met a Roman Catholic, never mind spoken to one. Until then, my only encounter with Roman Catholics had ended with me in hospital. Hardly a ringing endorsement for cross-community relationship building.

Maybe, I had grown up in a "Protestant ghetto" after all. I was so challenged by the changes in my life, I cried one evening wondering what I was going to do. I read a book entitled The White Rabbit by Bruce Marshall. It is the harrowing and inspiring story of the capture of one of Britain's top SOE agents in World War II and his refusal to crack under horrific torture. In his book Marshall writes "Swearing is a means by which the inarticulate raise themselves to illusions of grandeur." Memorising this helped me cope with life in the workplace. Understanding how other people's behaviour irritated me allowed me to deal appropriately with people who upset me.

The title Post Office Telephones was used until October 1969 when the Post Office ceased to be a Government department. This new division in the Post Office Corporation became Post Office Telecommunications with trademark yellow vans. The change from green vans was mainly for visibility reasons but the new image branding helped to reflect the changed identity and to show the telephone business was a separate part of the Post Office.

The next three years became a continuation of school. Only this was schoolwork with pay. The princely sum of £4 and 10 Shillings per week. In February 1971 that became £4:50 after decimalisation. TTAs' working days were spent between Belfast Technical College with campuses in College Square East, Millfield and the Old Town Hall in Victoria Street where we studied Telecommunication theory, Electrical engineering and Mathematics to achieve our Ordinary National Certificate. We then became students at the Ashby Institute to study for our Higher National Certificate and Endorsements in Telecommunications.

Our initial practical training took place at Killeen, the Post Office's technical training college at Fortwilliam Park, Belfast. We learned the step by step mechanical process from a telephone call initiated by lifting a handset to the call answered by the called party. We were taught how to climb telegraph poles, joint cables, wire up extensions, test lines and adjust mechanical switches called 2000 Type selectors. My first visit to a telephone exchange mesmerised me. The noise: there was nothing to compare with the intriguing mechanical noises of a busy Strowger telephone exchange; the smell of floor polish, the ozone and solder fumes. The pungent smell of sulphuric acid, when batteries were charging, was a cure for anyone with blocked sinuses.

To me, a telephone exchange was a huge Meccano Set on acid.

I had found my niche.

That was when I knew my ambition was to be an exchange Technical Officer.

My apprenticeship culminated in "Field experience" on external duties with Jointers and Pole Erection Gangs. Jointers did exactly what their job title implied. They joined cables. Either new cables had to be connected to the existing network or damaged cables replaced with new sections and tested to ensure all the connections were working correctly. The joints might be underground, in a road, a footpath or on a telegraph pole. I was assigned to work with a jointer called Billy Rennie. Billy was an ex-serviceman who lived in Berlin Street off Shankill Road. Being a "fellow Prod" meant we got on reasonably well together. He even took me to the Berlin Arms one day to introduce "his Youth in Training" to his friends. Fortunately, he only had one pint before he decided we should do some work. We were driving along Antrim Road, passing St. Gerard's Church, when Billy crossed himself. He noticed the confused look on my face and said, "Don't worry Stephen, I only do it for luck."

After Billy passed my jointing skills, I was transferred to a four-man external gang. The T1 gang manager and driver was Tommy. Tommy and his crew were all ex-servicemen and responsible for pole erection and supplying overhead cables. Their lorry had no mechanical aides. Holes for poles were dug by hand using narrow spades, ladles to remove soil and iron bars to break stones. Poles were invariably made from Scots Pine, pressure treated with creosote. The size and type of pole was engraved at the six-foot mark. 30L denoted a 30-foot Light. 30M a 30-foot Medium. This mark also helped gauge how much of the pole was below ground.

I was generally a "gofor" and tea maker while the men got on with the heavy work. "Stephen, gofor the coach bolts." "Stephen, gofor the drop wire." Except for the weather, I quite enjoyed working in the gang. The one thing that struck me, across all the external disciplines, was the pride the men took in their work. There was never anything slapdash or, "Sure that'll do," attitude. Their joint service record led to a sense of comradery; their good-natured banter made for good working relationships. Given the mix of men with different backgrounds and personalities, there was never a dull moment.

On a lashing wet day, we were parked on Earlswood Road waiting for the rain to stop to allow us to replace a damaged telegraph pole. Five of us were huddled in the front of the lorry when Harry announced he needed to go to the loo. He refused to step outside because it was raining heavily. Inside the cab, was a cast iron gas ring connected to a gas cylinder. On top of the gas ring sat "the bailer," not unlike a wok, used for making tea. Ignoring all our protests, Harry grabbed the bailer and relieved himself into it. He slid down the window on the roadside of the cab and tossed the contents out. Oooops! Splash. All over a cyclist in a yellow rain cape. Harry was speechless. Before he could think of what to say, the cyclist said, "Never mind son, it might have been pee."

The 30L pole we replaced is outside the house Brian Funston, the Vice Principal of Campbell College bought in 2005 to add to his property portfolio. He had great difficulty removing the varnish from the bannisters. I'll explain later.

Post Office Telecoms

As part of my three-year apprenticeship, I was assigned to a Subscribers' Line Maintenance group headquartered in North Telephone Exchange in Cliftonpark Avenue, Belfast. Initially, I was to "learn the ropes" by accompanying Line Maintenance engineers on their daily routines responding to customers' fault reports. Before the Internet, customers reported problems with their telephones to operators based in Telephone House. The operators knew, from the customers' number, which telephone exchange area they belonged to and passed the fault report to the relevant, local exchange Repair Centre. Each Repair Centre was manned by dedicated testers who would carry out initial tests on customers' lines. Although testing was quite basic by today's standards, testers could make accurate assessments of what was causing a customer's fault and assign it to the relevant linesman for that area.

North Exchange had three maintenance zones. North 1, North 2 and North 3. North 1 covered the Docks and as far as Antrim and Cliftonville Roads. North 2 covered from Antrim Road to Ballysillan and Silverstream. North 3 covered from Ligoniel to Aldergrove Airport.

I began my Linesman working experience with George Jackson who was responsible for line faults in North 2. George lived in Tigers Bay and was a huge bear of man. He had a fully-grown beard and could have played any Hollywood part made for Finn McCool. Yet with all, he was quietly spoken and gentle-natured. I enjoyed being taught by George and discovered parts of North Belfast I'd never visited before. On 10th November 1971, I was on Day Release when George was asked by control to go to the BBC Transmitter on Divis Mountain to investigate a fault on the landline to the site. After completing his work, he was travelling back to North Telephone Exchange when he was involved in a road traffic accident on Upper Springfield Road in which a pedestrian was seriously injured.

George gave all his details to the police who attended the scene but "Gentle George" wanted more assurance he wasn't in serious trouble. There was only one man to go to. Ian Desmond Nolan. A legend in Subscriber's maintenance circles. Then Ian was in his sixties, slightly built and always wore a long overcoat. Imagine a tidier version of Compo from Last of the Summer Wine. Because of his long years working in North 1, in and out of police stations repairing faults, he knew practically every policeman and was regarded as an oracle because of his wealth of knowledge and contacts. Delphi, for this Oracle, was the lounge bar in the Imperial Hotel, affectionately known as The Mint. The Mint was located on the corner of Cliftonpark Avenue and Cliftonville Road. Long gone now. When George arrived at The Mint, he found Ian in the company of Walter Moore, an RUC officer stationed at Oldpark Road RUC base. George described his accident and Walter assured him, given the circumstances, there shouldn't be any further action by the police.

The next day, Walter and his colleague Dermot Hurley were murdered by the IRA in the rear of a shop situated behind Oldpark RUC base. This was one of the first occasions that drove the reality of "The Troubles" home to me. "Gentle George" was devastated. By the time he returned to work, I had moved on to a different area. Eventually, George was transferred from line maintenance to the transmission staff in Telephone House where we would meet occasionally. Unfortunately, George wasn't the only P O Telecoms person to be affected by murder over the following years.

I moved into North 1 under the wings of I D Nolan and "Wee" Joe Devlin. Ian was the living epitome of "so laid back, he was horizontal." Daily, after collecting the day's faults from North Control, everyone on duty retired to the café in the Midlands Hotel on York Street. Ian didn't go anywhere until he had completed the Daily Mail Cryptic Crossword. One morning, 14 down had him completely stumped. "Right Stephen, time to go." I couldn't believe it. We boarded our van and Ian drove to E T Greens in the Docks. There was no lift and we climbed the stairs to the very top of the building. The smell of grain was suffocating as we walked the length of a narrow corridor to reach the office at the far end. Ian opened the door and said, "Good morning, Sean, what did you get for 14 down?" Clue: Decided, Determined. 8 letters. Answer: Resolved. Ian to a "T." He was delighted when he completed his crossword.

It's good to get one's priorities in the right order. I was Ian's pole climber. Ian had a phobia of climbing poles. He had been blown upside down on a pole outside Andrews' Motorcycle Shop in Gresham Street when his running nose transferred 75 Volts AC ringing current directly to his brain. His safety belt held him fast as his tool wallet emptied its contents into the street below. The last pole he climbed was outside the Limelight Bar on the corner of Dover Street and Shankill Road. He had just secured his safety belt when he had a wardrobe malfunction. Ian attributed "his accident" to a fresh pint of Guinness the thankful bar owner had served him for coming to fix his phone. From that moment, Ian always ensured he had a "Youth in Training" with him to climb poles when necessary.

Ian's career nearly ended with a bang, literally! On 22nd of February 1972, he stopped his van at the bottom of Eia Street where it met the Antrim Road. He was busy checking the traffic for a break to pull out when Tap! Tap! On his window. Ian looked to his side to find himself looking down the barrel of a gun held by a man wearing a balaclava. "Don't move," said the gunman. The rear doors of the van were pulled open, and a bomb was placed in the back of his van. "Take that to York Street Police Station," he was ordered. The bomb exploded, killing seven people including two members of the RUC. Ian was so well known by the police they knew he was innocent of any responsibility for the atrocity. Subsequently, Ian suffered from severe nervous twitches before he retired due to deteriorating health.

The next linesman I trained with was "Wee Joe." Joe Devlin was five feet tall and sat on a cushion to help him see over the bonnet of his van. Joe was middle-aged, quiet and unassuming. The largest customer he was responsible for was Gallaher's Tobacco Factory on York Street, at one time the largest tobacco factory in the world. After a day of working with Joe in the factory, we stank of tobacco. I could taste it for days afterwards in the back of my throat. Aunt Betty worked in the canteen and served us dinners at no charge. No charge, no taste. All I could taste was tobacco.

One morning, I accompanied Joe to fit a Ship to Shore telephone line at a pier where a tanker had recently docked. This involved fitting a coin box-operated telephone on board at a convenient place for the crew, running out the connecting cable with a plug connected to the local telephone distribution point fitted on the pier. When we ran out the drum of cable on the ship, there wasn't enough cable to reach the pier. Oh dear! Back to the supply depot for another drum of cable? "Hold on," said Joe. "I have an idea," and off he went to the Bridge. "Excuse me, Captain, any chance you could back her back fifty?" Well! No harm in trying. If the ship hadn't been docked, the Captain might have had Joe keel hauled. Joe appeared vacant at times. He didn't talk much and sometimes forgot where he was meant to be. I became his navigator and tracked where we were meant to be. If Joe remembered, he would drop me home on the way back to garage his van at Ballysillan Depot. I always carried bus fare. Just in case.

The last linesman I trained with was John Martin. This was March 1972, and I had recently joined the UDR. John was one of the first Catholics I worked with. He lived in West Belfast and held my life in his hands. Those were very dangerous days. Innocent people were murdered daily. I was a serving British soldier working with a Catholic in parts of Belfast into which I would normally never venture. I didn't know John's politics and trusted I didn't become another statistic. John tried to help by collecting me from home when I had been on duty the previous night. John was a decent man and a good engineer. He taught me never to judge people because of their religion. It transpired he had served in the army in the 1950s.

August 1972 saw the end of my apprenticeship. I was duly promoted to the rank of Technician 2A. All my fellow trainees were promoted as well. Some were appointed to construction duties, and some to internal maintenance duties. Someone thought I would make a good linesman and, I was delighted to join the subscribers' maintenance team responsible for the North Telephone Exchange area. However, there was just one other thing I needed to do.

Before I became an independent Subscriber Linesman, I had to learn to drive. Because Post Office Telecoms owned and maintained its own fleet of vehicles, I had to pass the Post Office's commercial vehicle driving test. This was more demanding than the standard driving test taken by the public. My lessons were taken in a Morris 1000 van. A sturdy old workhorse that was a common sight on the roads in the early 70s. I was given around ten lessons before my instructor directed me to report to the Ballysillan Depot one Monday morning in October 1972 to take my driving test.

As requested, I reported to the depot at 8 am on a bright, cold morning to find three other would-be linesmen waiting to sit their driving test. Gerry Fitzpatrick, Stephen Potter and Greer Sloan joined me to wait nervously for the driving examiner. Our examiner was Mr Carson. He was a legend in the Post Office Driving School. Mr Carson was renowned and feared by all trainee drivers. Dour, strict, and famed for his high failure rate. He wore a brown dust coat, a tweed cap, a pair of glasses and carried the ubiquitous clipboard. He was straight out of Central Casting for Carry On Driving.

"Right Potter, you're first," intoned Mr Carson. We all wished Stephen good luck as he got into the driver's seat and buckled up. Mr Carson clambered into the passenger seat and told us they should be back in around one hour. As it turned out, they returned in around 15 minutes. Stephen got out of the car with a red failure slip in his hand. We asked him what happened. "When I got to the junction of the Ballysillan and Oldpark Road, Carson asked me to use hand signals to indicate that I was about to make a right turn. I wound down my window, put my arm out, and changed to third gear." "Turn around, you've failed," shouted Mr Carson. "What? Why?" Declared Stephen. "You didn't have any hands on the steering wheel, you idiot." After a short debrief with Stephen, Mr Carson approached the remaining examinees.

"Right, McDonald. You're next."

Nervously, I climbed into the driving seat; I adjusted the mirror and my seat before putting on my seatbelt. "Off you go then," said Mr Carson, "Follow my directions and instructions." I did as instructed and relaxed more as our journey continued through Glengormley and on to Whiteabbey where Mr Carson told me to head back along the Antrim Road. He directed me to turn right and drive up the Cavehill Road, back towards our starting point at the Ballysillan Road depot. Near the top, on the left-hand side was a row of shops with a lay-by for customer parking. "Pull into the lay-by McDonald and park. I want to buy a packet of cigarettes," said Mr Carson.

I pulled into the lay-by, stopped the engine and released my seat belt. Mr Carson got out of the van and entered the newsagents. I was waiting, looking out the windscreen when I noticed another car at the far end of the lay-by start to roll back. It was a green Austin A40 and was gradually gathering speed, not towards me but diagonally towards the road. I looked in my mirrors and saw a school bus full of pupils from the Girls' Model driving towards the junction with Ballysillan Road. I started the van, put it in gear and drove into the back of the A40. BANG!! The closing speed with the errand vehicle was around 20mph. I was thrown forward and banged my head on the steering wheel.

I was sitting dazed and shocked when Mr Carson appeared outside the crashed vehicles shouting and calling me all the expletives he could think of. "Look, look what you've done. Are you mad or just crazy?" He bellowed at the top of his voice. "Stop shouting at that young lad" I heard someone say. "He's just prevented a serious accident. I forgot to put my handbrake on." The driver of the A40 had been alerted by the noise of the collision and realised what might have happened if I hadn't prevented his car from rolling into the path of the school bus. Mr Carson stood gobsmacked before he asked me if I could still drive the van. Yes, and despite the van being badly damaged I drove back to the depot.

I can still see the faces of Gerry Fitzpatrick, Greer Sloan, and Stephen Potter when they watched me drive through the gates and park the van. The front of the van was crushed, and the headlights were hanging on by their electrical connections. My three colleagues were doubled over, convulsed with laughter. Mr Carson and I extricated ourselves. Mr Carson, despite his reputation, appreciated the situation and, so that everyone could hear, said loudly, "Well done McDonald, that was an exceptional piece of driving. You have passed your driving test with flying colours" and handed me a green Pass slip. My three colleagues stared at me, speechless. I suspect I'm the only person ever to have caused a crash during their driving test and passed.

Another learner didn't fare as well as me in his driving test. Mr Carson took Billy Cameron on his test from the PO Telecom depot in Ballarat Street. Billy stopped at the exit to the Ormeau Embankment, looked left, looked right, and drove straight on into the side of a fully loaded Co-Op milk float. The milk float toppled onto its side and bottles of milk spilled their contents into the River Lagan. "Cameron, just reverse back in. You've failed." Billy is the proud record holder for the shortest driving test ever. Stephen Potter eventually passed his driving test. How? I don't know. He knocked a cyclist off his bicycle in Duncairn Gardens. The cyclist accepted his bribe of £5 to, "Keep it quiet." We joked he should have hit a Free Presbyterian; it wouldn't have cost him anything. He managed to reverse into a brand-new Bedford lorry in Ballarat Street. The lorry had just been delivered and still had manufacturer's stickers on the bodywork. He swept the debris under the lorry and drove off before anyone noticed.

So, now I was a fully qualified solo linesman with my own yellow van. I was assigned to North 2 which had a rich mixture of business and residential subscribers. However, one of the first maintenance calls I made was to the Army Operations room at Leopold Street Police Station to repair the landline. I was shown into the room which was a buzz of activity where a newly arrived Major was being briefed. A large map of N Ireland was displayed on a wall and the different coloured counties were being pointed out and described to the officer. Any questions sir? Asked the Adjutant. "Yes, what's that blue county in the middle?" Enquired the major. "Oh, that's Lough Neagh sir?" They mustn't teach geography at Sandhurst.

Coincidentally, in October 1972, a proud Mr and Mrs McDonald of 23 Woodvale Street, were added to the Post Office Telecoms list of residential customers. They had waited two years from their application for a telephone to be installed. A cream-coloured 746 Type Telephone, number 744772. I naively told the telephone exchange staff about our family's latest requisition before leaving to work on that day's faults. One of the faults I dealt with was on the switchboard at Ballygomartin Road Brick Works, now the site of a large Tesco. After repairing the fault, I was sitting in the driver's seat marking up my faults' diary when a loaded articulated lorry drove by and began turning left towards the exit to the main road. I realised the turn was too tight to prevent a collision. I unclicked my seatbelt and jumped over to the passenger seat just as the edge of the back trailer opened the driver's side of my van like a tin opener. The lorry driver couldn't see me in his mirrors and must never have felt the collision due to the tons of bricks on his lorry.

As soon as the lorry turned down Ballygomartin Road, I jumped back in the driver's seat, started the engine and took off after the lorry. I followed him down Crumlin Road flashing my lights, but he never stopped. All I could do was note the registration number and drive back to North Telephone Exchange. I parked outside the exchange on Cliftonpark Avenue, entered the exchange and went upstairs to the Area Engineer's office to tell him what had happened. "Whistlin' Bob" McCandless was a gentleman from the old school. Always dapperly dressed and gifted with a delightful quirk to his voice which made it sound as though he was speaking through a referee's whistle. I told Bob what had happened. He looked out his window, saw the van with its driver's side ripped open and asked if it was still driveable. Bob said he would arrange repairs; "In the meantime take young Sam Montgomery out with you and let him drive. He has just passed his driving test." We boarded the van and headed to North 3 to visit a customer on the Seven Mile Straight. "We've gone too far," I said to Sam. "Reverse into that gateway and head back the way we came," I instructed Sam. Sam did exactly what I told him and reversed into one of the large gate posts, buckling the rear doors so badly they were impossible to open. The only way we could access our tools and equipment was by removing the wireframe that separated the front and rear of the van.

What a day! It had another surprise for me when I arrived home. I opened our front door to find an orange bucket in the middle of the hall beside the telephone table. When I investigated the bucket, I saw it was three-quarters filled with water. Immersed in the water was our brand-new telephone. "Dad? Why is our telephone sitting in a bucket of water?" "Oh, hello son, I got a call from a chap in North Telephone exchange this afternoon. He told me the exchange was on fire and advised me to put our phone in a bucket of water." Considering the exchange was two miles away, I didn't know whether to laugh or cry. It had been one of those days.

My van was eventually repaired and I was in Crumlin Telephone Exchange one Friday afternoon near Christmas when North control rang me and asked me to go to the Pig 'N' Chicken Inn in Templepatrick. The control staff were holding their Christmas dinner there that Friday evening. They wanted the coin box repaired so they would be able to call taxis at the end of the evening. I arrived at the bar's car park just as it was growing dark. I parked and went into the bar to find the coin box. The repairs took some time. When I finished and returned to my van, it was around 6:30 pm and pitch black. I climbed into the driver's seat, switched on the lights, put the van into first gear and headed to the main road. BANG! My lights had shone over the top of a small boundary wall which I hadn't noticed. I surveyed the damage. There was no damage to the wall, but the front of the van had been pushed back so the edges of the bodywork were rubbing on the tyres. The noise was loud enough to attract a customer from the bar. He was a huge lump of a guy. He took one look, lay down in front of the van, grabbed the bodywork and straightened it towards him. I thanked him and headed back to Belfast.

Halfway back a red light lit on the dashboard. I continued driving and thought if I was going to take the van to the garage in Ballarat Street on Saturday morning, it would be better to park in Knock Telephone Exchange at Astoria Gardens, East Belfast. I made it to the exchange, parked the van and caught a bus to Newtownards. On Saturday morning at 8 am, I called the garage to tell them about the accident. The manager enquired about the details of the incident. When he learned there was no other damage and no one injured, he advised me to bring him 40 Woodbine. The van would be fixed, and nothing more said. I turned right at the lights on Sandown Road and drove up Knock dual carriageway. Halfway up the hill, there was a loud explosion. The bonnet flew up and hit the windscreen. I guessed the engine had seized. I followed a drop wire from a telegraph pole to a nearby house to ask the resident if I could use their telephone to call a breakdown lorry. I rang the doorbell, a bedroom window opened, and a man in pyjamas poked his head out and asked what I wanted. "Can I use your telephone, please? My van has just broken down." "What's wrong with the call box?" He asked. I was so shaken I walked past the public call box at the entrance to his house.

I was living in Newtownards towards the end of my time as a linesman. I was driving a 90cc motorcycle which made the daily journey from home to work very tiresome and very wet when it rained. I started taking my van home in the evenings and parked outside our new flat in Shackleton Walk, Westwinds Estate. Unknown to me, one of my parents' visitors to our new home was a friend of "Whistlin' Bob" and had innocently mentioned to him she had seen my van parked outside our flat. Bob called me into his office and told me he was aware I was taking my van home. He explained, in those circumstances, my van wasn't covered by insurance because I was "Out of area." Typical of Bob, there were no repercussions. He said he appreciated my reasons but asked me to make sure I always parked my van in the Ballysillan Road depot in future. Lesson learned.

A month later, I had parked my van and was travelling home, down Crumlin Road towards Ardoyne. A learner driver was indicating to turn into Hesketh Road. As I passed, I noticed in my rear mirror the driver had begun her turn. I knew she had been too quick and felt her car nudge my back wheel. That was all it took to send my bike into an uncontrollable wobble. As I fought for control, a double-decker bus was coming towards me. Eventually, the bike swung so violently, I flew over the handlebars. I smashed headfirst into the large, yellow Fares On Entry sign on the front of the bus.

I didn't lose consciousness. I lay staring up at the sky as faces appeared staring down at me. "He's not dead," I heard someone say. That was a relief. I heard someone else say, "There's an ambulance on its way. The police won't come. it's too dangerous." The ambulance appeared and I was stretchered into the back. The driver sounded the ambulance's emergency bells and set off for the Mater Hospital. The paramedic sat beside my stretcher and tried to convince me I was going to be OK. As I lay there, I did a quick inventory of my wounds and found nothing obvious. I thought to myself, "I think I'm OK."

We screeched to a halt outside the Mater's A & E department. The paramedic stood up and turned around to open the ambulance's rear double doors. At that moment, I stood up. When he turned back to me, he screamed "AAAAAAHHHHHHH!" He fell out the back doors and was knocked unconscious when his head struck the pavement. At this moment, two orderlies carrying a stretcher appeared. I helped them lift the injured paramedic onto the stretcher and take him into the A & E department. I left quickly before I had to answer any awkward questions. I let the paramedic explain everything when he woke up. As I walked passed the ambulance, I reached into the rear and collected my Stadium Safety Helmet, it was practically split in half.

I was asked to help in the Ormeau area because of a backlog of faults. I called to a house on Rosetta Road one Friday afternoon to visit a subscriber who had reported noise on her line. When the lady invited me into her hall, I noticed her telephone was an old Black 232. This was one of the oldest bakelite telephones still in use and had a built-in drawer at its base. I asked the lady if she would like one of our latest telephones. A TRIM phone. TRIM stands for Tone Ringing Illuminated Model. The dial was illuminated by a tube of radioactive Tritium gas. Linesmen joked they had sterilised half the men in Belfast by fitting TRIM phones. The customer was delighted with her new telephone and the clear line. On Monday morning, I received a call from control to confirm I had attended to this customer on Friday afternoon. I confirmed the telephone was still in the back of my van. I was advised to take another engineer with me and retrieve the telephone. This completed, we were instructed to open the drawer on the base of the phone Inside, was £100 in £10 notes. The lady's husband had arrived home after I left on Friday afternoon. He must have gasped in disbelief when he spotted the new telephone. "What's wrong with you?" Asked his wife. He had to explain why he had a hidden stash inside the telephone. I returned the money later that day and the gentleman gave me £10 as a reward.

The last subscriber's line fault I dealt with was Mrs Yarr who lived at the rear of the Post Office in Rose Lane Ends, Upper Ballinderry. It was a freezing, bitter, cold day and I had to climb the telegraph pole that served the premises to complete testing the line. It was so cold I felt my hands freezing to the steps on the pole as I climbed to the top to secure my safety belt. Tears welled in my eyes, and I shook so much I couldn't hold my tools. I finished and went into the premises to find Mrs Yarr baking soda bread on a griddle over an open fire. I checked the fault was cleared and her telephone was working properly. She must have seen the condition I was in. My hands were blue, and my face was frozen. I was hoping she would offer me a cup of tea. I hoped in vain. Before I left, I called control to report that the fault had been cleared. I was asked if I would like to work in Telephone House for two weeks to cover an engineer on sick leave. I didn't need to be asked twice.

Telephone House

Telephone House, at the corner of Cromac Street and May Street, was built between 1932 and 1935 as Belfast's first automatic telephone exchange. Initially, it was an L shape and an L-shaped extension in 1959 made it into a hollow square. When I arrived there in 1974, little did I know what "two weeks cover" would mean. It would mean two decades. I never did external work again.

My training began all over again as an exchange maintenance technician at the rank of Technician 2A. The ground floor of Telephone House housed the standby diesel generators and battery room. The Local and Trunk exchanges were spread over the first, second and third floors. The fourth floor housed cross-channel relay sets, a Crossbar exchange, the Measurement and Analysis Centre, the canteen and a coffee bar. The fifth floor was home to the manual switchboard room staffed by scores of operators. It was a fascinating place full of personalities and a continuous buzz of activity.

Clyde "Dinger" Bell was one of those personalities. Clyde was a champion scrambler and Technical Officer (TO) who worked on the second floor Local Exchange. A work colleague mischievously challenged Clyde he couldn't ride his motorbike from the ground to the fifth floor without placing his feet on the floor. On this epic attempt at fame in the annals of "Tele House," "marshals" were posted on each landing to ensure Dinger adhered to the rules as he attempted to ride his bike from the bottom to the top of the building. He succeeded and still holds the record to this day and undoubtedly, for all posterity. That sense of freedom and fun disappeared over the following years. The deteriorating security situation resulted in the building being guarded 24 hours a day by the British Army. It had become a target for the IRA.

The 15th May 1974 saw the beginning of the UWC strike. The Ulster Workers' Council organised a general strike across Northern Ireland between 15th May to 28th May 1974. The strike was called by Unionists who were against the Sunningdale Agreement, which had been signed in December 1973. The strike lasted 14 days and devastated Northern Ireland. Homes were left without electricity and gas; cars without petrol; goods and services such as bread, milk and post were undelivered; major roadways were blocked; businesses and shops were closed. The Lamp Room in Telephone House became my temporary home on occasions when I couldn't travel home because of paramilitary-manned roadblocks on main roads in and out of Belfast. This was the quietest room in the building with only intermittent clicking of relays to disturb the silence. One morning, I was stopped as I drove home to Newtownards by masked men on Bradshaw's Brae. "Get out of the car," someone ordered. "Where's your driving licence? Where are you going?" The leader demanded. "I'm going home," I replied and handed over my driving licence which still showed my home address as 23 Woodvale Street; I was nervous about explaining why I was driving to Newtownards. I'm still grateful this member of the Ulster Defence Association suffered from Dyslexia or couldn't read at all. He handed back my licence and waved me through the roadblock.

Despite deepening tensions between the two communities with more tit-for-tat murders, there was never any sectarian rivalry or bitterness amongst any of the staff in Telephone House. The rising violence created a shared experience of adversity amongst colleagues and helped foster a sense of unity and collective identity. Paradoxically, although violence is destructive, it brought people together through their shared experiences and emotions. That collective identity became sacrosanct, and no one was allowed to threaten it.

One person who did threaten to damage staff relations was a card-holding Communist by the name of Jimmy "The Red" McKeown. An engineer himself, he couldn't keep his politics and extreme views out of the workplace. It appeared he was deliberately trying to stir religious tensions amongst the staff in Telephone House. I finished my coffee break one morning and headed to the back staircase to return to work on the third floor. I couldn't believe my eyes and ears when I opened the connecting door. Jimmy Strachan and Wesley Davidson were dangling Jimmy the Red over the fourth-floor stairwell holding him by one ankle each.

One slip and Jimmy the Red would have been Jimmy in the Red all over the ground floor 80 feet beneath. Jimmy and Wesley were repeating, "You're not going to cause any more trouble, are you, Jimmy?" "NO! NO! NO!" Jimmy was screaming at the top of his voice. After further reassurance he wouldn't return to Telephone House, they hauled him back over the handrails to safety. True to his word, Jimmy never set in Telephone House again. I saw him months later on television, speaking in his new role as a Student Union representative. I don't know who else witnessed this incident but, shortly afterwards, high guards were fitted on the handrails to prevent anyone from "toppling over."

Wesley Davidson was the TO in charge of the fifth floor manual switchboard room. This was a hive of activity during the day, always buzzing with activity. Operators answered 100 calls, Directory Enquiries and 999 Emergency calls. The switchboards required constant maintenance; replacing cords, jacks and plugs was all in a day's work. However, Wesley was also an entrepreneur. His office was a mini–British Home Stores. His storage lockers were full of towels, bed linen, and anything else a discerning, busy operator required for a gift or her home. Why traipse into city centre shops when your local BHS is right next door? Wesley, flushed with the success of his household linens business decided to branch out in a different direction to a different clientele one Christmas. He decided to open a brewery.

He installed a pressure barrel with all its accoutrements inside a locker in his office. He added the ingredients from a Tom Caxton Home Brew kit he bought in Boots in Donegall Place. Homebrew and winemaking enjoyed a huge boom during the 1970s and 1980s. I only discovered Wesley's new business adventure when I arrived for work at 7:30 am one morning to complete routine checks before the exchange became busy.

Wesley met me at the door. "Thank goodness you're here Stevie. Quick, follow me up the backstairs." Out of breath, we reached the fifth floor and found a torrent of beer flowing out of Wesley's office and down the main staircase. The hallway stank of beer. The pressure barrel had burst and spilt its contents. We worked frantically with mops and buckets to clear up the flood before the operators' shift began at 8:00 am. We just about made it. "What's that smell, Wesley?" Some of the operators enquired.

I visited Wesley later in the day. He read a note the Area Engineer, Dominic Doherty, had left on his desk which stated that he had been made aware beer was being brewed on the premises. If that was the case, there would be serious consequences for those involved. Wesley screwed the note up and threw it in his wastepaper bin. "Hold on," I said, "That's not like any notepaper I've seen before." I retrieved the note and turned the written side over to discover the boss had written his warning on the Tom Caxton Home Brew label. Wesley took the warning seriously and diversified into wine and rum making instead. Wine was safer to store in glass gallon demijohns. Rum was the easiest of all. Take a large marrow, cut off the top, hollow out the inside, pack with Demerara sugar and replace the "lid." Hang the whole marrow in a wire shopping net, puncture the end and let it drip into your preferred receptacle. Boom Bang a Bang! Where's the party?

Another infamous character in Telephone House was Mr J W Poots, commonly known as Pootsy. Pootsy was in his mid-thirties, a Technical Officer, always sharply dressed in a suit or tweed jacket; he had a sharp wit and a fondness for alcohol which combined to create unforgettable memories for anyone who knew him. If anyone was looking for Pootsy and he wasn't on the second floor Local Exchange, they could look for him in The Black Bull, McMeal's, The Central, The Buttery, The Busman's, The Chester or The Garrick. Any Bar that was within a minute's walk from work. They would be unlikely to have found him in The International Temperance League Café beside The Black Bull. Pootsy admitted he was an alcoholic, but he functioned at a level where he was able to complete a day's work. Mostly!

On one of those "mostly" days, Alfie Kane, the Chief executive, was making a tour of Telephone House and speaking to staff on each floor. Jimmy was the worst for wear after a lunchtime session in a local hostelry. The Technical Officer in charge of Jimmy's workplace, Cecil Frizzell was concerned Alfie and Pootsy would meet. A quick phone call to "British Home Stores" on the fifth floor and Pootsy was spirited to Wesley's office and locked in a storage cupboard until the danger had passed. On another day, I was having a beer with Pootsy in The Garrick. We were discussing what films we had watched lately. I had recently watched Harrowhouse and explained to Jim I couldn't remember the name of the villain. To try and elicit some help from him, I prompted, "You must know the British actor who always plays the baddie." Suddenly, I remembered and told Jim the actor's name was Trevor Howard. There was a moment's pause then Jimmy said, "You're right about Trevor Howard always playing the baddie." "Why?" I asked. "Sure, he played the priest in Ryan's Daughter." I still laugh at Jim's sharp wit.

Pootsy said he would never fly. Travelling to BT's Training college in Stone, Staffordshire by boat and train required effort and could be exhausting but that's how Pootsy preferred to travel. On his way to Piccadilly Railway Station in Manchester to catch a train to Stafford, he called into a bar near the station at 10:30 am. "Sorry, we're closed," said the barman. "What time do you open?" Enquired Jimmy. "11 o'clock," replied the barman. "Any chance of a drink while I'm waiting?" Asked Jimmy. The barman laughed and poured Pootsy a double Bush. Jimmy made a similar enquiry in a bar on Achill Island several years later. "What time do you close?" Enquired Jimmy. "Is September, OK?" Replied the owner.

Eventually, Peter Cunningham, a Technical Officer in the same department as Pootsy, convinced Jimmy to fly with him to Manchester because they were booked on separate courses but on the same dates. Peter and Jimmy boarded the BAC 1-11 at Aldergrove, and the plane taxied for take-off. Jimmy was sweating profusely, and Peter was trying to calm him and make him relax. Wooosh! The pilot hit full throttle and the plane rocketed down the runway. The plane didn't make it to "Rotate." The pilot slammed on reverse thrust and the plane screeched to a halt. All the passengers were hurled forward in their seats, only their seat belts held them in place. Jimmy was a wreck. Peter probably wasn't too far behind him. Then the pilot announced, "This is Captain Black, my apologies for the abandoned take-off." The irony wasn't lost on Jimmy because the pseudonym "Captain Black" was employed by John White, the commander of the Ulster Freedom Fighters (UFF). One of the most notorious incidents involving this pseudonym was the double murder of Roman Catholic Senator Paddy Wilson and his Protestant friend Irene Andrews on 25th June 1973. The victims were hacked and repeatedly stabbed to death by UFF members. John White, aka "Captain Black," was convicted of this sectarian killing and sentenced to life imprisonment.

On the second attempt, the plane took off and landed without further incident at Manchester Ringway. However, Jimmy swore he would never fly again and cancelled his return ticket. His course was entitled SSMF No.2 and lasted two weeks. Over the middle weekend, he travelled with Peter to London; they booked into the Cromwell Hotel and decided to go to an Arsenal match on Saturday afternoon. They hailed a taxi, but Jimmy had drunk a few whiskeys and asked the taxi driver to stop outside Harrods. "Sorry, I need to go to the loo." He pleaded urgently. Peter advised Jimmy, "If you go in there, you will never find your way out again." And so, it happened. Jimmy found his way out, but a different way out and didn't make it to the match with Peter.

The only thing to do was return to his hotel and wait for Peter. "Taxi," called Jimmy. "Where to sir?" Asked the Cabbie. "The Cromwell Hotel please," replied Jimmy. "Which Cromwell Hotel Sir?" Enquired the Cabbie. "What?" Exclaimed Jimmy. "I know at least five Cromwell Hotels sir." "Let's start at the beginning and work our way through them," suggested Jimmy. At "the first" Cromwell Hotel Jimmy approached the reception and, by way of explanation said, "Good afternoon, my name is Jimmy Poots, can you tell me if I stayed here last night, please?" The receptionist checked her records and informed Jimmy he hadn't spent the previous evening on the premises. This repeated itself on his next call. He met with success on his third attempt. When Peter returned, he found Jimmy sitting in the Lounge Bar as if nothing untoward had occurred. When Jimmy looked up, he noticed he was the only white man in the bar. All the rest of the guests were black. He remarked to Peter, "How's that for a flush of spades." Jimmy had never heard of "Unconscious Bias."

At the end of the course, Jimmy made his way to Liverpool to join the overnight sailing to Belfast. During The Troubles, travellers to and from N Ireland were herded like animals into the recesses of travel ports and airports on the grounds of security. Green cards had to be completed on leaving the mainland and red cards had to be completed on entering the mainland. Subtle, wasn't it? Jimmy had already been searched and his baggage checked twice when he was stopped again just before the gangway to the ship. He had that type of face that attracted suspicion, especially after imbibing one or two to calm his travel nerves. The security officer asked for his ID and asked to check his holdall. The officer pulled out Jimmy's course folder and read out the title on the front cover. "SSMF No.2 What does that stand for?" He enquired. "It stands for Signalling System Multi-Frequency No.2," explained Jimmy. "Wow, that sounds complicated," said the officer. "Not half as bloody complicated as getting on this boat," was Jimmy's apt retort. Jimmy never made it to the mainland again.

In the early 1980s, news of impending digitalisation was circulating and the impact it was going to have on the analogue Private Switched Telephone Network. Engineers were being sent to Stone in Staffordshire to train on what was euphemistically known as System X. The Post Office Engineering Union was vehemently opposed to the new technology as it was viewed as a serious threat to jobs. The joke was an analogue exchange took 40 engineers to run, and a digital exchange only took one man and a dog. The man was there to feed the dog and the dog was there to bite the man if he touched anything. Work began on installing a System X Trunk Exchange on the first floor of the Seymour House extension to Telephone House. At the same time, work began to install a System X Local Exchange in City Exchange on Grosvenor Road.

Eddie MacDonald was a Technical Officer from Paisley, Scotland. He formed a breakaway union to the POEU called the Engineering Officers Technical

Association or EOTA for short. It was exclusive to TOs. His vision was that Technical Officers should be better rewarded for adapting to the new technology; it would then be up to the POEU to negotiate the restoration of differentials for the other technical grades. I believed the POEU couldn't see where the real threat to jobs lay.

On 1 October 1981, British Telecommunications, trading as British Telecom, finally severed its links with the Post Office and became a separate public corporation under the provisions of the British Telecommunications Act, 1981. In Belfast, the POEU was led by another card-holding Communist, Billy Somerset who opposed any attempt by the Thatcher Government to privatise BT. To my mind, the threat to job security didn't come from privatisation but from modernisation. I resigned from the POEU and joined EOTA.

Eventually, I was elected to the N. Ireland NEC of EOTA and made frequent visits to meetings in Belfast, Glasgow, Leeds and London. Despite EOTA's constant lobbying, BT never recognised it and was never involved in wage negotiations for its members. It was recognised at a local level and represented members in staff contract issues. The breaking point for me came when the POEU called a strike in 1987. Eddie MacDonald ordered EOTA members to cross picket lines. There was no way I was instructing N Ireland members of EOTA to cross colleagues' picket lines. In Belfast, every engineer knew every other engineer; they had worked together through the worst years of the troubles. EOTA members joined the POEU members on strike. It lasted two weeks. There had been several small fires in Telephone House caused by faulty switches and management was concerned there might be a major incident. In a total of 49 years of work, that was the only time I ever withdrew my labour.

Despite the POEU's opposition, BT was privatised in 1984. Thank you, Margaret Thatcher. All BT employees were awarded shares and allowed to buy as many as they wanted at 50p each. Shares rose to £17.50 each before the Dot.com bubble burst in the late 90s. However, this was a difficult time for me and I couldn't invest as much as I would have liked in the available share schemes.

By 1983, my relationship with Jennifer broke up and we decided to divorce. Two-hour lunches in The Garrick became more frequent and an evening's "craic" would sometimes last until closing. One lunchtime, I fell into "bad company" in the shape of Jim and Stan. No surnames to protect the guilty. They plied me with several pints; it would be a challenge to return to work. The telephone in the bar rang. Deirdre answered it and shouted over that the call was for me. "Phant" Stevenson had left the bar earlier to return to work. He called to say our line manager, Dominic Doherty, had been on the third floor and enquired where I was. He left instructions, I was to report to his office when I returned to work.

I arrived back to work at 2:30 pm. I sliced a finger with a sharp screwdriver; soaked up the blood with tissues and packed them into my mouth. When I entered Dominic's office, his secretary Edna took a double look at me. My mouth was swollen, and I was holding tissues to my face to prevent blood from running down my chin. "What happened?" Asked Dominic. I told him I had had a lunchtime dental appointment and the dentist made an emergency extraction. "Have you had a cup of tea yet?" Asked Dominic. I was back in the Garrick by 3:00 pm, much to the surprise of Jim and Stan. I didn't order tea.

I was oblivious to how reckless I was becoming. Liam O'Reilly was about to leave to get married. Following tradition, he was tied upside down from a travelling ladder between equipment racks and soaked with water and shaving foam. I was witnessing the festivities when I noticed Liam's wallet fall out of his trousers pocket. I picked it up, waved it under his nose and told him I would keep it safe for him. "I'll meet you in the Garrick when I get cleaned up," he said. He and three other well-wishers joined me in the bar after work. Two women who worked in Belfast Rates Office, three doors down from The Garrick, on Chichester Street came in. I discovered later they were best friends, Anne Largey from Cliftonville Road and Rhonda Ferguson from Ballyclare.

Over the following months, we met more often and our relationship grew steadily. Eventually, Rhonda moved into Ardgowan Street with me, and we set up home together. I was fighting the idea of settling down again with anyone and continued drinking while working in Telephone House and renovating our home in Ardgowan Street. Rhonda's best friend, Anne Largey, eventually married my friend, Alan McKinstry.

Often, this meant finishing 16-hour shifts and then spending the day wiring and plumbing. I was exhausted one afternoon when I climbed a ladder in the yard to reach the waste outlet from the bathroom. Halfway up, the ladder slipped, and I toppled backwards towards the ground. I had the time to say to myself, "This is going to hurt." I had the presence of mind to push my chin towards my chest, so the back of my head didn't hit the concrete first. Splat! My back hit the ground and I immediately jumped back on my feet. I steadied myself by holding onto the kitchen windowsill and waited for the shock to clear and pain to hit me. Miraculously, there wasn't any.

I have no idea how I didn't seriously injure myself. Only God knows. In 2021, I slipped on ice and fell. I broke five ribs and cracked the remainder. I never want to experience pain like that again. To keep Rhonda company in the evenings that I worked shifts, we bought a Shetland Sheepdog. Hilariously, the breeder's name was Jack Russell, and we collected the new addition to our family from his farm in Ahoghill. Cagney was the centre of attention wherever we took her; loved by all our family and friends. She was our constant companion for 17 years.

Rhonda and I made so many visits to Dawson Wright's Hardware Shop on Woodstock Road we became friends with Mr Dawson and his assistant Jim Cummings. Jim helped us immensely. When we had no car, Jim arranged delivery of larger purchases like our coal bunker and gas canisters for our Superser heater. Nothing was too much trouble for him. Jim was a real-life character. His nickname was "Boon." Just like Michael Elphick in the lead role of the TV drama, he wore a half-bowl safety helmet and goggles. He was the proud owner of a 900cc Kawasaki motorcycle and Rhonda accepted his offer one evening to, "Go for a spin." She returned shaken but not stirred.

In November 1984, someone suggested we collect money for Children In Need. Why not? Donations appeared to be for good causes. I decided Rhonda and I should dress up as a doctor and nurse. I went to the laundry at the City Hospital, explained my plans to the supervisor and left with a white doctor's coat and a nurse's uniform. As well as the white coat, I sported a headlamp from work and a plastic stethoscope. Rhonda looked the part in her nurse's uniform as we entered the Garrick on Friday lunchtime before the live BBC TV extravaganza that evening. We worked our way around the customers in the busy lunchtime period. I offered to take chest soundings, males and females. I only warmed the stethoscope if the "patient" offered a donation. There was a great sense of fun and plenty of craic. It all helped raise over £550.

I was back at work when someone hammered on our security door. I opened it to find Sammy Watson asking to speak to me urgently. He was one of our "donors" in the bar earlier. "Stevie, how much money did you and Rhonda collect at lunchtime?" I told him. "Leave it with me," he said. I had no idea what he meant by that. Ten minutes later, he was back and hammered on the door again. "Stevie, my friend is a producer at the BBC; he wants you to call him. He'll have you on TV tonight." I was relieved when I spoke to Sammy's friend. He explained he was turning people away who had raised £5000 and more. I apologised for bothering him. I walked around to Sammy in the Repair Service Centre and told him about my conversation with his friend at the BBC. Ten minutes later, Sammy came back again banging on my door. You'll have guessed by now we didn't have one another's telephone number. "Forget what he said, Stevie. The BBC will be at the Garrick at 6 pm this evening, to collect your donation. "Thanks for letting me know," I replied.

I called Rhonda and told her to meet me in The Garrick at 6 pm. Rhonda advised me to call Deirdre O'Neill. She and her husband Barney were the proprietors of that fine establishment. Deirdre thanked me for the "heads up." "That will give me time to have my hair done and change into something glamorous." We all gathered expectantly before our appointment with fame. At 6 pm sharp, the BBC arrived. BBC Radio. In hindsight, thank goodness the BBC hadn't sent a film crew. That evening, our Children In Need party in the upstairs lounge became known as "The Night of the Long Knives."

Any Friday evening in the Garrick Bar was busy with customers unwinding at the end of a working week. That Friday night seemed even busier than usual. The upstairs lounge was packed to capacity. Amongst the throng was Alex the Grate. So-called because his name was Alec and he worked for Aerocrete, a fireplace manufacturer on Shore Road. Opposite him sat Cesare Borgia aka Davey Connelly. Called Cesare for short because he was a body double for his alias in a popular television series at the time called The Borgias. That evening, they proved the saying, "When the drink's in, the wit is out."

Cesare decided to show Alex his new double-edged, balanced throwing knife. Alex reached out to take hold of the handle when Cesare pulled it back quickly. Unfortunately for Alex, his right hand was too close to the blade, and it sliced through his fingers and palm. There was a fountain of blood. Nurse Rhonda grabbed the injured hand and held it tightly to her chest saying, "There, there." Dr McDonald fainted. To think, one time I wanted to be a doctor. Cesare didn't return to The Garrick for six months just in case Alex the Grate turned up with a poker to show him.

That was the only time I supported BBC Children In Need. Now, I won't even watch it on television. I discovered it was funding an Irish Language group with paramilitary links in the Short Strand area of Belfast. The group had applied for funding to C in N because it had failed Government vetting procedures. I also discovered C in N is a funder of Educate & Celebrate. "Educate and Celebrate is a team of experts who help schools and organisations to become more LGBT+ friendly and inclusive." That's a quote from its website. To be cynical. It's only a woke, virtue-signalling platform for so-called "Celebrities." The same applies to Red Nose Day. More airtime for woke, so-called "Comedians." The National Lottery collected over £8 billion in the year 2023. £1.9 billion was spent on National Lottery projects. How much money is unspent? I haven't been able to find out. One thing is for certain, there's enough money to ensure no children are in need throughout the UK. We don't need BBC's virtue signalling. We certainly shouldn't be taxed to watch it. Especially now, during the Israeli-Gaza crisis, when it has proven to be institutionally anti-Semitic.

Everyone who frequented The Garrick could write a book about their experiences in that hostelry. During the dark days of The Troubles, it was a place of refuge for Catholics, Protestants and anyone who happened in. Life-long cross-community friendships were made that last to this day. Occasionally I ask myself, since I came to faith, if I had a choice would I do it all over again? My answer is probably, "Yes." I long for those dangerous, yet carefree days before wokery robbed us of our corporate sense of humour. No one will ever pop into the Garrick again for a quiet, late-night pint only to have their peace disturbed by Robin Hood and his Merry Men turning up in full costume along with Maid Marion and Rose Marie, the Irish pop singer. John Linehan was playing Robin Hood in the Christmas Pantomime at Belfast Opera House and decided to take the cast out after the evening performance. They must have been a sight walking up Wellington Place and Chichester Street. "Robin" had played the lead role for six weeks with his right arm in a cast after breaking it on a golf trip. Someone at the far end of the bar dropped and broke a glass. Robin Hood shouted, "Tell us again why you failed the interview for the Bomb Squad." The craic was ninety.

Speaking of bomb squads. Some enterprising engineers discovered how to make a very effective "bomb" using readily available materials in a telephone exchange. Bank contact cleaning tape came in large, cylindrical cardboard canisters. A small hole on one side allowed the bootlace-style abrasive tape to be pulled out to the required length and cut accordingly. Instead of using the tape for its designed purpose, the drum of tape was removed, the lid taken off, and the empty container's open end placed over a tin of floor cleaner purloined from the cleaner's store. The fumes were allowed to accumulate for around an hour before the container was removed and the lid replaced. A Selector's PG bulb with the glass removed, leaving the bare filament was pushed through the little access hole and long "jumper wires" were soldered to the bulb's contacts, ready for connection to a power supply. The "bomb" could be hidden under someone's workbench or chair. The best results occurred when someone was concentrating on adjusting mechanical apparatus, oblivious to all happening around them. One more wee tweak of that spring set; one more wee hair...... nearly there.........BANG. EXPLETIVE! EXPLETIVE! EXPLETIVE! No wonder, in all my years at Telephone House, I only had two weeks off due to illness. I was afraid of missing anything.

The first, second and third floor exchanges, Local and Trunk contained Main and Intermediate Distribution Frames. These frames ran almost the length of the rooms. These were where external lines cross-connected to the exchange side of the equipment. This was where lightning protection was provided and access for testing in and out of the exchange. The blocks were labelled A, B, C, D etc right the way to Z. The 27th vertical was labelled AA, the next AB etc; Then BA, BB etc to the end of the frame. Each vertical housed 20 blocks, individually labelled according to purpose. The higher terminal blocks were accessed by travelling ladders that ran the full length of the frames. Whoever was on duty at each floor's SFC (Special Fault Centre) acquired a local knowledge of the frame and was often asked to point out where a particular block could be found.

In one famous incident, Jimmy Metcalfe, all five feet of him was searching for a particular block on the third floor Trunk MDF. Having had no success, he approached Winston Wetherall, who was manning the SFC and asked the whereabouts of a block he sought. Winston was busy and directed Jimmy to, "Halfway up on the D side at eye-level." Jimmy came back to check Winston's instructions and he gave him the same directions. When he returned the third time, Winston became exasperated. "Come with me," he said. Jimmy followed Winston halfway along the D side of the MDF; with Jimmy directly in front of him, Winston reached down and hoisted him two feet. "There," he said, "I told you it was at eye level." Did anyone take offence? No. If Winston repeated that today, there's little doubt he would be marched to the front door with his P45. It's a sad indictment of modern society. Humour is dead. Jim said he always got the last laugh because he could buy child-sized clothes for himself. This meant he didn't pay VAT.

Like all good stories, they travelled fast in BT. The cleaner in Newry Telephone Exchange was comparing his "hard work" to the Technical Officer in Charge working on the Main Distribution Frame and complaining "Sure, all you have to do is run two wires from one side of the frame to the other, strip the wires and solder the contacts, anyone could do that." This banter repeated itself over several days. Eventually, the TO called the cleaner's bluff and invited him over to, "Strip the wires and solder the contacts," on a jumper wire he had run out between the Distribution and Exchange sides of the frame. There was a special pair of pliers to do this which ensured only the insulation was removed and the wire wasn't cut accidentally. Experienced engineers never used them as they tended to be ungainly. Instead, they all used basic BT-supplied side cutters.

If life was fair, the TO would have explained the use of the proper tool. You'll discover life isn't fair and the TO needed to make his point. "You do your job, and I'll do mine." Sure enough, when the cleaner tried to strip the insulation, he cut the wires as well. The gentleman in question was a keen cyclist and had been training for the first cycle race between Belfast and Dublin. Unknown to him, the other end of the jumper wire wasn't terminated on the MDF. Instead, it had been passed out a first-floor window and tied to his bicycle. The wire was holding his bicycle 15 feet above the car park. When it was cut, the Jumper wire whipped out of the frame and his bicycle crashed to the ground. The good news was it wasn't his Sports bicycle. If you cycle to work, make sure you secure your bicycle properly. You've probably upset a few car users who would relish the opportunity to watch you riding it with square wheels.

The fourth floor was undoubtedly the hottest place to work in Telephone House. On two sides of the floor were the Canteen and the Measurement and Analysis Centre; the other half housed the TXK4 Crossbar Exchange and racks of AC1, AC9 and AC11 relay sets. These provided cross-channel connections between Belfast and the mainland. The Technical Officer in Charge of the Crossbar exchange was Alec McLaughlin. Despite the heat, Alec always dressed immaculately in a suit and tie. Occasionally, he removed his jacket and rolled up his shirt sleeves. It was a pleasure to work with Alec as he taught me the workings of Crossbar. I enjoyed the work and immersed myself in the technical details. I helped clear outstanding faults caused by permanent wiring errors during the exchange's installation. Alec's daughter Marie was an operator in the fifth floor Manual Room. Marie married a TO, Peter Cunningham who later became my line manager.

Maintaining the relay sets on the fourth floor holds fond memories for me. The hybrid circuits in these sets used valves. The heat they gave off was formidable, especially when working on the uppermost racks of equipment. Simply because hot air rises. Not only did I enjoy the work, but I also enjoyed the company I worked with. Joe McIlwaine was the cleaner on this part of the fourth floor. Joe was quiet, humble and kept everything spotless. I looked forward to our tea breaks each morning. Joe would have tea and coffee made for 10 am with a table and chairs set up between the equipment racks.

We'd be joined by Alec, Tommy Rogers (TO) and Mickey Mullan (TO). I was the only Protestant on this staff and never felt excluded or not part of the team. There was always something to discuss. Joe was a keen gardener and inspired me to grow my own potatoes. He even taught me the intricacies of pigeon racing. At one time, Joe lived on Whiterock Road. One evening, after work, he answered his front door to someone collecting for the IRA. Joe had been an amateur boxer and the bloke at Joe's door received a severe right hook for his troubles. Joe and his family had to move and eventually settled in Lenadoon.

Mickey Mullan was quiet and unassuming. He was patient and encouraged me through my training on cross-channel transmission systems. AC1s were the oldest relay system; they were being gradually replaced with AC9s. Work was interrupted one Friday afternoon by a call from Liverpool. "Can you contact Dublin Adelaide, please? Tell them they've pulled out the wrong AC1 relay sets. No one on the mainland can call Southern Ireland and vice versa." I rang Dublin Adelaide exchange and explained Ireland was cut off from the mainland. I'll never forget the engineer's reply. In a Dublin accent, he said, "Ah, sure it'll do on Monday." You can never guess how people will react in an emergency. Some will baulk and back away; others will rise to the challenge and excel.

One example of this involved me and Rhonda. It concerned another exchange isolation. This time Belfast Cromac System X had suffered a catastrophic failure on a Friday evening around 8 pm, resulting in no telephony between Belfast and the remainder of the UK. PANIC STATIONS. The control centre called all available System X-trained engineers, but no one was available. I was off duty and not on call-out rota. However, the control manager used his initiative and called The Garrick bar, guessing correctly, there would be a suitably trained engineer on the premises. Dierdre O'Neill handed me the phone and the control explained the emergency. I explained I wasn't in a fit state and would need backup. Control told me to do whatever was necessary. "JUST GET THERE!" I hung up and shouted, "Rhonda, come with me."

Ten minutes later, after the doormen had let us in, we were standing at the control desk in the First Floor System X Trunk Exchange. The printer was spewing out reams of fault reports that showed the Central Processing Unit had failed on the main and standby sides. This was a nightmare situation. Rhonda was calm as we put on Zap Straps to prevent static electricity from causing more damage. I followed the directions in the Operations Manuals and shouted out the Power-down and Power-up sequences to Rhonda who dutifully followed my orders. One hour and two Slide-in Unit changes later, both CPUs were restored to service. Cause of fault: The Irish Sea.

All digital traffic between Belfast and the mainland was beamed across the Irish Sea from St John's Point in Co Down to the Isle of Man and onto the mainland via an 11 GHz radio link. Friday had been a particularly hot day. Water vapour rising off the Irish Sea caused interference to the signal resulting in thousands of simultaneous software fault reports that the processors couldn't handle. Well done Rhonda for restoring Belfast Cromac Trunk

Exchange to service after its worst-ever service failure. Due to circumstances, Rhonda never received the credit she deserved. Now, here it is in writing. Never too late!

My last conversation with Mickey was at the funeral of another colleague's father. Tony Denny's father had died in Australia while visiting family. It took weeks to repatriate his body and arrange the burial Mass at St Theresa's. Mickey and I chatted to one another after the service, while waiting for transport back to the city centre. A week later, I was at Mickey's Funeral Mass. He was killed in a car crash the following Monday morning on his way to work.

I last met Tommy Rogers in May 2016 when he arranged to meet some of his former work colleagues on a visit home with his brother. Myself, Greer Sloan and Charlie Walker met him in Café Vaudeville, Arthur Street. Tommy emigrated to San Francisco at the height of the Telecom boom to work for Cisco Systems and live the American Dream. Sadly, big job losses in the American Telecoms sector in the 90s, meant Tommy's dream never quite materialised. He found work in the construction industry, but years of hard physical work had taken their toll. I barely recognised him and we prompted him to speak louder his voice was so low.

When Tommy and his brother left, Greer, Charlie and I commented on how frail he looked. We mentioned that was probably the last time we would ever meet him. Eight years later, in June 2024, one of that company is dead. And it isn't Tommy. Charlie and his wife Marion were devout Catholics on their annual pilgrimage to Medjugorje when Charlie collapsed and died from a heart attack. I wonder if back in 2016, we knew one of us would die within eight years, would we have lived our lives any differently? What would I have changed? How should I live the remainder of my life now? How should you live yours?

Remember, the saying that a System X Exchange only required one man and a dog? A favourite memory of mine of Charlie is the summer evening he was on a callout to a PCM (Pulse Code Modulation) fault and gained entry to the System X Exchange to find me throwing balls of computer printout for Cagney, our Shetland Sheepdog. He burst out laughing and said, "I don't believe it. It's that one man and his dog." When I was called out, it was such a glorious evening, I decided to walk Cagney with me to Telephone House. Fortunately, I was first into the exchange the following morning. Cagney had pooped under the table holding the Signing-In book.

In the fascinating, ever-changing world of Telecommunications, while digital exchanges were being built, Strowger exchanges continued to develop too with full International Direct Dialling becoming available from 1982. The IDD exchange was situated on the second floor of Telephone House. Within days of the inauguration of IDD in Belfast, reports were filtering in of coaches taking people to Crumlin. They were queuing to use the public call box in The Diamond, a square in the middle of town. The kiosk contained an old A & B button-type coin box. Some "genius" had worked out that, by tapping the required number using the buttons, there were no "PIPs" and no coins had to be inserted. Considering calls to America cost the equivalent of £2 to £3 per minute, to many it made the journey and wait worthwhile to talk to Auntie Agnes in Chicago. No matter how good the technology is, someone can always "hack it." Same then, same today.

After the inauguration of the IDD exchange in Telephone House, I was called into an interview by the Technical Officer in Charge of the Third Floor Trunk Exchange. His name was Richard Harrison. A quiet, devout Christian of whom no one ever said a bad word. He was a great TO in Charge whose example encouraged staff to take pride in their work. Richard's wife had died of kidney failure, and he spent much of his free time raising money for the Northern Ireland Kidney Foundation. Richard began asking me technical questions about the workings of local and trunk exchanges. He encouraged me to be more specific in some areas and asked what my responses would be in the different scenarios he described. An hour later, Richard informed me I had passed my promotion board and was now a Technical Officer. I had reached the pinnacle of my career as far as rank was concerned. I hadn't reached my pinnacle regarding stupidity and I had plenty of role models to emulate.

Two of these were Noel Gellis and John Crozier. Friendly aliens from a different planet called Portadown. Somehow, a woman called Heather had married Noel and agreed to be his dogsbody for life. Outside BT, he was useless for anything. Heather did absolutely everything around the home. Heather went to London for a weekend to visit her sister. I answered the telephone to Noel on a Saturday afternoon. He explained that Heather was away and he wanted to know how to make chips. I told Noel it would be safer to order a Pastie Supper. Noel lived less than a mile from Portadown railway station. When he travelled home each morning, after a night shift in Telephone House, he expected Heather to pick him up at the railway station, drive him home and make his breakfast. One morning she wasn't there. A frustrated Noel rang home and said, "Heather, where are you? I'm waiting at the station." Heather replied, "I'm not there to pick you up because you took the car to work last night." Why are there so many likeable but useless men around? Why do women marry them?

Roll up, John Crozier. John was from Central Casting for Carry on Engineer. How could a man in his 40s be that naive and know so little about life outside his bubble of self-assurance? It made doing a 16-hour night shift with him in the Network Operations Unit entertaining and stressful at the same time. After testing for faults on a medical practice's digital switch in Warrenpoint, he called to speak to the doctor in charge of the centre. At one point, the discussion became heated and the doctor abruptly terminated the call. John turned to me and said, "Stephen, that doctor just called me an oaf. What's an oaf?" Further explanation isn't necessary. Now for the pièce de résistance. Part of our duties in the control centre was monitoring television feeds routed through BT's transmission cables. One afternoon, our attention was drawn to the BBC feed showing interference on a live broadcast from the Queens Club Tennis Tournament in Bournemouth. After the "noise" was cleared John pointed at the monitor screen showing a match in play and asked, "Stephen, who is that girl Stella Artois?" Back to the question, what is an oaf?

I must mention Geordie Wilson at this point. Geordie was "Van the Man" for Telephone House's central maintenance staff. He delivered replacement parts to digital telephone exchanges in and around Greater Belfast. After he had loaded his van with the spare slide-in units needed for the day, he would join us at our tea break in the canteen before he headed off on his rounds. George didn't realise his gift for Spoonerisms, a verbal error in which a speaker accidentally transposes the initial sounds or letters of two or more words. He was a natural in this field of entertainment. Some of his sayings are legendary amongst his BT colleagues and deserve a mention.

One morning, George explained he was taking annual leave to "Semtex" his house. Other famous sayings were when he asked for advice on preventing "compensation" from running down his windows and, "never put all your legs in one basket." My favourite happened when he had just returned from a holiday in Rome. I was curious what George, a card-holding member of the Con Club in East Belfast, made of one of the cultural capitals of the world. "What did you do in Rome?"

I enquired. George replied, "Simple, when in Rome I did what the Romanians do."

I'll finish this chapter of my career with a bang and a shaggy dog story. On 15th of July 1989, Telephone House was evacuated, due to a bomb scare. We adjourned to Magennis's Bar in May Street to await developments. In the middle of the packed bar, two locals threw punches at one other, reliving a recent Barry McGuigan fight they had attended. The barman came from behind the counter, pushed his way through the middle of the two "boxers" and shouted into the occupants of one of the booths, "No singing." Yes, they were crazy days. Then, BOOM! The windows came in around us. The scare turned out to be real. 250 lbs of homemade explosives had exploded outside Telephone House.

No one in the bar was injured and eventually, we were given the all-clear to return to work. On our way back, we were accompanied by a black and white Collie dog that had hidden in the bar. The doormen were too shocked to ask questions and let the dog through the security doors with us. The bomb damage was mostly confined to Seymour House. Telephone House was virtually bomb-proof and there was little we could do other than watch contractors clear the mess in Cromac Street.

Cecil Frizzell was the TO in Charge of the third floor Local Exchange. He was a dapper wee man, with a pipe permanently in his mouth, and proud of "His Floor," and staff. His face was a picture when he walked into the third floor locker room and found four engineers talking to a bedraggled dog. "Go on, give's your paw." Cecil just shook his head and walked out again. He had forgotten what he came in for. Then there was a discussion about who should take the dog home.

Stan McKnight won the debate. You'll learn more about Stan in the next chapter. The wee dog was a better judge of character than me. Stan took the stray home with him to Carrickfergus. The dog put up with him for a couple of days before it decided to make a run for it. Good decision. I wish I hadn't taken so long to have nothing to do with him.

In the last two years, serendipity brought my old colleagues from Telephone House back together again. We meet for breakfast on alternative months. It is always a pleasant morning catching up with one another and swapping memories. I won't name them in case I leave someone out. I know they won't take offence when I call them "Tubes." Like myself, their lives have unwound like the proverbial toilet roll that Richard Littlejohn compared to life, and now there's only the cardboard tube remaining. I use the term as a compliment. No one has ever worked with a better bunch of tubes. I am grateful to them all.

Doing The Dishes

Renovating our house and socialising took a considerable amount of money. I was also paying a court order for financial support for Jennifer and my two daughters Claire and Lorna. I needed another source of income. I approached Stan McKnight, another TO who I knew was installing satellite dishes and receivers, along with his brother Victor in their spare time. The business was named Satellite Ireland. My timing was perfect. Victor was leaving and Stan was glad of my offer to help. We worked well together; our reputation for good work led to more offers from people interested in Satellite TV. Often, it meant finishing a night shift, loading my car with tools and lashing a set of ladders onto the roof rack before heading out to do installations.

Sometimes we worked individually; sometimes we worked together on more complicated motorised installations. Occasionally, suppliers asked us to rectify work carried out by "cowboys." There was no shortage of them during the boom years of Satellite TV. Some installers drilled through double-glazing frames, to avoid the bother of drilling through a wall to feed cable from dish to receiver. The business wasn't our bread and butter, so we afforded time to ensure customers were satisfied with our work. We took pride in a job well done.

Our reputation spread and one evening, we were invited to a "hush, hush" meeting with a gentleman at the Stormont Hotel. After verifying our credentials, the gent introduced himself & informed us he was the Area Manager for SSVC. This stood for Sight and Sound Visual Corporation. The business supplied White goods, and TV services to the military. It had retail outlets in all the army bases in N Ireland. "Would Satellite Ireland be interested in Satellite TV installations for SSVC in Co Antrim and Co Down?" Surreptitious security checks had already been completed; we were good to go if we accepted the contract. We didn't appreciate what we were letting ourselves in for.

The military was a guaranteed source of work. When a regiment moved out of a base, they took everything, including Satellite systems from barracks and residential accommodation, with them. What we had installed, we might install again, six months later, in the same place as before. It was good for business and we only ever had one complaint. That was from Alexander Barracks, inside Aldergrove RAF Station. I had installed a SMATV. A Satellite Master Antenna Television (SMATV) combines Satellite and Terrestrial TV and distributes pictures and sound to multiple rooms. When I finished this job, I asked an officer to accompany me around each room in the barracks to confirm everything was working to his satisfaction. I left an invoice for the work before I headed to another location.

A month later, Stan was with me driving to RAF Aldergrove to install two systems, we planned to complete on-site that day. "Stevie, did we ever get paid for that SMATV you installed in Alexander Barracks?" He asked. "No," I replied. "Let's head there first," he said. The Duty Sergeant in Reception refused my payment request and said, "That system never worked." I explained I was the person who installed the system and Lieutenant Baker had confirmed it was in working order before I left. The sergeant ordered another soldier, "Corporal, go and ask Lieutenant Baker to come down to Reception." The corporal complied and disappeared to fetch my witness. On his return, he informed the Duty Sergeant that Lieutenant Baker was on duty and not available. "There you go then, we're not paying," he announced.

"Step aside Stephen, I'll handle this," said Stan. "Who's your best man?" Enquired Stan. The Duty Sergeant looked at Stan as if he was a mental case.

(He was quite correct in this assertion). Stan's wife had driven into a skip several years previously. As a result, one of Stan's eyes was fixed in a permanent watery stare because the associated eyelid couldn't blink. This afforded Stan a permanent menacing look. The one-eyed, unblinking stare suited the man who didn't possess any rational sense of fear and self-preservation. A one-to-one fight would be a walkover to the man who fought thirteen of The Chosen View bikers' gang on West Strand in Portrush the previous year.

"What did you say?" Asked the soldier. Stan repeated his challenge and added. "Bring out your best man. He and I will go out to the lawn. If I knock him out, you pay us. If he knocks me out, you've won a free installation." I just stood mesmerised. I couldn't believe what I was hearing. The sergeant checked Stan's eyes and said, "How much do we owe you?" That was a wise decision. His innate ability to avoid collateral damage should have earned that sergeant promotion.

RAF Aldergrove was one of the more accessible bases. We could simply drive there. Other installations were more challenging in terms of commitment and life expectancy. The Royal Commandos were stationed in Crossmaglen and required our services to watch Sky Sports when off duty. This required careful planning and a tight timetable. On this installation, The SSVC manager accompanied us to assess our on-base work. With my Citroen BX fully loaded with tools and equipment, he directed us to Bessbrook Mill. This was the helicopter hub for all military flights in and out of South Armagh. Colloquially, known as Bandit Country. We were security checked and briefed on arrival. Then we were directed to a landing pad to await the next flight to Crossmaglen. Our helicopter ride wasn't smooth, and I was relieved when we landed at our destination. We were told we had two hours before the helicopter returned to take us back to Bessbrook.

We co-opted off-duty soldiers who were happy to help. Stan and I erected the Satellite dish and made connections between the TV and receiver. Soldiers ran the cable between the two and made the installation as neat as possible. We powered up and tuned in the receiver. Everything worked satisfactorily. Another satisfied customer. The helicopter returned on schedule. We gathered our tools and boarded the aircraft. Stan and I sat in the two bucket seats against the rear bulkhead. The SSVC manager climbed aboard, placed the empty cable drum on the metal deck and sat on top. Directly in front of us, held by a safety harness to the roof of the cabin, stood a gunner manning a

7.62mm General Purpose Machine Gun. The gunner wore a flash embroidered with the motto "Paddy Don't Surf." This was a reference to the scene in Apocalypse Now where, to the music of The Ride of the Valkyries, American helicopters assault a Vietnamese village. Who said, "Humour is dead?"

The helicopter lifted off without any warning. The gunner leant out the open doorway as far as his safety harness permitted to gesticulate the universal two-fingered "Victory" sign to the locals below. No doubt, they returned the gesture in kind. "Bon-voyage, come back soon!" Our SSVC companion nearly returned to Crossmaglen sooner than planned. When we gained height, the pilot banked the aircraft 45 °. The cable drum he was sitting on slid towards the open doorway. He reached out frantically; I managed to grab his hands, just as he was about to fly solo. It was a great relief when the helicopter levelled out and we arrived safely in Bessbrook.

Another installation we carried out was for the Royal Marines stationed in Forkhill. We had flown in by helicopter and worked under time restrictions to ensure we finished and were ready for the scheduled return flight to Bessbrook. This Sunday afternoon, our return helicopter was overdue. I was concerned about what time I would return home. I strolled out to the landing pad at the rear of the barracks and watched a policeman practice his golf swing. He was hitting balls into the surrounding security fence. "Have you any idea why the helicopter is late?" I asked him, "Do you see that mountain over there?" He replied. "No," I said. "That's why the helicopter is late." To my relief, It arrived an hour later. The late flight meant we arrived at Bessbrook in the pitch-dark and lashing rain. I was tired and in too big a rush to get home. I thought the aircraft had landed. I didn't realise it was still hovering over the landing pad until I jumped out. Thankfully, I only dropped four feet to the ground. No bones were broken. Move along, please! Nothing to see here! I arrived home late and exhausted. Until then, I hadn't told Rhonda the extent of our work for SSVC because I didn't want her to worry. That evening, I owed her to tell her the truth.

I made frequent trips to One Flight, Army Air Corps at RAF Aldergrove and City Flight based in Holywood Army Barracks. It was 30 years since I visited Holywood Barracks with "Aunt Katie." I visited the home of a One Flight crew member in Aldergrove who couldn't record Satellite TV. The gentleman invited me in. All I had to do was tune his VHS Recorder to the receiver. "I couldn't follow the instructions," explained the customer as we chatted. He offered me a cup of tea and I asked him what his role was in the Air Corps. "I'm a pilot, I fly Wessex Helicopters;" we both burst out laughing. He couldn't "fly" a Sony VHS Recorder. The SAS had a presence at RAF Aldergrove in a hangar tucked away at the back of the base. I only made one call to them to realign their Satellite dish. When I returned to the car, several tools had vanished. I couldn't afford to go back a second time.

The SSVC outlet in Aldergrove was managed by a formidable English woman named Denise from Burton on Trent. She knew everyone on base and was a wealth of useful information. I don't use the word "formidable" lightly. Denise survived the Kegworth Air Disaster on 8th of January 1989 when British Midland Airways Flight 092, a Boeing 737-400, crashed onto the motorway embankment between the M1 motorway and the A453 near Kegworth, Leicestershire while attempting to make an emergency landing at East Midlands Airport. The next week, she flew on an RAF flight to Brize Norton. Denise didn't do Post Traumatic Stress Disorder.

With constant work from SSVC, 24-hour, 7-day rotas in BT and doing home renovations, I worked 16-hour, sometimes 20 hours a day. I self-medicated with Caffeine, Nicotine and Alcohol to keep the wheels turning as one day rolled into the next. In 1987, I used my Satellite Ireland earnings to take Claire and Lorna to London, for a weekend. We stayed in the Regent Palace Hotel and, saw Starlight Express in the Apollo Victoria Theatre. It was an expensive and enjoyable challenge, to keep two young daughters entertained for a whole weekend. Breakfast was £25 each; they only ate cornflakes.

Around this time, Stan moved to a new house. He and his partner invited me up to have, "A wee chat," one evening. Stan asked if I would allow him to use Satellite Ireland's funds to make necessary renovations to their new home. He said that, in return for my permission, he would make me a full partner in the business. I agreed.

Business and work continued. Rhonda and I began searching for a new house. We were in a better financial position to apply for a larger mortgage. We were working hard and "burning candles at both ends," sometimes oblivious to what was happening around us. We were shocked back to reality on the morning of 24th of February 1988. We turned on the BBC news to hear "Frederick Starrett and James Cummings, both 22, were killed by an IRA bomb as they arrived to close the security gates at Castlecourt in Royal Avenue. Our dear friend "Boon" had been murdered while on duty with the UDR.

That tragic news might have been the catalyst that convinced us we should marry as soon as possible. Life was too precious and uncertain to delay our plans any longer. We made the necessary arrangements to marry in Gretna Green on 6th of September 1989. We packed our little Citroen Visa, boarded the ferry with Cagney, our Shetland Sheepdog, and drove from Stranraer to Silloth in Cumbria on 4th of September. It was pitch dark when we reached Solway Firth. There was a heavy sea fret, which cleared intermittently, as the road undulated up and down, between peaks and troughs. On a peak, our headlights shone over the mist and it appeared we were flying over clouds. In a trough, the mist reflected our headlights at us. It was the strangest car journey I've ever been on.

We reached our rented accommodation after midnight. It was bone-chillingly cold and we rushed to unpack our car and get into the warmth. I wondered why the gravel path to the front door appeared so bright as there was no exterior lighting. I looked up and caught my breath. The mist had cleared and revealed the Milky Way stretched, from horizon to horizon, in all its majestic glory. The light from billions of stars in our galaxy was lighting our path. This was the first time I had seen the Milky Way. I doubt I will see it again in such splendorous detail.

The next day, we visited the Lowther Arms in Mawbray. The visit lasted longer than we intended. The owner was struggling to install new lighting over a brand-new pool table. I volunteered to help and retrieved my tool kit from the car. An hour later, everything was working. The owner and his wife were very grateful and a party atmosphere developed when we told them we were marrying the next day. We were still groggy when we set off for Gretna Green the following morning and arrived on time for our appointment with the Assistant Registrar, Mrs D Taylor. She asked who our witnesses were. Ooops! We didn't have any. "Quick," she said, "Go fetch the couple who have just left." Our wedding was witnessed by two Indian Doctors from Cambridge, Mr and Mrs Sharma. An Estate Agent we had met in the Lowther Arms took our photographs. At some point during the previous day's festivities, he had volunteered to be our photographer and travelled to Scotland to honour his promise.

Now for our Honeymoon. Because I'm a great romantic, I took my new wife to Sellafield Nuclear Power Station. Not exactly though! To my disappointment, we were only allowed into the Visitors Centre. When Rhonda and I stood in the middle of a mock-up Nuclear Reactor, we just had to sing, "I'm in the middle of a chain reaction." That was the start of our week's stay in Cumbria, visiting the Lake District. For the second week of our Honeymoon, we stayed in Skipton and toured the Yorkshire Dales. Our rented house was on a very steep street; I didn't trust my handbrake so I put bricks behind the rear wheels each evening. Just in case......

We drove some demanding routes while touring through the two National Parks. Fortunately, we had no mechanical issues until our ferry docked in Larne. We had just disembarked when the gearbox seized. We managed to drive home in second gear. The next day, our friend Phil Holland called to welcome us back. I mentioned the car and he said he might be able to repair it. He replaced a broken link the next day for £8.00. Phil was "a raker" in the true sense. He burnt all his candles at both ends at once. We always enjoyed his company and craic. However, we lost contact with Phil when we moved house in 1993. But God had plans.

In Spring 2022, I was walking Marley through Ballyhackamore when I heard someone shout my name. I turned and, said, "Paul?" I couldn't remember his name. It was nearly thirty years since we had last met one another. He gently corrected me and introduced me to his wife Caroline, standing beside him. Once we had formalities completed Phil said, "Stephen, you might not believe this but I've come to faith in Christ." Wow! Phil was surprised in return to discover his old drinking buddy was now an Ordained Elder in the Presbyterian Church. Phil and Caroline accepted my invitation to visit Bloomfield Church and are now regular attendees. Caroline has jumped right in. She joined Presbyterian Women and is a member of the Welcoming Committee. They are dear friends and we are blessed that God brought them into our lives.

Our daughter Rebekah was born on 12th of March 1991. Rebekah spent the first six weeks of her life in Intensive Care at the City Hospital suffering from a Pneumothorax and a cleft in her soft pallet. Rhonda spent every moment with her while I carried on as best I could at home and work. When Rebekah finally came home, she had no sleep pattern and required special bottles to help her swallow her daily feeds. Rhonda and I took turns going to bed so one of us could nurse and feed her through the night. I had contacted local taxi firms previously to ask their drivers to rap customers' doors rather than sit outside and sound their horns. In other words, follow the Highway Code. We were pestered often in this respect and one morning, "I lost it." At 1.00 am, Rebekah fell asleep in my arms, I dozed off too then, HONK HONK, right outside our house. When I "woke up," I was standing beside the taxi. I had Rebekah in my left arm and the driver's throat grasped in my right hand. "I'm sorry mister, I'm sorry mister," he stuttered. I was fortunate he didn't report me for assault. I realised I was living on my nerves.

I was assembling a Satellite dish at home preparing for an installation the next day when our door rapped. It was someone from the East Belfast Mission inviting people to a Gospel rally, taking place the following weekend. I'm ashamed of what I said to this "brave" man. I scolded him for having the audacity to ask me along to any Christian event. "I had no time for any religion," and chased him up the street. He had twanged my one remaining nerve. One day, I will apologise to him.

We installed our largest SMATV system in the Military Wing of Musgrave Park Hospital, Belfast over the weekend of 25th and 26th of September 1991. On Saturday the 2nd of November 1991, a bomb planted by the Provisional IRA exploded in the Military Wing. Two British soldiers were killed, and nine others were wounded. Two children, a five-year-old girl and a baby of four months, were also injured by the blast. I waited to be taken in for questioning. Surely, we must have been suspected of involvement, but my fears never materialised. A hospital porter was eventually charged with the two murders.

Later, the same year, our SSVC manager & friend welcomed a visitor from England to his Lisburn office. The visitor was the SSVC Director responsible for N Ireland. He informed him he was giving him a month's notice as his services were no longer required. True to his Scottish roots, our friend told the director what he could do with his notice, put his coat on and walked out. This was the harbinger of the demise of SSVC. Within a few months, all its retail outlets closed and staff were redundant. All requests for white goods and services would be handled by the NAAFI organisation already present on all the military bases. Satellite Ireland had no connection with NAAFI and our work for the MoD ended.

Stan drove us home one evening from an installation we had just completed in Whiteabbey. We took the opportunity to discuss what direction to take the business considering developments with SSVC. During our conversation, I mentioned our partnership. Stan replied, "Partnership, what partnership?" I reminded him about the verbal agreement we made that allowed him to carry out work on his new house. "I don't remember that conversation," he said. Despite my protests, he continued to deny any knowledge of our agreement. After everything we had been through together, literally risking our lives for the sake of the business, I was completely devastated. It wasn't about money, there wasn't a great amount in the company's bank account; it was the act of betrayal that hurt. I was a fool and too trusting not to have asked for a written agreement. People and money again. They're seldom a good combination. That was the end of our "partnership" and our friendship.

It was time to move on physically and leave the past behind. Our move to Irwin Drive in the spring of 1993 proved stressful and difficult but nowhere near as difficult as forgetting the past.

In the next chapter Northern Telecom, I mention Doug Riley's mantra "The customer comes first." This emboldened BT staff to go the extra mile to ensure customer satisfaction at every level, whether in Sales, Construction, or Maintenance. An incident occurred, which gained me a reputation for being able to deal with awkward customers. The awkward customer in this case was the Postmaster of Woodstock Road Post Office. I have huge sympathy for Postmasters caught up in the Horizon Scandal, but this Postmaster was an obnoxious character. He was referred to me because he was complaining about nuisance telephone calls. I called him; he was irate. "Every time he answered his phone no one spoke to him." He refused to cooperate with me, saying he didn't have the time.

Taking Doug's advice to heart, I informed my manager I was leaving Telephone House and drove to the Post Office on Woodstock Road. When I entered, I joined the queue for the counter. There were three people in front of me. While I was waiting, the Postmaster leaned over to the assistant on the adjacent till and waved a Scottish £5 note in her face. He chastised her saying, "How many times have I told you not to accept these notes?" The assistant was visibly shaken. When I reached the counter, I asked if he was the gentleman who had reported nuisance calls on his telephone. He said he was. I showed him my security pass and informed him I was the engineer he had been ignorant with on the phone. He refused to open the slotted screen to hear me more clearly.

Eventually, I convinced him I had set up an automatic trace facility on the line. All he had to do when he received a nuisance call, was press "1" on his keypad. This would hold the call and trace it to its point of origin. I asked him if I bought a book of stamps and posted threatening letters to someone, would it make sense for that person to blame the Post Office for selling stamps? "I suppose not," he reluctantly admitted. Within two days, I solved the problem. The Post Office Control Centre at Milton Keynes was inadvertently sending test signals to his security alarm connected to his main telephone. He never said thank you. I reported him to the Post Office Customer Services' HQ in Glasgow. I sent a letter detailing everything that happened including how he treated his staff. Within weeks, he was no longer in charge of the Woodstock Road Post Office. No one wants anyone to lose their job and I trust he was offered a less stressful position within the Post Office.

I received a reward for showing initiative and my reputation spread. One morning, I received a call from Brian Nixon in the Repair Service Centre asking if I would deal with another difficult customer. He forewarned me, "Be prepared to take abuse." "Send it over," I said. The fault report appeared on my Customers' Service System screen. This was a computer-based customer fault recording program that traced the actions taken by staff on a given fault. The customer in question was Mrs White of North Boundary Street, complaining that her customer's coin box telephone wasn't working properly. I tested her line and couldn't detect any fault. So, I suspected the problem was with the mechanism on her telephone. I called Mrs White, and she was able to answer me. I said hello and introduced myself. I explained someone would need to visit and check the mechanism on her phone. She advised me, in her broad lower-Shankill vernacular, that I could, "Take my telephone and shove it where the sun didn't shine," followed by a string of expletives about the inconvenience this was causing her. Charming to meet you too madam.

This was before GDPR and Freedom of Information requests. No company was concerned about someone demanding to know what information the business held about them or what computer records were stored against their details. So, on 13th of October 1994, I tapped the following into my computer:

"Linesman required to visit subscriber's premises. Line tested OK. Customer unable to make outgoing calls. Suspect faulty coin mechanism. Change coin mechanism. Advise Linesman to take new mechanism, a stun grenade and fully charged cattle prod. When customer answers door, pull pin on grenade and lob it into hallway. Step over comatose customer and swap coin mechanism ASAP. If customer stirs before this job completed, zap with cattle prod, complete job and get to blazes out of premises tout de suite."

I completed the fault report and dispatched it to the Repair Service Centre for allocation to a Linesman. Brian Nixon approached me when I was queuing for tea in the canteen the following day.

"We killed ourselves laughing when we read your advice for the linesman. An engineer visited her and Mrs White's telephone is working now. Were you watching the news last night?" Brian asked. "Yes, I was," I replied. "Did you watch Gusty Spence announce the loyalist ceasefire?" He asked. "Yes, I did, I was glad to hear it," the conversation continued. "Did you see the man sitting beside Gusty?" Asked Brian. "Yes, I did." "Do you know who he was?" "No," I replied. "That was Mr White." Brian laughed when he saw the stunned expression on my face. John White aka Captain Black. So much for life imprisonment. I'm relieved he never got in touch with me.

The Sky Was The Limit

Our first challenge:

Running was my main pastime from Cross-Country days at the Boys' Model and I joined Buster McShane's Gym in Newtownards, managed by his son Michael. At the age of 30, I was never fitter in my life. I had exhausted the musical talents I thought I possessed and, had given up hope of playing guitar or piano anyway well.

I mentioned Alan "Joey" McKinstry earlier. Alan and I turned 30 in January 1983. We decided to celebrate three decades of life by doing three things we would never do again. First, was the Belfast Marathon, second, the Mourne Wall Walk and third but not least, a Parachute jump.

Together, with Tom Black and Kevin Weir, we began a rigorous training programme including daily lunchtime runs from Telephone House, May Street up to Forestside, along Knock dual carriageway, down Cregagh and Woodstock Roads, along Albertbridge Road, down Cromac Street and back to Telephone House. On weekends, I ran from home in Pinecroft Avenue, Newtownards to Greyabbey and back again. I was running approximately 100 miles every week and enjoying myself.

May Bank Holiday Monday 1983, saw the start of the second Belfast Marathon. The four of us were among 4,000 starters who set off on the 26-mile Marathon route around Belfast. There was a party atmosphere and, due to the beautiful weather, spectators thronged the entire route, cheering the runners. On Ravenhill Road, a family had moved their living room, including a television and standard lamp, and placed it on the footpath. Four spectators sat on the settee and cheered us as we ran past. I didn't have the breath to laugh, I could only wave at them. I ran non-stop and crossed the finishing line at Maysfields Leisure Centre in 4 hours 4 minutes. Not too Craigavad!

Several days later, I was sore. It felt as though I was sitting on broken glass. I set a mirror on the loo, bent over, spread my cheeks and spotted what I thought was a blister on my bum. That made sense after all the running without greasing my moving parts beforehand. Taking medical matters into my own hands, I boiled water and used it to sterilise a needle. I went back to the bathroom and assumed the same position. I gingerly guided the needle towards the blister. I was set to administer the Coups de Grace when our doorbell rang. I abandoned proceedings, dressed and went to the door. Guess who? Dad had called to see how I was. I explained my predicament and he offered to take me to A & E for proper diagnosis. Unbelievably, it took three doctors to identify the problem. The third doctor was an Egyptian. He declared, "Mr McDonald you 'ave de piles," and smiled. I was sent home with instructions to rest and apply ice to my nether regions. I couldn't help but wonder what would have happened if I had punctured that "blister," come pile. The bathroom might have needed repainting. Might I have bled out? Only God knows. I thanked Him for Divine Intervention. He would intervene again before we completed our trio of events.

We had no ice-making facilities at home. For the next few days, I lay on my tummy in bed with a half-pound bag of Bachelors Frozen Garden Peas jammed between my bum cheeks. I hope this revelation doesn't put you off your greens. You'll not see Captain Birdseye doing that in TV commercials. "Arr, arr mehardies." I can't remember if we ate them when they thawed. I couldn't take any more time off work and returned after two weeks on sick leave. I was determined not to tell any of my colleagues the truth about why I had been absent; the banter would have been merciless. One morning, at coffee break, I was sitting with Terry Neeson, who mentioned, "You don't look very well, is there anything wrong?" Terry agreed he wouldn't repeat what I told him to anyone. To my surprise, he told me his brother was a doctor at Newtownards Hospital; he would call him on my behalf. An hour later, Terry told me Connor was expecting me at Newtownards A & E. I asked Terry how I could show my appreciation. His advice was to buy Connor a box of 20 Embassy Regal cigarettes.

As promised, Connor was expecting me. He accepted my gift of cigarettes and invited me to undress so he could inspect the matter in question. Lying on my tummy, Connor began to probe around my nether regions. Pain shot through me. I instinctively twisted around and threw a punch at Connor. "Wow! Wow!" Shouted Connor. "Relax Stephen don't move. Those piles are fighting back. I'm going to get a surgeon to look at you." I lay there expecting a middle-aged bloke with bifocals and grey hair to appear. I was still on my stomach when the surgeon arrived. The first thing this beautiful 30-year-old female saw was my bare bum peeping out of my hospital gown. She said, "Hello Stephen, do I know you from somewhere?" Pain and laughter make strange bedfellows.

"Right," she said, "You're not going home, take this letter up to Male Surgical." I walked slowly and eventually made it to the ward. I handed the Ward Sister the surgeon's notes and she directed me to a free bed. I staggered over to the bed, braced my arms and leaned on it to catch my breath. Behind me, I heard, "Huh! You think you're bad?" My bed neighbour was the Head Gardener from Castle Ward on Strangford Lough. I'll not mention his habits. They would definitely put you off your greens. I was so eager to get away from him that, following my surgery, I signed myself out of hospital.

When I discharged myself, I drove straight to Millfield Technical College to sit my HNC in Telecommunications examination. I had studied for this over the previous three years. Somehow, word was out about my predicament and, when I entered the examination room, the adjudicator Ray Lunn, offered me his cushion to sit on. Everyone seemed quite amused. I opened the exam paper and read it. I must have been studying a different subject. I only realised then my mind was completely mush. I wrote the date, signed my name, waited for the minimum of 30 minutes, handed in my paper and "Got out of Dodge."

Ray Lunn arranged the resit of my HNC examination a month later. To my great relief, I passed with Endorsements in 1986.

Our second challenge:

In 1956 the Youth Hostel Association of Northern Ireland organised the first "Mourne Wall Walk" encouraging the public to walk the length of the Water Commissions Wall that encloses the rain catchment area. The wall is a gruelling 22 miles long with 10,000ft of ascent. Walking it in a single day is a considerable feat. Only a few walkers participated in the first year, but news of the event spread by word of mouth. By 1960 there were nearly 150 walkers. In 1962, numbers increased to 250. In 1967, 500 turned up for the 10th Anniversary walk. Numbers increased annually. In 1977 almost 2,000 walkers took part with 1,512 completing the event. The record was broken that year for the best finishing time by Jim Hayes, a 30-year-old man from Comber who finished in 4 hours, 11 minutes and 30 seconds, beating the previous record by minutes. In 1979 3,000 people applied to participate. By 1984 there was serious concern about the damage so many walkers were doing to the fragile Mournes environment resulting in the Youth Hostelling Association cancelling the walk in the name of conservation.

I'm proud to boast, between 1981 and 1983, I completed the Mourne Wall Challenge on three consecutive attempts in the 12-hour allotted time space. I have the badges and certificates to prove it.

Alan and I set off at 8.00 am from the Quarter Road, Silent Valley starting point and made our way steadily up the track towards the summit of Slieve Binnian. On completion, we learned our friend and work colleague, Martin Hanvey was one of the last walkers to begin the challenge around 10.00 am. Halfway up Slieve Binnian he heard someone calling for help. He followed the cries and discovered an injured walker with a broken leg; his face and hands bloodied by his fall.

Martin returned to the assembly point as quickly as he could and reported the situation. An emergency call was made, and Martin was asked to return to the injured party and guide in the RAF Rescue helicopter. The helicopter and Martin reached the casualty at the same time. He helped stretcher the lad onboard the aircraft and the winchman invited Martin to travel back with them to the First Aid tent. It was too late for Martin to recommence his walk.

On landing, Martin bid farewell to the casualty and crew. He walked to the reception tent and Martin described what happened next. "I was standing in my dirty gear, carrying my rucksack and holding a cup of tea and slice of lemon cake when I heard someone gasp in an English accent, "Ahh no!" I turned to see a slight figure in running gear and track shoes who asked me, "How long did it take you?" I realised immediately this bloke was a Fell Runner. Practically, a professional mountain runner, out to claim Jim Haye's record. Thinking quickly, I looked at my watch and answered, "Oh, I got in about 10 minutes ago." The Fell Runner's face was a picture of devastation. I let the guy stew in misery for about 10 minutes before admitting the truth." As far as I'm aware Haye's record of 4 hours 11 minutes and 30 seconds still stands.

Exhausted after our 12-hour trek, we were met at the finish by another friend and work colleague, Greer Sloan, who had agreed to drive us home after a visit to the Brook Cottage Hotel to celebrate our achievement with other friends and their wives. It turned out a rather late night due to the two types of high spirits flowing. On leaving, we couldn't see Greer's Citroen 2 CV and found it lying toppled on one side. After some exertion, four of us pushed it into an upright position. Unbelievably, it started the first time and off we headed to Belfast with someone asking Greer to open a window to let in some warm air. I owned a 600cc

Citroen Dyane at the same time which I enjoyed driving. Greer borrowed my wheels to get his 2CV through the MOT because his tyres were worn. Michelin X tyres were specific to the Citroen Dyane and 2CV models. They were expensive to replace.

Our third and nearly fatal challenge:

Having finished our first and second challenges, we continued with our plan to complete a parachute jump. This would be the climax of our Three Decades Three Challenges celebrations. Alan and I asked Gerry Gettenby to arrange our jump with the Wild Geese Parachute Club near Garvagh, outside Coleraine. Gerry was an Executive Engineer, and member of the club, who had advanced to Freefall. Our jumps would be on Static Lines from a height of 2,000 feet.

Eventually, our appointment with Destiny arrived one Wednesday in September 1983. Gerry, Alan, myself and another colleague, Paul Shortt were given instructions on how to enter and leave the aircraft. We were shown how to pack our own main and reserve parachutes. This gave us confidence in the opening of the chutes because we had seen how they were packed and how the release mechanism worked. So far so good. Take-off was planned for 1.00 pm. With nervous excitement and anticipation, we strapped on our parachutes, listened to final instructions and proceeded to board the plane and connect our Static Lines. They would automatically open our chutes when we jumped from the plane, a Cessna 182, adopted for parachute jumping. In other words, a Cessna 182 without doors.

The four of us crouched behind the pilot as he started the engine, taxied to the end of the field and made his final checks before he opened the throttle and sent the plane hurtling down the grass runway. As we reached take-off speed, Phutt! Phutt! The plane's engine stopped, and we ground to a halt at the end of the runway. We unhooked our Static Lines, disembarked and walked back to the Portacabin. What had happened? Everyone was disconcerted. Dave Penny, founder of The Wild Geese, offered us his apologies and, walked to the plane where the pilot was inspecting the engine.

We found out later that week what had happened. Outside, down one side of the club's Portacabin, was a line of jerry cans filled with Lycoming O 540 engine oil for the plane. Down the other side of the Portacabin was a line of jerry cans filled with diesel for the club's Land Rover. Our pilot had filled the plane with diesel. There was enough Lycoming in the plane's tanks to take us to the end of the runway. Any more and we could have been 50 to 100 feet off the ground when the engine failed. Our parachutes wouldn't have been much use. Even today, all these years later, I find it hard to appreciate how close we came to meeting our deaths that day. I believe Divine Intervention occurred again that day. We packed up and headed home with an invitation to return the following Friday and complete our jumps.

The following Friday the four of us returned to the Wild Geese and found the pilot was still cleaning diesel out of the engine's 12 carburettors. Paul, Alan and I decided not to hang about and informed Gerry we were going for an early lunch to the pub in nearby Garvagh. We had just finished our second pint and were about to start a third when Gerry popped his head through the door and asked, "Have you boys been drinking?" "No, no, we innocently replied." "Come on then," said Gerry, "They've got the plane going."

We arrived at the plane, put on our Main and Reserve parachutes, listened to final instructions and boarded the plane. I "volunteered" to go last forgetting that last in meant first out. Oh dear! This time we took off without incident and, as I knelt behind the pilot, I watched the altimeter climb steadily towards 2,000 feet at the same rate as butterflies in my stomach. At 2,000 feet, I was tapped on the shoulder to indicate it was time to exit. There's nothing quite like stepping out of a plane to stand on a little platform, hang on tightly to a wing strut and wait for a nod to let go. Perhaps, without the Dutch Courage I had imbibed, the plane might have had to land with me still gripping the strut for dear life. Who knows?

When I "got the nod" I let go and watched the plane recede above me. On leaving the plane, our instructions were to count, "One thousand, two thousand, three thousand, check canopy." I only remember shouting "Aaaaaaaaaaaaaaah!!!!!!!" There was an abrupt tug, I looked up to see my canopy fully deployed above me. Phew! As I drifted towards the Drop Zone, I came within earshot of Dave Penny who was using a megaphone to direct me to which of two toggles to pull to ensure I touched down in the Drop Zone. I heard, "Right toggle Number One, right toggle Number One, for f???'s sake, right toggle Number One." I can't explain why I kept pulling the left toggle. I was never left-handed. My right brain seemed to have taken control of my body. I unceremoniously and uninvitedly landed in a farmyard about a quarter of a mile from where I was supposed to land. It was a mercy I didn't land on the busy Carrowreagh Road and get run over or land on power lines. I gathered up my chute and walked back to the airfield. The instructor completed my Jump Log and added, "I didn't hear you count." No comment!

Our companion that day was Paul Shortt. Paul worked on the Transmission team in the Repeater Station at Telephone House. Alan and I counted our blessings and never jumped again. Paul was bitten and took up parachute jumping as a serious pass time. He qualified as a skilled, display Freefall Parachutist. two years after his debut with The Wild Geese, Paul died during a display in County Offaly when his main parachute didn't open, and he couldn't reach his reserve. A careless mistake cost Paul his life.

It's a testament to how well staff in Telephone House worked together that, regardless of religious background during the bad years of The Troubles, we all attended his funeral at The Good Shepherd Chapel on Ormeau Road. Until then, we hadn't realised he was a Roman Catholic. The choir sang Ave Maria that day. It would have wrought tears from an atheist. It was a sad day and a tragic loss.

An Ill Wind

I mentioned before, we moved to 12B Shackleton Walk on Westwinds Estate in Newtownards in 1972 on medical advice after Dad's accident. Mum and Dad settled in quickly, but I found it strange not having a front door, living on the first floor beside two other flats. I never felt at home or had a sense of belonging. I had left my previous life on Woodvale Road behind, along with all my friends. It was difficult to keep in contact with them and, over time those friendships gradually withered away. We joined Strean Presbyterian Church, and I attended most Sundays, more from habit than any commitment. Mum and Dad adjusted quickly to their new church and congregation. Soon, they were popular members of Strean Indoor Bowling Club.

One evening, Charlie and Anna Cunningham invited us for supper to their dairy farm on Anderson's Hill off Crawfordsburn Road outside Newtownards. This was the first time I met them along with their son Dessie and daughter Jennifer. We spent a pleasant evening getting to know one another. Dessie worked on the farm with his Dad while Jennifer was a secretary at Northern Ireland

Carpets. Later that year, Jennifer and I began dating. We were engaged by the end of 1974 and married in Strean Presbyterian Church on 27th September 1975 by the Reverend George Eagleston. The signs didn't auger well for our future together.

Before our wedding ceremony my Grandmother "Day" whispered something I will never forget. "Stephen, you're going to tie a knot with your tongue, you won't loose with your teeth." How did Day know our marriage wouldn't last? The weather was atrocious, the worst day of the year. There was a break in the rain as we left church that allowed our photographer to take a couple of photographs. When we arrived at Clanbrassil House in Cultra for our reception, it was lashing rain again, and the sea was crashing over the seawalls. It was disconcerting considering we were due to sail to Liverpool that evening and next morning, travel by train to Torquay where we would begin our week's honeymoon.

Rodney and Mary McCurley were two guests. I had worked with Rodney since I joined the same staff in Telephone House. Mary, his wife, was a supervisor in the fifth floor Manual Room. Rodney approached me and asked how Jennifer and I planned to get to the Liverpool ferry after the reception. We gladly accepted his offer of help and left the reception with Rodney and Mary around 5.00 pm. They lived on the Colinbridge Road in Glengormley. Mary made a light tea for everyone, and we left around 7.00pm. Rodney drove an Austin Mini at the time. Our suitcase was in the boot; Jennifer and I clambered into the back seat. Mary sat in the front passenger seat and off we went. It was twilight as Rodney drove along Antrim Road and turned down Serpentine Road.

Suddenly, there was an almighty crash and the car's windscreen disintegrated when a young woman came through it and sprawled across Rodney and Mary's knees. Mary and Jennifer screamed; Rodney and I were too shocked to do anything. We all scrambled out of the car but weren't sure about moving the casualty. Someone called the emergency services; the police and ambulance appeared quite quickly and managed to extricate the casualty from the car and place her on a stretcher. Paramedics assured us she had regained consciousness and appeared to have only sustained a broken leg. The woman explained she was running across the road to catch a bus when Rodney's car hit her.

The police noticed the confetti covering the car's floor and asked Rodney where he was travelling to. Rodney explained all that had happened that day and he was driving the newlywed couple to the

Liverpool ferry. I can't remember if Rodney was breathalysed but it wouldn't have served any purpose. Rodney had been teetotal all his life. He might have been better off drinking beer as his doctor blamed his ulcers on all the Coca-Cola he drank. A burly policeman appeared beside Jennifer and me carrying our suitcase. He threw it into the back of the police Land Rover and told us to climb aboard. Rodney saw our hesitation and said, "Stephen I feel bad enough as it is, if you don't go, I'll feel even worse." As soon as we clambered into the back of the Land Rover, the police jumped aboard carrying their rifles and submachine guns. The driver put on his lights and sirens, did a U-turn on the road and headed for the docks as fast as the Land Rover would go.

After leaving Serpentine Road, we joined the recently opened Foreshore Section of the M2. This was the first time I was ever along this new motorway section and I will never forget it. We raced along at top speed towards the ferry terminal, where the Belfast Weir is today. When this section of the M2 opened to traffic in May 1973, it was the widest motorway in the British Isles with two 10-lane sections. A long queue of passengers was waiting to enter the terminal when our Land Rover screeched to a halt outside. The police disembarked and "stood guard" as we climbed from the Land Rover grasping our single suitcase. I could imagine what people were thinking. "Who are they?" "Are they being deported?" "What have they done?" "Isn't he a dodgy-looking character?" We thanked our escorts and were ushered to the front of the queue; we passed our security checks and boarded the ship. What else could go wrong?

We found our cabin. It had a bunk bed. I took the top and Jennifer took the bottom. Our cabin was next to the hold. There had been a dog show that Saturday in the King's Hall. It sounded as if every dog in Britain was returning home that evening. WOOF! WOOF! WOOF! WOOF! All night long. It wasn't exactly the wedding evening either of us had anticipated. Guess what was number one in the Pop Charts that day! Sailing by Rod Stewart. You couldn't make it up.

Our two daughters Claire and Lorna were born on 23rd October 1980 and 29th April 1982 respectively and turned our once quiet home into Bedlam. Like all daring children, the girls had begun to collect their fair share of cuts and bruises. The worst accident happened when pushing them in their double buggy along Frances Street one Saturday morning. The front wheels of the pram caught in a concrete rain drain that ran the breadth of the pavement. Forward momentum tilted the buggy over and dumped the girls headfirst onto the pavement. It happened so quickly the girls couldn't put their hands in front of them to cushion the blow. I heard the dull thud when their heads hit the pavement. The girls were too shocked to cry. By the time we arrived home, Claire and Lorna had "boiled eggs" growing out of their foreheads and their eyes had begun to blacken. Jennifer and I were afraid to take the girls to hospital in case we were accused of child cruelty. The lumps and black eyes made them look cute though.

This is a difficult part of my memoir to write. It refers to incidents and personal feelings that Jennifer and I tried to forget as we moved on with the rest of our lives. Within four years, cracks appeared in our marriage. We had realised we didn't have a lot in common. We had married for the wrong reasons: not true love. I had married to get out of Westwinds Estate by any means possible. As tensions rose between Jennifer and I, arguments increased and became more serious. Subconsciously, I was pushing Jennifer away. I remember the date and time of our worst argument. We were living in Victoria Crescent when it happened on 27th August 1979 at 5.00 pm. News had just broken of an IRA bomb attack on the British Army in Warrenpoint and the assassination by the IRA of Lord Louis Mountbatten while on holiday in Sligo. I can't remember what we were arguing about but Jennifer kept on at me despite the news reports. The news made our differences seem irrelevant to me and I lost my temper.

The Narrow Water Ambush, also known as the Warrenpoint Ambush, took place that infamous day at 4.40pm During this incident, the Provisional Irish Republican Army ambushed a British Army convoy near Narrow Water Castle, located outside Warrenpoint. The attack involved two large roadside bombs. The first bomb targeted the convoy itself, while the second was aimed at incoming responders and the Incident Command Point set up to deal with the aftermath. IRA volunteers hidden in nearby woods fired on the troops, who returned fire. 18 British soldiers lost their lives, and over 20 were seriously injured, making it the deadliest attack on the British Army during The Troubles. An English civilian was killed, and an Irish civilian was wounded by British soldiers firing across Carlingford Lough after the first blast.

In all our rows and arguments, there was never any physical abuse. However, in this instance, it came very close. One of our naff wedding presents was an ostentatious bedside lamp made up of a lampshade mounted on an onyx body atop a brass base. You can guess it was a considerable weight.

214

When I was in full voice, Jennifer lifted the lamp from the bedside unit and threw it at my head. I saw it coming, frozen to the spot, I couldn't do anything. It was my good fortune the lamp was still plugged in. The lamp stopped abruptly an inch from my face and fell to the floor. We couldn't argue any further as we were laughing too much.

Even bad moments can work in our favour if we don't withdraw and face difficulties and challenges head-on. I don't enjoy arguments. I suppose no one does. I need time to think, gather information and form responses when I argue I'm not nimble minded enough to think on my feet and have often thought of something I wished I had said after the event. I become so frustrated I believe it's better to "Get out of Dodge" as quickly as possible and find somewhere to think. This happened one Sunday afternoon in 1982. I was due to start night shift in Telephone House at 8.00 pm but stormed out of the house around 5.00 pm, during another argument with Jennifer. I needed time to think.

There was no point in driving directly from Newtownards to Belfast, I would have been much too early for work. Instead, I took the long way out via the Crawfordsburn Road to where it meets the Belfast to Bangor dual carriageway. I drove towards Belfast. When I approached the Folk and Transport Museum at Cultra, I noticed two hitchhikers standing under the bridge to avoid the rain. They were facing away from me and wearing rucksacks bearing Maple Leaf flags. One was broad-shouldered, and I assumed they were a Canadian couple hoping for a lift to Belfast. Hitchhikers didn't have much success in those days because of The Troubles. I was sure it was safe to stop and offer them a lift. After all, I was in no hurry. So, I pulled over.

I was nearly right on both counts. They were two sisters from Toronto, Judy and Sue Hastie, hoping for a lift into Belfast. Sue happened to be burlier than her sibling. There wasn't much space in my Citroen Dyane, so Sue sat up front and Judy sat in the back with their rucksacks. "Where to?" I asked. Their answer was ambiguous so I asked again, "Where would you like to go?" Again, they prevaricated. The penny dropped! I said, "I'm a Protestant, does that help you?" Judy and Sue laughed. "Yes, it does. We want to hear the Reverend Ian Paisley preach in The Martyrs' Memorial." I explained I was early for work and could take them there. We chatted along the way, and I learned they were touring Ireland for a month. They were both amicable and easy to get along with. So far so good.

We arrived outside the Martyr's Memorial around 6.30 pm. Sue got out of the car and spoke to a lady wearing her Sunday best about to enter the church. "Excuse me, madam. Is the Reverend Ian Paisley preaching here this evening?" The woman replied, "I'm sorry love, he's in Toronto. "The three of us dissolved into laughter. The tears tripped us. Our friendship was cemented. "Where to now?" I asked when we all got our breaths back. "We need somewhere to stay," they answered. I found them a B & B off Ormeau Road and arranged to collect them the next morning when I finished work.

I collected them on Monday at 8.30 am. It was a bright, clear morning and I didn't feel too tired, so I drove the girls to Carrick Little in the Mourne Mountains. The sisters were keen walkers and agreed to my suggestion to climb Slieve Binnian and return via Wee Binnian and the Head Road. And off we went. The walk took longer than we anticipated. Halfway into our walk, Judy informed me she was asthmatic, and we had to stop quite often to let her catch her breath. We returned to the car in lashing rain. It was typical Mourne's weather. If it's not raining, it's going to rain.

We had enjoyed our hike and the sisters had taken dozens of photographs. We were exhausted by our exertions and the girls were happy to call it a day. I found a house on Bryansford Road advertising B & B. Judy knocked on the door and enquired if there were any vacancies. The owners invited her in to check the rooms. She returned to the car and asked me to come in. Inside she whispered, "Stephen, are they Catholics or Protestants?" I've no idea why she wanted to know but her query was easily solved. There was a copy of the Irish News lying on the hall table. Using my extraordinary powers of deduction, I whispered "They're definitely Catholics." Is Northern Ireland is the only place in the world where someone can tell another person's religion by the newspapers they read?

They told me they enjoyed their overnight stay with "the Catholics" when I met them again on the return leg of their tour of Northern Ireland. By then, Jennifer and I were on speaking terms again and were delighted when Judy and Sue accepted our invitation to stay with us for the remainder of their holiday. We stayed in touch with one another for a while when they returned to Canada but inevitably, we lost contact. To Judy and Sue, thank you for the fun and laughter.

Despite everything, I never regretted leaving Westwinds Estate. Belfast was changing rapidly due to urban redevelopment during the 70s and 80s. Displaced families were relocated to new estates in Greater Belfast and rural towns. Unfortunately, people brought their problems and loyalties with them; estates became divided by tradition and religion. Westwinds became predominately Protestant. There were a few Catholic families, but they kept a low profile and didn't draw attention to themselves. Drugs became an issue on the estate and where there are drugs there are paramilitaries. I hold them all in total contempt for what they did to my friend and work colleague Jackie Anderson.

Jackie was a cleaner on the third floor Local Exchange in Telephone House. I knew Jackie well as we shared lifts to work together with another colleague, Ray Fitzsimmons. Jackie was a simple soul with seven children. On holiday to Newcastle, Co. Down his family had to book two B & Bs. There wasn't one large enough to accommodate them all. Eventually, Jackie and his wife separated, and he lived with his oldest son in Westwinds. Unknown to Jackie, his son was carrying out break-ins on the estate. When police did nothing to investigate, victims turned to paramilitaries for help.

One evening, Jackie answered his door. Several masked men asked, "Are you Jackie Anderson?" Jackie replied "Yes." The three "local heroes" proceeded to beat Jackie within an inch of his life with hammers, leaving him permanently disabled and unable to work again. None of the idiots had checked Jackie's son was named Jackie Anderson as well. Jackie moved to Hornby Street in East

Belfast where his remaining family cared for him. Up to 2018, I would see him limping along the Lower Newtownards Road on his Zimmer frame. I stopped one day and spoke with him. He was polite as always, but I don't think he recognised me. Sadly, he has passed away. Another victim of violence no one was ever held to account for.

Trust, Rust and Isopon

To my great regret and shame, I lost touch with another couple but for a completely different reason. I'll end this chapter with one of the greatest regrets of my life. One I'm still ashamed of. Perhaps, God in a miracle of grace, will allow me to say, "I'm sorry" someday. Our neighbours at 8 Victoria Crescent were a newly married couple, Clifford and Lorraine Henry. Clifford was a scientist who worked for the N. Ireland Water Service. Its headquarters was in the building that is now Marks & Spencer in Donegall Place, Belfast. Lorraine worked around the corner in Ulster Bank Headquarters.

From the moment we met, we became firm friends. Clifford and Lorraine, like Jennifer and myself, were newly married and setting up their first home together. We were continually decorating and making alterations to our homes which necessitated a continual exchange of advice and the requisite tools to do the jobs. We came close to disaster on two occasions.

Kenneth and Barbara were our other neighbours in number 4 but we called them Ken and Barbie. Just like their Mattel plastic effigies they were the "Body Beautiful" types and jogged together in matching tracksuits and headbands. Ken was a fireman based in Belfast. He was embarrassed when he came home one afternoon to find a fire engine from Newtownards Fire Brigade at his house, pumping water down his chimney. Our houses were all heated by gravity-fed, glass-fronted, coal-fired boilers in our living rooms. Ken and Barbie's chimney had caught fire and another neighbour called the fire brigade. Unfortunately, Jennifer and I shared their chimney flue and suffered some water damage. We didn't have flooring or fitted carpets and the damage was easily rectified.

A week later, our house caught fire. I finished decorating our living room one evening and went to inspect my handy work the next morning. I opened the living room door and couldn't see anything. I thought I was dreaming and rubbed my eyes. I still couldn't see anything in the room. Then, I realised it was smoke but there was no smell. I opened windows and doors to circulate fresh air and began investigating what was happening. When I lifted the mat in front of our boiler, I found a hole burnt through the floorboards, exposing the foundations underneath. I assumed that unnoticed, a lump of hot coal had fallen off the ashpan when I decoked the boiler the previous evening before bed. The mat had prevented oxygen from feeding the fire and the damage was confined to two floorboards. We never understood why we didn't smell the smoke. Maybe, we both had blocked noses. We considered ourselves fortunate we didn't have a serious fire. We didn't have smoke detectors. I doubt many homes had them fitted then as the first domestic fire alarms only began selling in the early 70s.

For men of the Baby Boomer generation, like Clifford and myself, it was important to understand car mechanics and the basics of bodywork. Few working-class people could afford new cars and most drove "Bangers" as they were lovingly nicknamed. Our first Banger was Jennifer's Morris 1100 which we scrapped shortly after we moved to Victoria Crescent. Our next car was a Triumph Toledo 1300. The starting motor jammed regularly so I carried a one-pound hammer in the boot. A good tap on the motor with the hammer helped to free it whenever necessary. An accident in my Toledo resulted in the most challenging repair I ever performed on a car.

I was driving home one winter's evening from Jennifer's parents when I lost control of the car on Anderson's Hill due to black ice. Thankfully, no one was coming in the opposite direction as the car spun through 180 degrees and slammed into the grass bank on the opposite side of the road. I was still able to drive back to Charlie and Anna's farm and park in an outhouse. On inspection, I discovered I'd bent the steering rack. Over the next few days, I bought a new steering rack, sought mechanical advice, bought a Haynes Manual for the Toledo that detailed individual components and borrowed the requisite tools.

The main tools to change a steering rack are a two-pound hammer, a ball-joint breaker, and a good right arm. I removed the damaged rack and fitted the new one. I replaced the front wheels and proudly announced my accomplishment. However, when I took the car for a test drive, I discovered the steering rack wasn't centred. This meant when turning left, I could turn on a sixpence. When turning right, it would have taken the length of Newtownards Airport runway to complete the turn. I managed to remove the rack, centre it, and replace it in half the time I had taken before.

All cars had mechanical idiosyncrasies but one thing they all had in common was rust. Lots and lots of it. While I worked on mechanical issues with British-built cars, Clifford continually patched up bodywork on foreign-made ones he preferred to drive. His Alpha Romeo was a stylish addition to his driveway. However, it was a rust bucket. He was an expert in the application of Isopon and glass fibre. He would sand it to a smooth finish with Wet and Dry sandpaper before applying aerosol paint over the patched-up bodywork. The colour never came close to matching that of the original bodywork. The door sills had completely rusted away, and Clifford made new ones from sheet metal, cut to size, shaped and pop-riveted into place. We even managed to pass MOT checks because checks of a car's body structure and chassis didn't begin until 1977. We shared common pride in our abilities to keep our cars on the road.

One time Clifford owned a 1969 Saab 96. Most weekends he spent tinkering with the engine and repairing the bodywork. It was a stylish car and made the Renault 4 that I drove look like a box on wheels. Clifford mentioned his Saab needed a new carburettor and thought he would cut his losses and move up to a Saab 99. I asked him if he would sell his Saab to me as I disliked my Renault 4. He happily agreed. He practically gave me the car for the princely sum of £50.

After a few phone calls and enquiries, I discovered a breakers yard in Jerrettspass that specialised in Saab parts. I managed to buy an automatic carburettor for a Saab 96. On my return, I borrowed Clifford's tools and fitted the carburettor to the engine block. After tweaking and priming with petrol, the engine fired into life when I turned the ignition key. The Saab 96 was way ahead in technology. It had a flywheel that played a crucial role in maintaining the engine's momentum, balancing the crankshaft, assisting with engine startup, and helping to transfer power to the drivetrain.

One Saturday afternoon I had to travel to Belfast, and I'll never forget what happened. I had worked on my car in the morning and left my Post Office Telecom stencilled leather tool wallet lying on the front seat of the Saab. Just before Knock junction with Upper Newtownards Road, I undertook a driver doodling along at 20mph. I kept driving towards the city centre and had just crossed North

Road junction when I heard a police siren behind me. I looked in my mirror and saw a motorcycle policeman waving me over to the side of the road. I pulled over opposite Knock Fire Station and the policeman parked his motorcycle in front of me.

I was confused when he asked me if I knew why he had pulled me over. I said I didn't know. He explained I had undertaken a slow driver outside Stormont Presbyterian Church and asked me why I was in such a rush. From the corner of my eye, I noticed my PO tool wallet and realised the officer had spotted it too. I said, "I apologise, officer, I'm a telephone engineer and in a rush to get to Telephone House. I just received an emergency call at home to tell me the 999 boards aren't working." "Right, follow me he said." He mounted his bike, started the engine and put on his siren. I followed him down Newtownards Road and onto Albertbridge Road at around 90 mph.

He pulled over onto the traffic island in Cromac Square and watched me as I pulled up at the rear gate to Telephone House. I got out of the car and pressed the intercom. Charlie Burnside answered the intercom. "Who is it?" "It's Stephen McDonald," I replied. "What are you doing? We weren't expecting you in today." Charlie said.

"Please Charlie, just let me in, please," I pleaded. I felt relief when I heard a buzz, and the automatic gates began to open. I looked over to the policeman and gave him a thumbs up. He nodded back and then gave me a salute. Very decent of him. I still sweat when I think about what might have happened if he radioed RUC headquarters to check my story. I would have been on a bread and water diet for at least six months as a guest of Her Majesty's Prison Service.

Clifford was a Jazz enthusiast and owned an impressive collection of 78s vinyls which were the predecessor of 33s or LPs (Long Players) as they were better known. He played them on an old gramophone he kept in his living room. He was also the proud owner of a Thomas Edison cylinder phonograph and some cylinder recordings. Phonograph cylinders were the earliest commercial medium for recording and reproducing sound. They were commonly known as "Records" during their heyday around 1916.

I already had an interest in folk and blues music. The 70s were Bob Dylan, Tom Paxton, Woodie Guthrie, Pete Seiger, Joan Baez and Carly Simon years. All protest and social justice songs. Anti-Government, anti-Vietnam War, anti-establishment, anti-capitalism, basically, anti-everything. Everyone had their axe to grind. Just like today. Nowadays, however, all the whingers and malcontents use anti-social media to bleat about their "anti." It was far more civilised and engaging when people protested in song. I engaged so well with Tom Paxton's music, I have a photograph taken in 1980, of Tom holding Claire when she was three months old. I took the photo with a borrowed Russian-made Zenit B SLR 35mm camera that didn't have a built-in light meter. Hence, the photograph is underexposed. I travelled to Corrymeela where he'd been invited to give a concert to celebrate its work as Ireland's oldest Peace and Reconciliation organisation. The Roman Catholic Bishop of Derry, Edward Daly, in his regalia complete with biretta, was sitting in the front row along with three nuns. I wondered what they were thinking when Tom sang his song called "Not Tonight Marie." You can listen to it on YouTube and confirm my suspicion that Tom was anti-religion. As all Christians should be.

Clifford's enthusiasm and knowledge drew me into the Jazz scene, and I began visiting venues with him. (Gigs wasn't a word yet). I got to know local jazz legends like Rodney Foster (Trombone), Jackie

Flavelle (Bass), Trevor Foster (Clarinet) and George Mullan (Trumpet), to name a few of the talented musicians who continued to play and entertain audiences throughout the violent years of the 70s and 80s. One evening, I took a colleague from Telephone House to hear the Rodney Foster Jazz Band playing at the BP Social Club in East Belfast. Phillip Stevenson was known as "Phant" to everyone. He was the only person I knew who could drink a pint of beer in a single gulp. And he often did.

On this occasion, he was suitably primed when he approached Rodney during an interval, and I saw him whisper into Rodney's ear. Rodney stepped off the stage and came over to me. He said, "Stephen, I think you and your friend should leave." "Why?" I asked. "Your friend just asked me to play Stranger on the Shore," he replied. "What's wrong with that?" I asked. Rodney replied, "That's like taking a pencil into a joiner and asking him to sharpen it for you." I began to suspect some Jazz musicians were quite aloof about their niche. So, we left and I can't remember ever going back. Phant never went back either. He died at the age of 30 on his friend's sofa. He told his friend he didn't feel well after returning from a fishing trip they had been on that morning.

Clifford joined me on my last visit to a Jazz concert. We went to hear The Garrick Showband at the Strangford Arms Hotel in Newtownards. I was completely out of my depth. This wasn't music to me. To my uneducated ears, it sounded like musicians playing the wrong notes. Michael Garrick's musicianship extended to choral works, liturgical pieces, and big-band scores. On this occasion, the musicians were improvising and composing pieces contemporaneously. Too intellectual for me. I couldn't hear the emperor's new music. Jazz and I parted company that evening.

Jennifer didn't share my musical tastes and, as time progressed, we realised we had no common interests. We couldn't admit that, as far as a happily married couple was concerned, we were living a lie. We mistakenly believed our relationship would be fine if we made a fresh start. After Lorna was born in 1982, we moved to 8 Pinecroft Avenue, Newtownards where we set up our new home. Just before we left Victoria Crescent, tragedy struck Clifford and Lorraine when their first child was stillborn. I remember how traumatised they were, made worse by a bureaucratic mix-up that meant they received their son's death certificate before they received his birth certificate.

After our move, we met our new neighbours sooner than we anticipated. On our first evening in Pinecroft, Jennifer reversed our car into the neighbours' car directly opposite. The accident was dealt with amicably. After that shaky beginning, everything was fine for a while. We were busy working, decorating, and coping with two loving, mischievous, little girls. I was left to babysit them one Saturday morning. I was working in the dining room and wondered why it was so quiet. I discovered why when I entered the living room to check what Claire and Lorna were up to. They had emptied the contents of our writing desk onto the living room floor; then poured a two-pound bag of Tate & Lyle sugar over the contents. After the shock and clean-up, I laughed. It's a sweet memory.

It was inevitable that our marriage began to suffer because we didn't spend any quality time together. Both of us were content to lead our own lives. Jennifer was very independent and carried on with life, while I became more caught up in work and the after-work drinking culture that many Telephone House colleagues enjoyed at that time.

We were like two similar poles on a bar magnet. The closer we tried to become, the more we pushed one another away. Eventually, Jennifer began socialising too, telling me she was meeting old school friends. I stayed out late and made excuses for my erratic behaviour. Now, as well as living a lie, we were lying to each other. Our bond of trust was broken. We couldn't fill the cracks or treat the rust in our marriage and began sleeping in separate bedrooms. After two years of waking up with only Bubbles our cat for company, I knew our marriage had reached the point of no return. We both agreed to remain friends and file for divorce. Our Decree Absolute was granted on the grounds of "Irreconcilable breakdown of marriage."

The hardest part of any marriage breakdown is the impact on children. I consoled myself with the excuse that Claire and Lorna were too young to understand and would quickly adjust to me not being home. I knew they would be well looked after. Despite our issues, Jennifer was always a loving mother, and I was confident she would do her utmost to raise Claire and Lorna as best she could.

Time proved Claire and Lorna were resilient and adapted well to life with a single parent. Lorna was the first McDonald ever to obtain a university degree. Through sheer determination and willpower she graduated from Sheffield University with a BA in Business Administration in 2003. She has a big heart, is a hard worker and recently set up a new home with Jonny Caldwell, a golf professional, in Donaghadee. I'm delighted we're growing closer as the years progress.

Claire excelled in her work in the Retail sector. She has an empathy for people and rose to Senior Regional Manager for B & M with responsibility for the North of England and N. Ireland. However, that meant spending too much time away from her family and football commitments so she asked to be demoted. No rat race for Claire. No corners either. Claire tells it as it is. Sometimes, she lands a few surprises and I admire her determination to work through whatever life throws at her. Claire is stoical with a capital "S."

I spent some nights sleeping in my car parked in Groomsport Harbour as I tried to work out what to do next. My cousin, Edward was involved in a property business, and he arranged my purchase of a terraced house at 91 Ardgowan Street with a £500 deposit.

I described earlier how I came to meet Rhonda. By the time I moved into Ardgowan Street, I had pressed my self-destruct button and began drinking more often. There was no shortage of pubs in Belfast to go to for a change of scenery. There were 66 bars, all within a twenty-minute walk from the City Hall. If that wasn't enough, there were pubs and clubs within a five-minute walk of Ardgowan Street. I was desperate for help and companionship. Despite having drinking buddies, I was quite lonely. Rhonda was a good listener who didn't judge me and empathised with my situation. Our relationship deepened and, with Rhonda's love, support and encouragement, I began to rebuild my life. After 40 years together, I'm blessed she still prays for me daily.

After my split with Jennifer, Clifford and Lorraine invited me to join them for a meal in a Great Victoria Street restaurant. I was too drunk to have a proper conversation. The last thing Clifford said was, "I've had enough of this." They both stood and walked out. That was the last time I saw them. At the time, I didn't care. It was all about me. The Lord knows I care now.

Old Soldiers Never Die

Old soldiers never die,
Never die, never die,
Old soldiers never die,
They simply fade away.

My UDR service ended abruptly in 1973. By then, I was a Post Office Telecoms Linesman working out of North Telephone Exchange on Cliftonpark Avenue, adjacent to Girdwood Barracks. I was working on the switchboard at Ligoniel Mill when another Linesman arrived to tell me I was needed at home as quickly as possible, Dad had suffered a serious accident at work. North Control sent John Martin; they didn't want to give me bad news by phone. Before, WhatsApp and texting, messaging was generally face-to-face. I drove home to learn Dad had lost his left hand in a guillotine at work, in the Belfast Newsletter.

Dad, with his detached hand in a bag of ice, was rushed to Ulster Hospital at Dundonald where surgeons operated to re-attach his hand. Microsurgery was in its infancy and their endeavours proved unsuccessful. The best they could do was place a spring inside the remainder of Dad's palm which allowed him some grip. To help

Dad recover, doctors advised our family to move out of our "troubled area" and find somewhere more peaceful to live. Within a short period, we uprooted from Woodvale Street and moved to Westwinds Estate, Newtownards. This is when I resigned and collected my "Honourable Discharge" papers from the UDR.

Eventually, the Newsletter admitted negligence due to a faulty guard on the guillotine. Dad was awarded £8500 compensation and Captain Henderson, the Chairman of Century Newspapers, offered Dad a job for life as a Proofreader. My parents could have bought a detached house for that amount in 1975. Jennifer and I bought our first house, a brand new, semi-detached chalet Bungalow in Victoria Crescent, Newtownards for £6400. A detached Bungalow in the development was £8000. Our first mortgage was £64 per month; we worried if we could afford it. Dad and Mum were never money conscious. They were always generous to a fault and gave £1000 each to me and Elizabeth. I used the gift to help buy a Triumph Toledo 1300cc to replace my old Saab 96.

Mum and Dad were keen bowlers and joined Ards Bowling Club and became friendly with Lily and Jim McKernan. Jim was a UDR veteran and member of the British Legion. I found Jim a real pain. He was loud and bumptious. Lily hardly got a word in. I would avoid him if I knew he was visiting my parents. However, I do have to thank him for persuading my father to join the British Legion. Dad had never been a member until Jim explained to Dad what the potential benefits might be. Thank you, Jim. In 1990, my parents were offered a British Legion flat in the recently converted Savoy Hotel on Donaghadee Road in Bangor. I was greatly relieved. Westwinds was becoming a grim place to live as paramilitary and anti-social behaviour became more prevalent.

Mum and Dad loved their new home surrounded by other ex-servicemen and their wives. A bonus was they were only a short walk from Ward Park where they enjoyed long days playing in bowling tournaments. In 1992, Rhonda, myself and the new addition to our family, Rebekah took Mum and Dad to Yorkshire on holiday. We had booked a holiday rental in Long Preston, and I was disappointed with the state of the house when we arrived. As I considered what to do, someone knocked on the front door. Our next-door neighbour welcomed us to Yorkshire with, "Move your car, you're on our property." I called the letting company and they moved us to a beautiful house in Farnhill where we spent the rest of our holiday in the Yorkshire Dales.

In 1994, Rhonda spotted an advert in the Belfast Telegraph placed by David Ashe. This wasn't the same David Ashe from Woodvale Street. David was organising a 50th Anniversary trip to the French Landing beaches for D-Day Veterans. Dad was surprised and delighted when we told him we were sending him back to Juno Beach. On his return, he said, "I was in more danger than I was 50 years ago. They tried to drink me to death this time." Over time the other residents in The Savoy passed away. The Savoy was taken over by Clanmill Housing Association and, apartments were rented to the public. As typical, changes are seldom for the better.

The warm, friendly atmosphere was gone, and a change of warden didn't help. Around this time, I joined the British Legion. I was a member of the local Sydenham Branch but gave up attending because I suspected paramilitary links. I was content to pay my annual membership fees directly to the Legion's headquarters to support its important work. I joined the Victory Services Club along with Rhonda in 1996. Membership is open to ex-servicemen and their families. I had to produce my army Discharge papers and, proof of ID to gain membership. The VSC is situated on Seymour Street, near Marble Arch in London. The concierge says on entering, "Welcome to your London home." Indeed, it felt like home on several occasions.

In 1999, through the British Legion, I obtained a ticket for the Annual Festival of Remembrance, in the Royal Albert Hall. I wore my dress uniform and N. Ireland Service Medal and was seated close to Her Majesty, Queen Elizabeth II. What a powerful, emotional evening it proved to be. The band of the Royal Marines introduced the event playing Hymn For The Fallen. The drums alone brought tears to my eyes. The words of a poem found written on the wall of a cellar in Cologne where Jews had hidden from the Nazis were read out:

"I believe in the sun
even when it is not shining
And I believe in love,
even when there's no one there.
And I believe in God,
even when he is silent.
I believe through any trial,
there is always a way
But sometimes in this suffering
and hopeless despair
My heart cries for shelter,
to know someone's there
But a voice rises within me, saying hold on
my child, I'll give you strength,
I'll give you hope. Just stay a little while.
I believe in the sun
even when it is not shining
And I believe in love
even when there's no one there
But I believe in God
even when he is silent

I believe through any trial
There is always a way.
May there someday be sunshine
May there someday be happiness
May there someday be love
May there someday be peace...."

It proved to be an evening I'll never forget. When I returned to the VSC, I was approached by a guest who asked me, in a Geordie accent, if I was from Belfast. "Yes," I replied. He said, "I spent five years in Belfast during the 80s." "Whereabouts?" I asked. "Top of Divis Flats," he laughed. We immediately became friends. "Come and meet my Dad," he said. We walked from the vestibule into the lounge bar where he introduced me to his father, a WWII Veteran. After our introductions, I learned his Dad had been a member of the Eighth Army, the "Desert Rats." A survivor of the Battle of El Alamein. El Alamein saw the Allied armies defeat Rommel's Afrika Korps. This was a major turning point in WWII.

The eve of Remembrance Sunday's parade at The Cenotaph was rumbustious in the VSC. A reminder of the high spirits enjoyed by veterans made it into the Daily Mail. A gentleman, slightly the worse for wear, decided a stroll would help clear his head. He walked along Seymour Street and turned the corner into Connaught Square. I believe the gentleman in question knew exactly where he was going and what he intended to do. Tony Blair and his family bought a house in Connaught Square in 2004 for £3.65 million to add to his property portfolio. It was guarded 24 hours a day, front and rear, by police at taxpayers' expense. After the invasion of Iraq in 2003, initiated on the premise of Weapons of Mass Destruction and supported by falsehoods, lies and fake dossiers Tony "Bliar" wasn't held in any esteem whatsoever by members of the British Armed Forces. They and Iraqi civilians were only "little people;" they didn't matter.

Our gentleman stopped at Blair's house and climbed steps towards the front entrance. He didn't ring the bell. Instead, he unzipped his trousers and urinated on Tony's doorstep. A policeman appeared, put his hand on the man's shoulder and asked him to desist. Every man reading this knows, that after a few beers, once you've started, you can't stop. And so, it proved. My hero was arrested and taken to Paddington Green Police Station where he spent the rest of the evening reflecting on his act of defiance. He shared the reason he was incarcerated with his cellmate who passed the story to someone else. They contacted Richard Littlejohn at the Daily Mail who wrote about the incident in his Tuesday column.

This is how Littlejohn finished his article. "Now Tony Blair knows how the rest of us have felt since he came to power." If I knew who this man was, who demonstrated his disdain for Tony Blair in such a diuretic way, I would shake his hand. After he washed it, of course.

On Sunday morning I travelled by bus from Marble Arch to Whitehall. The assembly point for the annual Cenotaph March Past is Horse Guards Parade, the ceremonial parade ground, and location of Trooping the Colour each year on the Monarch's official birthday. I was in uniform when I boarded the bus at Marble Arch; the driver refused to take my fare. On a later visit to the Cenotaph, I went by taxi and the driver refused to take my fare, saying it was a token of his appreciation of the armed services.

There is no better place to remember the sacrifice made by earlier generations than London on Remembrance Sunday. There's a palpable air of reverence around the assembled veterans and spectators. The reverence is magnified when the bands of HM Royal Marines and the Central Band of the RAF play Elgar's Nimrod and a hush descends over the assembled crowds. No one pushes or shoves; there's a stillness and sense of anticipation; everyone present wishes to demonstrate they don't take freedoms for granted. There is no experience comparable to marching past the Cenotaph with veterans from different campaigns, flanked by smart ranks of the Royal Navy, accompanied by the band of the Royal Marines in view of Her Majesty and Royal entourage, standing on the balcony of Richmond House.

In 2001 Rhonda and Rebekah accompanied me to London where I joined members of the UDR Regimental Association to march past the Cenotaph on Remembrance Sunday. We stayed in the Victory Services Club for the weekend and dined in a Moroccan restaurant on Friday evening. Before we left for dinner, we were sitting in the vestibule when an elderly gentleman was helped through the front entrance by a lady, we guessed was his nurse. I remarked to Rhonda and Rebekah, that the gentleman was probably a WWII Veteran; wouldn't it be great, if we had an opportunity to talk to him sometime? By then, few WWII Veterans were remaining. This gentleman was in his 80s and frail looking.

We returned to the club around 9 pm and, joined other residents in the lounge for the Victory celebrations. This was the last occasion our compere led the sing-along. The lady in question led the celebrations at VSC on VE Day 1945 and every year afterwards. This was her Swansong. To my surprise, who was there? My Geordie friend with his father, whom I met two years previously. As we made our way to their table both stood to greet us as I introduced Rhonda and Rebekah. What can you say when an old, Eighth Army Desert Rat stands to greet your wife and ten-year-old daughter? I can't describe it adequately even now. "Humbling," is the best I can do. Can there be any better company for a night in London?

Every year, on this weekend, a collection is made amongst residents and staff of the VSC for the Earl Haig Fund. The proceeds are collected by members of the Gurkha Regiment stationed at Buckingham Palace. It is well known that Irish, Scots and Welsh Guards Regiments alternate guarding the palace. Less well-known is the Gurkha Regiment is the only one in permanent residence. Spot on time, two Gurkhas in immaculate uniforms, appeared to collect the proceeds of the appeal and deliver a special thank you message. I hope the photograph I took of Rebekah between two smiling Gurkhas turns up someday. It's in a box somewhere.

The next morning Rebekah left us and went downstairs on her own. When we caught up with her, she was in the reception area sitting beside the elderly gentleman we had noticed the previous evening. Rebekah was in conversation with him and, when she saw us, waved us over to join them. Our guess was proved correct. He was a WWII Veteran. He had served in The Queen's Own Regiment. Rebekah mentioned her Granda Bill was a D-Day Veteran and landed on Juno Beach. "I was there that day," replied our friend. We were gobsmacked. Our elderly friend landed on Juno Beach on 6th of June 1944, the same time as my father. He explained, that when his regiment fought their way to Bernières bodies were already piled six feet deep. There were over 1200 Allied casualties on Juno Beach that day. The Americans suffered the greatest number of casualties when 2400 men were killed and wounded on Omaha Beach. These included 12 pairs of brothers along with a father and son.

Our gentleman was wounded later that June and invalided to N Ireland where he eventually married the nurse who helped him recover from his wounds. Their wedding was in the Slieve Donard Hotel in Newcastle. My last meeting with him took place later that afternoon. I was heading back to our bedroom and entered the lift to find a couple already on board, standing at the rear. I pressed the button and, just as the doors closed, a hand appeared through the gap and forced them open again. The hand belonged to the gent's nurse who ushered him into the lift to stand facing me. The guest at the rear enquired in an American accent, "Going up sir?" "Oh, I sincerely hope not," replied the gent. We doubled up in laughter. It's a question we all will find the answer to someday.

Dad was delighted when I recounted this story to him. He was so proud of his granddaughter; he told me he would like his medals passed to her eventually. My Dad, the old soldier, succumbed to prostate cancer in Dundonald Hospital on 18th February 2006. The previous evening, I had bought a voucher to watch Manchester United play Liverpool on the bedside TV/Phone apparatus fitted in each bay. I set everything up to watch the match together the next day. In hindsight, I believe Dad knew he wouldn't live through the night. He said, "No fear here son." Later, he said, "Son, take your mother home." Mum didn't want to leave him, but Dad insisted and eventually, she agreed to let me take her home. As we were about to leave, Dad called me back to his bedside and whispered "Son, when you get home take that coat off and run the iron over it." I replied, "Dad when I get home, I'll take this coat off and run the car over it." The last time I saw Dad alive he was laughing. His anchor held to the very end; he entered the Lord's presence wearing a smile but no shoes. My mum bought me every coat I owned over the previous 20 years. It was a family joke. They were all brown.

The one I was wearing that night was a particularly hideous shade and Dad hated it. I never wore it again.

Dad lay in his coffin in stocking soles. We had forgotten to give Russells' Undertakers of Bangor his shoes. Dad was a lifelong Manchester United fan and often bantered Rebekah about supporting their arch-rivals Liverpool. Rebekah had inherited the McDonalds' sense of humour and took the opportunity to place a Liverpool Supporters' scarf in her Granda Bill's hands before his coffin was closed. We were recounting this to family and friends in the waiting room when Mum arrived. She went to the receptionist and said, "Hello, have you got my Bill?" The receptionist replied, "Mrs McDonald, don't worry about that today, we'll look after all that in due course." An old soldier and a good man, I was blessed to call Dad and Father.

We travelled as a family to London again for Remembrance Sunday in 2008. This time we brought Muriel, Rhonda's Mum, as part of her 70th birthday celebrations. We did the sights and visited Westminster Abbey, the London Eye, The Imperial War Museum and the Victoria and Albert Museum. It was a busy weekend. As usual, on Saturday evening we retired to the lounge for the Victory Celebrations Sing-along. Again, we proved you can't help falling into good company in the VSC. On this occasion, we sat beside RAF personnel stationed at RAF Coningsby in Lincolnshire, home of the RAF Memorial Flight. In their company was a 90-year-old, former Lancaster Bomber's rear gunner.

At the bar, I spoke to a young man and asked him, what had brought him to the VSC. The club had been recommended by a friend, because of its friendly reputation. He was there with his pregnant wife, expecting their first child. His wife had gone to bed earlier. I noted his German accent and enquired where he was from. "Cologne," he replied. Cologne was reduced to rubble by 35,000 tons of bombs dropped on the city by the RAF in 262 separate air raids. Amazingly, the only building to survive was Cologne Cathedral. We exchanged pleasantries and I explained to Dietrich there were some guests he should meet. I introduced the young German to the gunner of a Lancaster Bomber who helped destroy his city and tried to kill his relatives. What a moment! When the gunner and young German hugged one another. Like I said, what a place!

On Sunday morning, Rebekah asked if she could wear her Granda's medals to the Cenotaph. There were very tight security checks as we neared Horse Guards Parade. A young female police officer stopped Rebekah and asked her whose medals she was wearing and where she was going. The WPC smiled as Rebekah explained why she was wearing her Granda's medals and she was going to watch her Dad march past the Cenotaph. The officer told Rebekah to wear her Granda's medals with pride and waved us through the security barriers. I went to the rear of the parade ground, to join other UDR Association members. Rhonda and Rebekah went to find a vantage point to watch the parade. Unable to find a suitable place, they tried to find me by walking through the Horse Guards Arch entrance to the Assembly point. "Stop, shouted a policeman. "You can't come through here." A Guards' officer appeared from behind; looked at Rhonda and Rebekah with her ribbon of medals and barked, "Let them through." In Horse Guards, the police defer to the army.

My generation has had the privilege of rubbing shoulders with people who understood the value of sacrifice and duty throughout two World Wars and later. Rhonda's father, Raymond served in Palestine during Partition in 1948. Another departed old soldier. Those people are all gone, everyone. Now, you will never be humbled when a Desert Rat stands to greet you or listen to a personal account of what it was like to land on a Normandy beach. But you can honour their memory, defend their legacy, and pray you are never called to make the ultimate sacrifice. I never marched past the Cenotaph again. I wouldn't feel safe In London now, wearing my UDR dress uniform and medal. I have been back several times over the past years. A great city has changed out of all recognition. You can make up your mind if it is for better or worse.

For the last 25 years, I have organised Bloomfield Presbyterian Church's annual Service of Remembrance to remember fifteen members of our church who died in WWI and eight who died in WWII.

"Their names will live forevermore."

Dover Street

Dover Street ran between Shankill and Falls Road. Number 54 stood on the corner of Dover Street and Upper Cargill Street. It had three floors; the top one we called the Attic. There was no bathroom, just an outside toilet and a coal bunker. This was home to Granny, Granda Kirk, and their daughter May. This house was a second home to our family, relatives and friends. "Day" was called Day simply because Mum's cousin, Hazel couldn't say, "Granny" when she was young and called her, "Day." That was her name for the next 90 years.

People obtain nicknames by different means. My friend in British Telecom, Alan McKinstry, lived in Dunraven Park. His father was painting the living room when Alan let their budgerigar, Joey out of his cage. After a few laps of the living room, Joey fell into a two-litre tin of best Crown Magnolia emulsion and gave himself an unexpected makeover. Alan lifted Joey out, gave him a quick wipe down and drove him to Cedar Lodge Veterinary Clinic on Knock Road. Alan gave the receptionist the patient's name and the reason for his visit. He then sat down and proceeded to read a magazine. Eventually, someone called out, "JOEY

MCKINSTRY." Alan didn't respond, "JOEY MCKINSTRY." Again, Alan didn't respond. For a third time, "JOEY MCKINSTRY." At this, a Chinese man waiting with his pet dog leaned over and nudged Alan and said, "You, you Joey McKinstry?" The penny dropped and Alan took Joey in for treatment. Alan made his next mistake when he shared this story with his colleagues in Telephone House. He became "Joey" McKinstry from then until the day he retired. Joey, the bird that is, made a full recovery but had an aversion to paint. He tweeted about it.

Rhonda and I nicknamed Rebekah "Gordo" after Gordon Cooper in The Right Stuff. He fell asleep waiting for the launch of Faith 7, the last Gemini mission. He was the last American ever sent into space on his own. The control centre had to wake him by shouting, "GORDO," over his intercom so he could start the launch. "Uhh, uhh." OK Control, we're good to go. Starting countdown sequence." Rebekah's response when we tried to awaken her sometimes. "REBEKAH! REBEKAH!" "Uhh, uhh." I don't recall Rebekah ever launching out of bed.

Dover Street stirs many memories and stories told by my parents. My mother was Hazel Kirk by birth. She was the oldest of four sisters. She had two brothers Jackie and Edward. Mum was born on 26th March 1921 and was six months off her 101st birthday when she passed away. May was born in 1923 and never walked her whole life. May wasn't born disabled. She contracted Polio at the age of two. She was sent to the Institute for The Disabled at Stricklands Glen in Bangor where an unsuccessful operation ensured she would never walk.

My father-to-be, William (Bill) McDonald, lived at 103 Westmoreland Street which joined Dover Street where Harry Millar's shop stood. He and Mum met at church in the late thirties and began dating. One evening, during The Blitz in 1941, a German incendiary fell through the roof of 54 and set the attic on fire. Bill ran into the house, scooped May into his arms and carried her to safety. He ran back in again and carried the incendiary out to the street before extinguishing the fire and saving the house. Mum told me, "That's when I decided to marry him." At one point, May was evacuated and lived on a family-owned farm in Dervock. She didn't return to Dover Street until the end of the war.

It is impossible to explain what May meant to me, Elizabeth and our wider family. Elizabeth and May became particularly close and a deep, loving relationship lasted all their lives. Mum, her sisters and brothers worked and the children were left with May during the day. All she had was a pair of wooden crutches with padding where they rested under her arms. May cooked, did the washing, sowed, knitted and helped Day with the daily housework. Once a week, she polished every piece of silver and brass and put them back on display.

Going to bed entailed May pushing herself up backwards one stair at a time and hoisting herself onto her bed. In the hallway sat May's chariot covered with a blue tarpaulin. Basically, it was a three-wheeled bicycle. A chair between two wheels with a drive wheel in front, connected by a chain to handles within reach of the driver. There were only three gears. May peddled her bicycle by hand up and down the Shankill and Woodvale Roads, to and fro between our respective homes and shops. Wearing her Sunday hat, she would pedal down Upper Cargill Street to the Elim Church in Melbourne Street whose Pastor was Mr Griffith.

I only realised lately why May wasn't a Presbyterian like the rest of our family. There were too many steps at the entrance of Townsend Presbyterian Church, so it was much easier to go to the Elim and wheel herself in from street level. Occasionally, I'd accompany her; I heard people speaking in Tongues for the first time. I thought how holy do you have to be to do that? The singing was more engaging than the Presbyterians, with hymns like Living In Beulah Land and When The

Roll Is Called Up Yonder, I'll Be There. I still love to hear these hymns sung.

Just Imagine the amount of upper body strength it must have taken to pedal May's chair by hand and support herself on crutches for long periods doing chores. May was a skilled seamstress and, when relaxing, always had a pair of knitting needles clicking away in her hands. V necks, polo necks, jumpers, and Aran cardigans were made regularly for whoever in the family most needed some style. Sometimes, she asked me to sit on the pouffe stool, where she rested her feet, take hold of a ball of yarn while she unwound the end and wrapped it around her outstretched arms to make a loop ready for knitting. Knit one, purl one. May must have had the patience of a saint and might have embarrassed some of them with her work ethic.

May helped establish the Disabled Christian Fellowship in Northern Ireland. She knew, from experience, the difficulties and challenges facing disabled people in everyday life. Above all, she loved to share her faith in Christ. Meetings she arranged presented opportunities to provide practical advice and share her "Walk of Faith" with the growing number of regular attendees. From a young age, the youngsters in our families were accustomed to people with different disabilities, calling into Dover Street to talk and share a pot of tea with May.

One was Peggy Mann. Peggy dressed like it was the depths of winter, topped off with a thick woollen hat. The lenses in Peggy's glasses were so thick when she looked directly at you, that her eyes appeared four times their normal size. She had an infectious laugh, and we always enjoyed her company. Another visitor lived right next door at 52. Jim McClure and his Mum would call in to have a cup of tea and catch up on the latest news. Jim suffered from Cerebral Palsy and was non-verbal. Again, we youngsters were always happy to keep him entertained and could tell from his reactions he loved the attention and friendship. I have no idea how Jim's mother coped with his needs that allowed him to live at home. I'm sure those visits with us in Dover Street must have been a well-earned moment of respite.

Eventually, Day and May had to leave Dover Street in the mid-seventies after it was vested, as part of the Belfast Urban Redevelopment Plan. This plan had huge implications for the people living on the Shankill Road. When the West Link was built it effectively cut off a whole community and led to a diaspora which is the cause of many of our current social problems.

Belvoir Park

Day and May moved to a bungalow at 7 Kirkistown Walk, Belvoir Park in 1966. In effect, Dover Street just moved to a different postcode. Some Sunday mornings I would mitch church. After BB Bible Class, instead of going to church with the rest of the company, I would quietly leave by the back entrance and, walk to Belvoir Park. I left at 11:30 am from Townsend Street and covered the five miles in time to share dinner with Day and May.

May loved animals. There was always a pet in Kirkistown Walk. The first pet was a cat named Bubbles, then a Miniature Poodle named Lucy, followed by a Red Setter named Bruce and, finally a Cairn Terrier named Cindy. My favourite was Bruce. Bruce was a beautiful, gentle giant of a dog I loved taking for a walk. I mean miles. One Sunday it was raining heavily. So, I put on my motorcycle wet gear and set off with Bruce towards the Giant's Ring. Halfway there, Bruce decided he'd had enough, sat down and wouldn't move. When I gave up trying to coax him to walk, I turned around and faced the direction of home. He stood up and, proceeded to walk beside me. A clever, wet dog.

On another Sunday walk with Bruce, I was passing Milltown Baptist Church. A young lad, seemingly "fired up" after a sermon, stopped me and asked me if I was saved. I can't remember my answer, but I don't think my reply was polite. I was very anti-religion in any shape or form at that time and I resented being questioned about my beliefs or lack of them. I had a similar encounter later in life when living in Ardgowan Street. A volunteer from East Belfast Mission rapped my door to ask me if I was saved. I'm sure his friends were horrified when he described being chased up the street by a madman from 91. I'll apologise to them one day.

As time passed, Bruce proved too big for May to cope with. May's niece, Hazel Welch volunteered to give him a new home. I heard later Bruce accompanied Hazel's daughter to school each morning and, one morning, attacked a stranger who attempted to pull the child into his car. Bruce became a local hero in Rathcoole.

I separated from Jennifer in 1983 and moved from Pinecroft Avenue to Ardgowan Street in East Belfast. I had no car and bought a bicycle from a colleague at work to help me get around. I cycled to Belvoir Park to tell Day and May about my separation. They were very "religious" and I dreaded sharing my situation with them. There was no condemnation at all from either of them.

They shared their love and understanding and sent me home with a pound of butter, a jar of marmalade and a box of tea bags. Granny Kirk passed away on 27th November 1987, aged 91 in Belfast City Hospital. She is buried in Roselawn Cemetery with her daughter May and cousin Maureen Thompson. Their grave plot is adjacent to Day's daughter and son-in-law, Violet and Tommy Philips. Their son George is buried with them.

There was nearly another death in the family when my Dad managed to have Cindy run over by a car when he took her for a walk around Belvoir Park. He let her off her lead and she took off across the road in front of an oncoming car. To Dad's and the driver's relief, Cindy went under the car and came out the other side unscathed. Phew! We never told Aunt May about Cindy's close encounter with death.

Rebekah was four when Dad and I took her to Belvoir Forest to let her ride her new bicycle. We had Cindy with us and walked her beside Rebekah as Dad and I caught up on recent events. At some point, we looked around and there was no sign of Rebekah. She had disappeared. We heard a little voice shouting, "Help, help," and found Rebekah and her bicycle lying twenty feet down an embankment in a thick bed of nettles. We both clambered down and managed to untangle her.

When we arrived back at Kirkistown Walk, Rebekah was covered in a red nettle rash all over her body. She was not a happy child and grassed me and Dad up to her Mum and May for allowing her to fall into a bed of nettles. Calamine lotion was found and liberally applied by her Mum. Although the rash cleared within a few days, she still reminds me occasionally about my dodgy parenting skills.

Like Dover Street, there was always family and friends in Kirkistown Walk. It too became the focal point of our family. I enjoyed my visits immensely and decorated the bungalow one summer while I waited to begin a new job. I was papering May's bedroom in 2001 when I received news to report to Campbell College. I was to start work as a technician in the school's Technology and Design Department.

After Day died in 1987, May lived independently in Belvoir Park for another fourteen years. She took up new hobbies of painting and sowing tapestries. The completed tapestries were framed and given to family members who expressed a wish to own one. There are two still in Irwin Drive and Edward has several that May completed over the years. As time passed, May became frailer but never needed the assistance of carers. Due to a unique bond of love built over the years, family and friends were always concerned for May's welfare and ensured she was comfortable and well looked after.

This remarkable woman's story doesn't end here. May's life continued to unfold in ways no one could have anticipated. In The Lion King, Elton John sings about The Circle of Life. Our family was about to witness May complete her circle and prove her truth to these words by Tim Rice.

From the day we arrive on the planet
And blinking, step into the sun
There's more to be seen than can ever be seen
More to do than can ever be done

Some of us fall by the wayside
And some of us soar to the stars
And some of us sail through our troubles
And some have to live with the scars

Fogged Mirrors

This is a strange title for a chapter. One I find difficult to write because it doesn't truly reflect who my sister Elizabeth was. The beautiful young woman I grew up with, loved, argued and fought with, whose beauty and charm were stolen from her. She was robbed of the opportunity to reach her full potential in life, caught short by tragedy. Please read this chapter as a tribute to Elizabeth.

Elizabeth was a happy carefree young woman. She played hockey for Glencairn Girls' School and was a budding pianist. She was a great cook and enjoyed baking. Her cakes were a real treat. She loved drawing and enjoyed copying her favourite cartoonist Rowel Friers' drawings from the Saturday Night's editions of the Belfast Telegraph. Elizabeth was popular with her contemporaries and made friends who lasted her lifetime. Liz's greatest gifts were a generous heart and the ability to see the good in everyone. She was always on the side of the underdog.

Her academic life suffered when she was caned at school for errors in her homework. Mum remembered the day she arrived home with red welts on her legs where the cane had left its mark.

Dad or Stevie reported the incident to the Headmistress, but the damage was done. Elizabeth hated school and couldn't leave soon enough. The same damage was done by her music teacher, Miss McDowell, who cracked Elizabeth's knuckles with a ruler whenever she played a wrong note. Miss McDowell was the organist at Woodvale Presbyterian Church and continued to play there until she was 100 years old.

Liz wasn't doing well at school for a more sinister reason. Years later, when her life was unravelling, Liz confessed to Mum, Dad and myself that she'd been abused at her after-school job in the butcher shop at the junction of Enfield Street and Woodvale Road. I can't describe the impact this revelation had on our family. We had moved from Woodvale Street some years before and the shop had changed ownership. I'm vague on the details because, as a family, we've tried not to dwell on what we should have or shouldn't have done. "If onlys" .... keep you awake at night.

Elizabeth began full-time work in Brands & Normans shoe shop in Queens Arcade, Belfast in 1965. She proved popular with customers and staff. She was nominated for Start-Rite Shoes Shop Assistant of the Year which she won in 1967. It was a beautiful shop, and I called in occasionally to say hello. Elizabeth and her boss "Fergy" became friends inside and outside work and Fergy was a frequent visitor to our home. The average working wage around then was £30 per month. I know because I had begun casting my eye over job advertisements in anticipation of leaving school.

At the beginning of 1969, Belfast had a vibrant nightlife with dance halls and bars on practically every corner. The Plaza, The Piccadilly Line, The Starlite, The Boom Boom Rooms and The Abercorn were some of the popular entertainment attractions. The city centre was so busy in the evenings that there was a plan to introduce an all-night bus service. Riots and the burning of buses in August 1969 ended that. Elizabeth's life changed one Saturday night when she and her friend Nan Taylor went to the Orpheus Ballroom, inside the huge Co-op building on York Street.

Frank Craig was a sheet metal worker from Braniel and worked in Shorts Aircraft Factory. To Elizabeth, Frank's USP was his height. At six feet tall he was three inches taller than Liz. Elizabeth's previous suitors had been vertically challenged; she was determined to marry a man she could look up to. It transpired she would only ever do this in the physical sense. At 16, I couldn't verbalise my first gut-felt impression of Frank. To me, something felt off. Now, I know my gut was telling me that Francis Carvil Craig was a cold, narcissistic, miserable control freak. That's not a shining reference for someone planning to marry my sister.

There's little point in describing how Frank manifested these qualities. I wish Mum and Dad had intervened and advised Elizabeth she was about to make a huge mistake by marrying Frank. Christian parents can be too understanding, too deferential, too damned nice to want to interfere in their children's lives. Predators will always take advantage of those they believe are naive and inferior to them. At a terrible cost.... so, it proved when Elizabeth married into the Craig family.

And what a hideous family it proved to be! It consisted of Mr and Mrs Craig, Frank, his brother Ronnie and his sister Meta. I didn't like any of them. Sometime after Frank the elder passed away, the Widow Craig brought "her partner Tom" to cohabitate in the family's house in the Braniel housing estate. It was a council house the family had procured through a Rent-to-Buy scheme with the Housing Executive years earlier. The "partnership" lasted about a dozen years, until Mrs Craig's death around 2008. Ronnie, wanting his share of the house, gave Tom one week to vacate the premises. He didn't consider the time and devotion Tom had shown to his mother throughout her illness, up to her death. This elderly man was ruthlessly and callously put on the street with nowhere to go.

It transpired Meta owned the house. She sold it and didn't give Ronnie a penny; Frank was deceased by then. Meta took great delight in recounting the whole story to me before she left for Lakenheath where her husband served in the USAF. She didn't have any time for either of her brothers. Lovely people! The kindest thing I can say about the Craig family is "Frank was the best of the bunch."

Elizabeth's first glimpse of Frank's dark side came on her honeymoon. He took control of the money she had saved for their trip to London. Matters worsened when they moved into their first rented flat in Glandore Avenue, off Antrim Road. "Keep the lights off," "What did you buy that for?" I'm delighted to report that, on one occasion, when he criticised the amount of time and gas she consumed making dinner, Frank wore steak and kidney pie when Elizabeth emptied the pot over his head. Good for her! More gravy anyone? Eventually, they moved to Tullycarnet before moving to Beaufort Walk in Westwinds, Newtownards. By then, my niece Frances and nephew Phillip were born. I'm Godfather to them both.

Elizabeth's arrival in Westwinds marked the beginning of a rapid decline in her health. She had no control over what she spent and Frank found fault with everything she did to make their house a home. Everything was too expensive. "That's my money you're spending." "You should have asked me first before you did that." "There's too much water in the kettle." "That oven uses too much electricity." Eventually, "Why did you invite them?" "Tell them to leave now." I witnessed this when Frank ordered Elizabeth to tell neighbours and two friends from her former workplace to leave their house one evening. I was embarrassed, I can only imagine how Elizabeth felt. Is it any wonder she found solace in alcohol? Who could blame her? Some abusers aren't as fortunate as Frank. Some are murdered for far less.

By 1980 Frank was a constable in the RUC and became part of the Special Patrol Group. This was dangerous work and for personal security reasons, Frank moved his family out of Westwinds Estate, which was being taken over by Loyalist paramilitaries, to a private house in Birch Drive off Rathgael Road in Bangor. I've been honest about how I thought of Frank and the Craig family, but I must qualify what I have written.

Despite, faults and idiosyncrasies, Frank Craig was probably the bravest person I've known. We travelled together one evening to see 2001 A Space Odyssey doing a rerun at the Curzon on Ormeau Road. Frank drove and parked off Primrose Street, close to the cinema. As we exited the car, Frank noticed smoke coming from a house adjacent to where we parked. "Call the Fire Brigade," he shouted. This was before mobile phones. While I traced telephone wires from poles to houses, Frank kicked in the front door, and disappeared inside. By this time, I had found a neighbour with a telephone who allowed me to call the Emergency services. The first neighbour I tried slammed the door in my face shouting, "Nothing to do with me." When I returned, Frank was carrying an elderly man from the burning house. The man shouted, "My dog, my dog." Frank sat the man down gently, ran back into the flames again, and returned with the man's dog. We still made it in time for the film's awesome introduction. Also Sprach Zarathustra.... check it out. Does anyone smell smoke?

When I worked at Telephone House, Brian McGuire was one of the Area Engineers. Not a popular boss but never my direct supervisor. His family owned Locksley Furnishings in Dunmurry. One sunny day four members of the IRA decided to raid the premises and steal any cash on the premises. Why not? They did have a certain standard of living to maintain. Unbeknownst to

269

them and, to their great chagrin, Frank was off duty and driving past the showroom when he heard the fracas. He saw hooded men running across the car park and stopped his car, drew his weapon and shouted warnings to the robbers, who immediately began shooting at him. Frank wounded two of the would-be robbers, captured one and the fourth escaped. Later, Frank's inspector commended him for his marksmanship. Frank replied, "Why? I wasn't trying to wound them." Frank received a bravery reward for his actions. Rumours have it he lost the reward after he delivered some overzealous questioning of the robbers in Castlereagh Holding Centre. Maybe, this is why I enjoy Jack Reacher books by Lee Child.

Frank's moods and tempers continued to become more erratic and unpredictable. I was standing beside him in the kitchen at Birch Drive when he announced the burgers, he was grilling had turned purple, and threw them in the kitchen bin. Frank was beginning to hallucinate and wouldn't admit it. Frank and Liz's marriage was effectively over the night Liz called me from a call box to say Frank had thrown her out of the house. She came to live with Jennifer and me in Pinecroft Avenue until she could find somewhere to live.

Frank sold the house in Birch Drive and bought a house in Carrowdore. There, he met a woman called Madeleine and she moved in with him. When Frank's mental and physical health began to decline more rapidly, he was diagnosed with an advanced brain tumour and moved to Belfast Hospice on Somerton Road for palliative care. The dripping insincerity from this woman is still vivid in my mind. All she was interested in was getting Frank's house. With Ronnie's connivance, there was probably money in it for him somewhere, Frank's last will was that Madeleine kept the house.

In his last days, Frank sent word to an old colleague from Shorts Aircraft Factory who was an ordained minister. He visited Frank and told us Frank had made a deathbed confession. Well, it's never too late! The "beautiful" Madeleine wouldn't let Phillip or Frances collect any of their belongings or family mementoes from Frank's house. I know Madeleine cuckolded Frank and her lover was ensconced in Frank's favourite chair before his body had time to cool. A brave man? Undoubtedly. An idiot? Absolutely. He disenfranchised his children and cut them off from their inheritance to give it all to a lying cheat. All to prevent the only person who ever truly loved him from inheriting anything. A tragedy of epic proportions!

Eventually, everyone in the family suffered because Elizabeth abused alcohol. I wept for

Frances and Phillip, listening to their parents arguing and shouting daily. When Frances was old enough, she left home and made a new life in England. Phillip took up residence with Granda Bill and Granny Hazel in their British Legion flat in the Savoy apartments. Dad didn't live long enough to know Phillip changed his name from Craig to McDonald by Deed Poll as a token of his love for his grandparents and the support they gave him.

On leaving school, Phillip went to England and joined the RAF as a Dog Handler. Now, he works for Police Scotland. While he waited to start work there, Phillip's civilian work had an inauspicious beginning as a security guard at the Edinburgh Tattoo. After a shift, he returned to his office to find someone had stolen his coat. His father and grandfather would be extremely proud of what he has made of himself. He is married to Louise, an Equine Veterinarian and they have two children, Eliza and William. Eliza is named after her Grandmother Elizabeth. William is named after his Great Grandfather William. I hope they adopt "Liz" and "Bill" in tribute to their Grandma and Great Grandpa.

Elizabeth's drinking continued for the next twenty years. My parents were constantly worried about her. Shamefully, I had become calloused in my attitude towards her and was getting on with my own life, making my own mistakes. I had enough concerns of my own. During this time, Elizabeth tried to commit suicide three times and was a regular patient in Newtownards Hospital Psychiatric Unit. She was a patient in the Cuan Mhuire Trust's clinic in Newry on three occasions. The last time I drove her there she tried to throw herself out of the car. Those were desperate days. While I had practically given up on Liz ever being cured, Mum admitted she frequently took a walk in Ward Park at midnight so she could scream at God. "God, where are you?" "Do you hear my prayers?" "What are you doing for my daughter Elizabeth?" And……. God was listening.

On the last occasion Liz tried to commit suicide, she was admitted to Newtownards Hospital. Following her treatment, she was discharged and I visited the Psychiatric Ward to collect her and drive her home. By then, Elizabeth was living in a house in an area of Bangor nicknamed The Bullring, adjacent to Clandeboye Football Club. When we arrived, I wouldn't go in. I was angry with her, for all the pain and heartache she was causing, especially for our parents. I threatened Liz with an Exclusion Order if she went near Mum and Dad ever again. In a fit of fury, I threw my car keys at her. To my horror, they hit so hard the fob broke. I left her standing in the rain, shaking. Some brother I was!

I left for home and joined the A2 dual carriageway heading for Belfast. I was in the outside lane and the car's wipers were working hard keeping the windscreen clear. In the distance, I noticed a figure at the side of the road thumbing a lift. During those years of The Troubles, no one stopped to give strangers a lift. I berated myself over how I'd treated Elizabeth and thought, "I've let one person down today; I don't want to let anyone else down." So, I indicated and pulled over, stopping a short distance before the hitchhiker.

When the hiker climbed into the passenger seat, I said inwards, "Dear God, not another one." From years of experience dealing with Elizabeth and her drinking friends, I knew my random guest was another alcoholic. We said our "Hellos," he placed his bag between his feet, and we started towards Belfast. He told me his name was John and was heading to Lisburn. I explained I was going to Belfast and could drop him off in the city centre. He asked me to drop him in Holywood. That seemed strange and I repeated my offer to drop him in Belfast. I remember verbatim how the conversation went all these years later.

Me: If you're going to Lisburn, why do you want off in Holywood?"

John: "Stephen, if you drop me off in Belfast City Centre I'll have to walk to Botanic Railway Station. If I do that, I will meet people on the way who I don't want to meet."

Me: Who? Why?

John: "Stephen, I'm a recovering alcoholic and those people I mentioned are friends who will want to take me for a drink, and I don't want to do that."

At this point, I "opened up" and explained to John what had happened between Elizabeth and myself. John reached into his bag, pulled out a Bible and said, "Stephen don't give up on your sister because God didn't give up on me."

A shiver ran through me, and I still get goosebumps recalling that meeting. I ended up driving John home to Dromara. It was a catharsis for me to speak to someone who truly understood what Elizabeth and her family were going through because of her addiction. John gave me a card for the Stauros Foundation, the Christian organisation that helped him in his fight against alcohol. The charity states, "It extends the hand of fellowship to those who have alcohol or other drug-related problems, with the view of helping them recover. Stauros promotes the Christian message of Jesus Christ as the means of that recovery." I wasn't a

Christian then, but I knew that meeting, that Sunday evening, was ordained by God. God's reply to Mum for screaming at Him. I wouldn't want Mum screaming at me either.

From that moment, there was a great weight off my shoulders. We weren't alone. God was in our situation and knew our pain. I knew and trusted that changes were coming. I thanked John profusely. He prayed, we bid our farewells and I headed towards home. I hadn't realised the passage of time until my mobile rang. Rhonda enquired where I was and what was taking so long to drop Elizabeth home. I cried when I replied, "I've just given Christ a lift to Dromara." After enquiries and assessments, Elizabeth was accepted as a patient in Ballyards Castle.

Two of the charities' volunteers had a great impact on Elizabeth and they became close friends. Thank you, Pamela and Roy Brown, for witnessing Christ's love for Elizabeth and guiding her to recovery. Roy is now the General Director of Stauros; you can find his and Pamela's testimonies on the internet. However, the war was far from over. Elizabeth lapsed and was readmitted months later for a second programme of treatment. The second time she returned home, there was a short period when her life appeared to be returning to normal...and then...the downward spiral to self-destruction began all over again.

Somehow, I didn't lose my conviction that God was still at work, and we resolved to help and support Elizabeth in whatever way we could. Again, God would prove faithful to His word.

2 Corinthians 1:3-5

Blessed be the God and Father of our Lord Jesus Christ, the Father of mercies and God of all comfort, who comforts us in all our affliction so that we will be able to comfort those who are in any affliction with the comfort with which we ourselves are comforted by God. For just as the sufferings of Christ are ours in abundance, so also our comfort is abundant through Christ.

God wasn't finished yet.

In spring 1999, I was working one Sunday afternoon in the Network Operations Unit in Telephone House when I answered a call from Dad. He said, "Stephen, Elizabeth came for dinner as promised but she's talking funny." I replied, "Come on Dad, what did you expect?" "No son," he replied. "She was sober when she arrived this morning, I know she hasn't drunk anything, and she only began slurring her words after she finished her dinner. I'm going to call the doctor."

"No," I said, "Call an ambulance." An ambulance arrived a short time later and the paramedics stretchered Elizabeth from the flat and delivered her to the A & E at the Ulster Hospital in Dundonald.

Medics were wheeling Elizabeth into the Casualty Department when a passerby took one look at Elizabeth and ordered the paramedics to turn around, put Elizabeth back in the ambulance and take her to the Neuro Surgical unit at the RVH. "Put on your Blues and Two's, go as fast as you can, I'll be right behind you." This gentleman was one of the top Neurosurgeons in N.Ireland. After he operated on Elizabeth, he explained Elizabeth's life was saved by about 15 seconds. She had suffered a massive brain haemorrhage and her organs were shutting down one by one. There was damage done. Elizabeth was left partially paralysed down her left side and effectively wheelchair bound. God at work? Yes. Elizabeth lost her addiction to alcohol and never drank again.

The hospital would not discharge Elizabeth until she had a care package. To that end, I searched for a nursing home, that would accept Liz as a permanent resident. I went around different homes in Bangor convenient enough for our parents to visit as they no longer owned a car. The average age of home residents appeared to be 80 to 90. How could I put my beloved sister, who was only 51, into a place where she would be surrounded by dementia and incontinence? Watching TV all day would add nothing to her quality of life. In my opinion, watching daytime television, is the equivalent of signing a digital Do Not Resuscitate order. Who would want to be defibrillated back to life to catch the end of Bargain Hunt? I'd rather die.

The last home I visited was Kingsland Care Centre in Ballyholme. I felt wretched. There was a vacancy for Liz, but I hadn't agreed to accept it on her behalf. I was driving up Old Bangor Road towards the dual carriageway when I felt this compulsion to pull over and stop the car. I said aloud, "Lord, tell me what to do." Instantly, I heard Him say "Call Aunt May." Her number was 645817. When Aunt May answered I explained what I was trying to do for Liz and, the reservations I had about committing my sister to an "old people's" home. May advised me to check if the N.I Institute for Disabled was still open. This is where May had spent part of her childhood which I mentioned earlier on Page 55. To my surprise, the NIID was open and still in Stricklands Glen, just around the corner from where I was parked. Wow!

Within a month of that call, final assessments had been made, interviews and forms completed;

Elizabeth was discharged from the hospital to become the latest resident in the institute's beautiful premises in Stricklands Glen which overlooks Belfast Lough. What a turnaround! The staff were incredible, caring and loving. Most, if not all, were Christian. The residents were a mixture of ages and disabilities, and Elizabeth became popular and loved by staff and residents alike. Elizabeth hosted the celebrations for Dad's 80th birthday in the Common Room. Two of the nurses were sisters. One played the piano and the other the harp. We had a beautiful afternoon of entertainment, dancing and songs. All the residents, staff and our family were invited. Uncle Stevie leaned over to me and whispered, "This is one of the best days of my life."

By 2001, Aunt May was becoming less capable on her crutches; it would just be a matter of time before she fell. Enquiries were made, interviews completed, and May was accepted as the latest person to take up residency at the Stewart Memorial Care Home in Stricklands Glen. And so……. just as in Elizabeth's childhood, she and Aunt May were back together again. Elizabeth's life improved further when independent living apartments were built beside the main residence and she was allocated her own home with views over Belfast Lough. It would have cost a small fortune to buy. Elizabeth's apartment became the new Dover Street, where May, Mum, Dad and family would gather most Saturdays.

All the above "Miracles" helped make up my journey to faith. I spent time with Liz reading the Bible and praying with her. She eventually became self-mobile when she took delivery of an electric wheelchair. Now, there was no stopping her. Elizabeth, in common with other women, was a born shopper. Her pièce de résistance was a hideous dining room suite she bought on a trip to Springhill Shopping Centre. It looked like something out of the Spanish Inquisition that Tomás de Torquemada used to extract confessions from his victims. On her own initiative, she began attending Bangor Elim regularly on Sunday mornings. Over time, the Lord did a work of grace in Elizabeth, and she was Baptised in Easter 2010. I was quite nervous for her. I'm not sure Elizabeth appreciated the risks of the combination of water and electric wheelchair, but it all went well. Elizabeth's name was added to "The Book of Life." Revelation 20:12.

Eventually, Elizabeth's paralysis became more pronounced; she was effectively bedridden. Nevertheless, during the crazy financial bubble of the mid-noughties, Elizabeth convinced an M & S Card representative at Bloomfield Shopping Centre that, despite her mobility issues and unemployment, she was able to service a credit limit of £5000. Somehow, by another miracle, she understood and "signed" the credit agreement. The card subsequently arrived through the post. I wonder how much commission the salesperson made for falsifying Liz's signature.

TV shopping for someone with limited faculties meant Elizabeth believed all the hype used by the presenters to describe the latest gadget and tat they were promoting. It also meant she could not remember what she had bought. She ended up with five George Foreman Lean Grill Machines. The grills were distributed around the family. I used ours once. The food tasted awful because all the fat had been drained from it. Our "George" ended up in the "Small Appliances" skip at our council skip. More boxes appeared regularly containing bric-a-brac of all sorts.

Name a household gadget and Elizabeth had one, two or three of each. Electric tin openers, Espresso machines, binoculars, ornaments of Laurel and Hardy and garden gnomes. Elizabeth didn't have a garden. "Because I was a Christian," she bought me a Bible off some TV shopping channel. It must have been the Billy Graham All Things Holy Channel. It turned out to be a Pulpit Bible. It was a beautiful book whose cover was embossed with gold leaf but too big and heavy to carry. It's now part of Bloomfield church's library. I was reluctant to intervene and take her card away; what other pleasures had she left in life? I kept note of her credit card bills and ensured I paid them on time.

Elizabeth's Immobility brought on a host of other ailments; she was in constant pain from bedsores and, at one stage, suffered from gangrene in her feet because of her poor blood circulation. Eventually, in 2015, she was moved to Scrabo Isles Care Home in Newtownards to receive 24-hour nursing. There, and in Stewart Memorial, carers and nurses often commented, "Elizabeth never complains." I never once heard Elizabeth complain about her life or blame anyone, including Frank for her situation. Continued chest infections lead to pneumonia setting in and Liz's transfer to the newly opened Inpatient Ward Block at the Ulster Hospital. Her health continued to decline; family and friends were able to visit day and night because Elizabeth had her ensuite room. We spelled one another around the clock. Phillip was with her when she passed quietly into glory on the morning of 26th September 2017. Liz is buried with her Mum and Dad in Clandeboye Cemetery, Bangor. Plot EX 1577. Their gravestone reads, "Safe in the Father's hands."

Amen to that.

The Circle Of Life

Aunt May continued to live in the Stewart Memorial Care Home at Strickland's Glen but there were changes in the air. Inevitably, those changes weren't for the good of the home's residents. After a change of ownership and management, new staff with a different work ethos ran the home. Residents, who lived on the premises most of their lives, were allocated to other homes throughout Northern Ireland if they were assessed to require too much nursing care. Those without family members to fight and argue their case for continued residency were dispatched to anywhere a place could be found for them. One long-term patient was sent to Londonderry and died within a short time. A regime of profit before care was enforced mercilessly. What was going on?

Step up Edward Phillips, my cousin, fearless nemesis of authority and May's "favourite nephew." In common, with all our family and relatives, Edward loved "Kirky," deeply. Edward was a self-made businessman, who possessed the expertise and experience, together with the time and resources to advocate for his beloved Aunt May. What transpired when Edward "took on" the management of The Stewart Memorial Care Home and the RQIA warrants a separate book to do Edward's efforts, not just for May but all the residents, proper justice. I know Edward has the details of every conversation, letters, minutes of meetings and reports meticulously logged and catalogued.

When he called into May's room one afternoon, instead of taking a seat, he sat on May's bed and found it saturated with urine. He didn't leave until her mattress was changed. This was the manifestation of the drop in standards of care over a relatively short time. Incredibly, on another occasion, he noticed all the residents' bedroom doors had been fitted with automatic closure devices. On enquiring the reason for these, he was informed, that in the event of a fire, the doors would close automatically to keep residents in their bedrooms until rescued by the Emergency services, or someone announced, "All clear!" After another legal tussle with the home's management, all these devices were removed "for the patients' wellbeing."

At another management meeting, in a scene straight out of Law & Order, when a member of the RQIA had been invited to arbitrate, Eddie provided evidence that proved management had been lying in their responses to his written enquiries about

May's level of nursing care. He identified the guilty parties sitting around the table. One manager was forced to resign. Eddie suspected that each of the charity's Trustees had been offered £5000 as an incentive from a prospective buyer to ensure the premises were completely vacated by April 2016. Justice doesn't come cheaply, and Edward was faced with looking at a potential legal bill of £500,000 if he took the trustees to court for malpractice and lost.

Edward realised what was about to happen and began searching for another care home for Aunt May. After several visits with residents and staff, he decided that Carnalea Care Home in Bangor West would best suit her and offer May the required level of care. With the help of Dr. Kelley Greer, May was offered Dr. Kelley's mother's room after the lady passed away. This proved to be just in time. Edward received a curt call one morning. "Come and get your relative now." May wasn't even addressed by name. May Kirk was the final resident to leave the Stewart Memorial Care Home in February 2016.

And so, at the age of 93, May settled into her new life and surroundings at Carnalea Care Home where she enjoyed the company of other residents and regular visits from her family. Mum lived independently in the Savoy Apartments in Bangor and travelled once a week to visit her sister. Gradually, May became more senile, and her mental decline was exasperated by the Covid 19 Pandemic which closed the home occasionally and interrupted our regular visits. Sometimes, when allowed into the building, we had to sit behind Perspex screens and were denied any physical contact with May.

By 2018, we were deeply concerned about Mum's ability to continue living alone. We suspected she wasn't eating well and noticed a decline in her general well-being. I began enquiring about the possibility of finding a place for Mum at Palmerston Care Home in East Belfast. It had a good reputation and was only a short drive from home. I was emailing Palmerston when Rhonda said, "Stephen, bring your Mum to live with us."

Rhonda's concern for her Mother-in-law moved me to tears. Until then, I never appreciated just how deep that love was. Mum agreed to our suggestion and moved in with us at Irwin Drive in October 2018. Within a year, Mum was struggling with our stairs and fell twice in her bedroom. After her second fall, I had to call an ambulance as I couldn't get Mum up on her feet again. Dementia gradually took hold and Mum lost track of time. She began getting out of bed during the night; it would be only a matter of time before she fell down the stairs.

We spoke to the Care Manager at Carnalea Care Home who knew Mum and our family well from our regular visits to Aunt May. With her help and assistance, Mum became May's next-room neighbour in July 2020. Rhonda and I felt relieved but our home seemed empty without her. However, it wouldn't be empty for long. Throughout Mum's time there, we had to deal with COVID restrictions when visiting, right up to her 100th Birthday celebrations on 26th March 2021. It was a wonderful celebration, tinged by the continuing isolation rules that didn't allow our family to be present altogether with Mum and May.

The home was decorated beautifully for the grand occasion. A band played familiar tunes and some residents danced the afternoon away. The local press was there to record the event for posterity and congratulatory cards were received from Her Majesty, Queen Elizabeth II, and the Irish President, Michael D Higgins. Because Mum was born in March 1921 before the Partition of Ireland in May 1921, she was awarded the Irish Centenarian Bounty which amounted to £2500. Mum was especially pleased with the congratulations card from the Moderator of the Presbyterian Church in Ireland, David Bruce.

Mum collected her crown on 15th November 2021. May collected her crown on 4th January 2022. 1 Corinthians 9:25

In their later years, the circle of life brought Elizabeth, Mum and May together again and, through them, a unique bond was established between family and friends which remains to this day. God is good and faithful.

Their circles were completed.

Psalm 100 : 5

For the Lord is good and his love endures forever.

His faithfulness continues through all generations.

In-laws and Bad Laws

The breakdown of my friendship with Stan was the added incentive I needed to try and move on. But how? The challenges of finding somewhere to move to and selling our house in Ardgowan Street appeared daunting. I took Cagney for a walk one Friday evening to try and work out how to make our hopes a reality. I felt a deep peace and calm when we reached Ravenhill Park. At that moment, I knew our plans to move house would be realised. I realise now it was a "God moment."

It marked the beginning of a very stressful time looking for a new place to live. We had installed a new kitchen, a new bathroom, new doors, new plumbing and electrics and we were quite proud of what we accomplished, considering we started with four bare walls. However, it was only a terraced house in the middle of a busy thoroughfare between Castlereagh and Woodstock Roads. There wasn't much interest when we put it up for sale. I asked the Housing Executive if they planned to vest homes in the area due to urban redevelopment. They assured me there were no such plans.

We found a detached house at 26 Irwin Drive for sale. It was a four-bedroom property owned by an elderly lady, Mrs Hill. The house was built in 1938 and it appeared there hadn't been much work done to the property since it was built. There was an asbestos-roofed garage and the old "backyard" toilet had been boxed in. Mrs Hill's brother had done all the outside work and nothing was square. The heating was an old gravity-fed, glass-fronted, solid fuel boiler, the same type as I had issues with in Victoria Crescent. The lack of work on the property worked to our advantage as the asking price of £48,000 was within our budget.

We agreed to buy but explained to the purveyors the need to sell our house first. Eventually, a young couple showed interest in our property at our asking price of £20,000. They were first-time buyers, and their building society sent a surveyor to inspect our home. We needed to show planning permission for our kitchen extension which took a considerable time to obtain. Then we were told we would have to replace our roof tiles because they were made from asbestos. Again, this took time to organise, and Mrs Hill and her family were threatening to pull out of our arrangement because we were taking too long to arrange our mortgage.

To ensure our house was sold, we completed the necessary work and practically gave the house away by dropping the price to £15,000. Three years later, the Housing Executive vested the houses in Ardgowan Street. The young couple who bought our home made a profit of £15,000. After the stress of moving to Irwin Drive, I told myself, "Next time I move it will be feet first."

We began renovating our new home and the work continued for 25 years. We managed financially only because Rhonda was able to work full-time. Muriel retired from McNinch Solicitors in Ballyclare and became our full-time childminder. In August 1993, we were progressing with the work and, settling into our new neighbourhood. Just when all appeared to be going well, I received a call which would shatter our lives and plans. Jennifer phoned me to say she had been in a road accident. On her way to work, her car was stationary at a road junction when another motorist collided with her. The impact had left her paralysed down one side and unable to work. The person who caused the accident was able to walk away without injury.

Jennifer explained she had gone to the DSS to seek assistance they asked her for my National Insurance Number. I sympathised with her and gave her my NINO. I thought no more about the phone call until four weeks later. I was preparing to go on a month-long BT course to Stone in Staffordshire when a letter arrived through our letterbox. It was from the Child Support Agency informing me that my court-ordered monthly support payment for Jennifer and the children was now under their auspices; their calculations showed my payment had increased from £350 to £900. This meant we could no longer afford our mortgage and would lose our new home.

The Child Support Agency (CSA) was established in 1993 with the passing of the Child Support Act 1991. Its primary purpose was to facilitate child support arrangements between separated families without involving the courts. However, the CSA faced significant criticism due to its complex rules and accumulation of arrears. This led to some historians labelling it as, "Arguably the greatest fiasco of the century in British social security policy." It took nearly 20 years for politicians to address its failures. In 2012, the CSA was abolished and succeeded by the Child Maintenance Service.

Too late for many fathers. But hey! Who cares? Let's move on and create another fiasco.

So much for hindsight, but no one would listen when I appealed my case in writing to Peter Robinson MP, John Major PM and Alistair Burt, Minister in charge of the Department of Social Services. My efforts proved a total waste of time. My life was encapsulated by a mathematical formula that was set in stone. Each gentleman above responded by sending me a copy of The Formula.

The wearing of seatbelts became compulsory in January 1983. How would drivers have responded if they were fined for not wearing a seatbelt in December 1982? That's effectively what the Child Support Act allowed. It punished fathers retrospectively. It punished fathers who were easily found because they were PAYE and deducted payments directly from their wages. It didn't pursue absent fathers and those who wouldn't co-operate with the agency. I knew a "father" with three children to three different women and didn't pay support for any of them. I remember reading of fathers committing suicide, two alone in Northern Ireland because they couldn't meet the financial demands put on them by "The Formula."

Don't forget, the driver who had wrecked this havoc on all our lives had walked away scot-free. They might have lost some of their no-claims bonus, but it was hardly life-changing. How was this diabolically cruel law given the Royal Assent? That's what my Executive Engineer, Winston Weatherall asked when I asked him to make me redundant because I couldn't afford to work any longer. My only option was to make myself unemployed to claim benefits and housing support. Why didn't some highly paid Government panjandarum see this law was an ass? The DSS supported Jennifer; now it would have to support two of us. Our situation was Kafkaesque, you couldn't make it up. Rhonda and I were at our wits' end and losing sleep. This was more stress. The only person who did anything to help us was Jennifer. As I mentioned before, thank the Lord, we separated as friends.

Jennifer telephoned to say she didn't realise the consequences of going to the DSS; she added she didn't want us to lose our home and was withdrawing her claim for maintenance. Rhonda and I were greatly relieved, but the CSA wasn't finished with me yet. Because I was now on their system, it cost me £300 to remove my case from their database. My case must have been flagged up a greasy pole somewhere. I was asked if two CSA Staff Officers could call out to speak with me. I agreed, and a week later two Staff Officers and assorted box files were sitting in our living room. I can't remember the exact conversation, but I remember how embarrassed they were when I explained the predicament the CSA placed me in by its blind application of mathematical formulae. Suitably chagrined, they apologised for the stress Rhonda and I had been through; they assured me my details would be removed from the CSA database as quickly as possible. They were true to their promise, and I haven't heard from them since.

I trust you are never on the wrong side of a bad law or an in-law, for that matter. Unfortunately, Thomas White and 2920 other people are still in prison because they fell foul of "Sentences of Imprisonment for Public Protection," created by the Criminal Justice Act 2003 and introduced by the Labour Government in 2005. This was another fiasco which was abolished in 2012. However, the changes made were not retrospective. Current IPP prisoners continue to serve their sentences and will only be released when the Parole Board assesses them as suitable. Thomas's indefinite sentence for a mobile phone theft has left him with severe mental health problems after 12 years in prison. When you read this, check if he's still in prison.

The Hate Crime and Public Order (Scotland) Act came into effect on 1st April 2024. This is a very appropriate date for a law introduced by a bunch of fools called the SNP. Andrew Neil labelled it, "An Orwellian Nightmare, introduced by clowns." He wrote, "It is the equivalent of a modern, secular blasphemy law for the Wokerati." Imagine living in a world where sitting in your living room and saying, "Men can't be women," could result in the police logging a "Hate Incident" against your name. Imagine, too, that your legally protected right to express such an opinion counted for nothing, because all that mattered was whether the person who heard you perceived it as offensive. In time, this too will prove a fiasco and be abolished. I wouldn't risk a holiday in Scotland until it is.

And still, after a huge corporate cover-up, legal malfeasance and the misleading of Parliament, over the conviction of 900 Sub-postmasters, between 1999 and 2015 for theft, fraud, and false accounting, only two people have been interviewed under caution for their part in the Horizon IT Scandal. To date, no one has been punished, for sending innocent people to jail. Yet, Thomas White has served 12 years for stealing a mobile phone. Like I mentioned before the "little people" don't matter. I believe it's a sad indictment on our modern society that many "little people" no longer know or care that they don't matter.

X Marks The Spot

Despite union opposition, the transition from the Strowger electro-mechanical telephone exchange to the System X digital system occurred during the 1980s and 90s. Specifically, the first System X exchange was brought into service in 1980. Over the subsequent decades, System X was progressively deployed to replace approximately 70% of the old analogue exchanges in the BT network in Northern Ireland. The remaining 30% of exchanges used Ericsson's AXE digital system 1.

During the same period, the TXE and TXK families of electronic and electromechanical exchanges were gradually withdrawn. The last TXE2 exchanges, (Ballycastle, Llandovery, and Ramsbury), were also closed on 23rd June 1995. The last TXK crossbar exchange, at Droitwich, was withdrawn in 1994. The UK network became totally digital on 11th March 1998 with the closure of electronic TXE4 exchanges at Leigh-on-Sea and Selby and their conversion to System Y (AXE 10) and System X, respectively.

Throughout the 80s, Strowger engineers were selected to be trained on the new digital system and processes. Some, who were nearing retirement or had family commitments, passed on the opportunity because they didn't want to spend months at the BT Training College in Stone, Staffordshire. I was fascinated by the whole "technology thing" and eager to take advantage of retraining.

The nearest village to the training school was Yarnfield. During WWII, Yarnfield was designated by the US Army as Army Air Force Reinforcement Depot Allied Air Forces Station 594. Barracks, named after Royal Navy Admirals, Duncan Hall, Beatty Hall and Howard Hall, were built in 1938 to accommodate munition workers working in the Royal Ordnance factory in Swynnerton, one hour's walk away on the other side of Cold Meece. As the war progressed, the barracks were all occupied by the United States Air Force, which used the site as a transit camp for its personnel. The General Post Office took over the buildings after the war, and the G.P.O. Engineering Department Central Training School opened in Yarnfield in 1946. A new training block was erected on the site of Howard Hall barracks and opened in 1969. This is where I would spend a considerable time of my career as a Technical Officer; through my Strowger days in the 1970s and my System X days in the 1980s and 90s.

Alan "Joey" McKinstry drove us in his Vauxhall Viva to our first course in Stone in the autumn of 1974. When disembarking from the ferry in Stranraer, a hump in the ramp ripped the silencer off his car's exhaust. It gave the engine a throaty roar but it could only deliver a top speed of 50mph. It made the long drive to Carlisle, then down the M6 to Staffordshire seem interminable. Our journey nearly terminated prematurely when my chauffeur took the wrong exit on a roundabout and headed down an off-ramp from the M6. I shouted, "Alan, why are all those cars flashing lights at us?" Whooops! Irish drivers! Eventually, we arrived safely and were allocated our rooms in the student accommodation blocks.

The next time we travelled to Stone was in November 1978. We decided to go by plane. Fly Belfast to Manchester; then a bus to Manchester Piccadilly Railway Station; then a train to Stone. It was a taxi ride from Stone railway station to Yarnfield where the school was situated. The training block was a fascinating place for me. Working replicas of different types of telephone exchanges were accommodated within the building. We were taught theory and how our type of exchange operated in the classroom and working models.

With Strowger, it was possible to follow a call from beginning to end through every contact and wire. We spent time in our working replica of a Trunk Exchange where our instructors could imitate faults with the flick of a switch at a master control panel. It was challenging and fun at the same time to work with engineers from all over the UK to identify faults. People we hadn't met until the beginning of the course, soon became friends, drinking pals and pranksters.

One day I noticed people having a chuckle everywhere I went. I discovered why when I took my coat off in the dining room to hang it on the back of my chair. Someone had pinned a notice to me which read, "Hit me with your shovel Mick." This was a reference to my Irishness and Ian Dury who was top of the charts with Hit Me With Your Rhythm Stick. Chief suspects were Howard Pau from Grimsby. The funniest Chinese person I've met. Shandra Kalahari, a Pakastani who took a shine to one of the school's secretaries and Tony Allen, our token Englishman who was so laid back he was horizontal. When the four of us met, we could have used the services of a translator; we spoke four dialects of the same language.

One evening in the school's club Shandra admitted how much he was attracted to Sophie, one of the ladies who worked in the administration office. As it happened, she was working as a part-time barmaid that evening. We all gently bantered Shandra and encouraged him to go up to the bar and invite Sophie out. Credit to him, off he went and spent around ten minutes in conversation with her. Eventually, he came back and sat beside us again. Before we could ask him, what happened, Sophie appeared beside him and said, "Sorry I can't go out with you Shandra but I'll play a song for you on the jukebox as a way of apology." Off she went to the jukebox and made her selection. She played Bright Eyes from Watership Down. Shandra led the chorus of laughter.

We didn't realise we were about to be stranded in Yarnfield because of The Winter of Discontent. The Winter of Discontent was the period, between November 1978 and February 1979 in the United Kingdom remembered for widespread strikes by private, and public sector trade unions demanding pay rises greater than the limits Prime Minister

James Callaghan and his Labour government imposed to control inflation. Some industrial disputes caused great public inconvenience, exacerbated by the coldest winter in 16 years. The school was closed early because there was no coal to fire the boilers.

However, Alan and I were permitted to stay as we couldn't change our flight arrangements. We spent a whole week on the campus reading and chilling in the TV rooms. There were separate rooms for BBC1, BBC2 and ITV. We only went to the pub once. Alan didn't appear for breakfast the next morning, so I went to his room to find what was keeping him. I rapped on his door. No answer. The door wasn't locked, and I let myself in to find Alan asleep on the built-in desk. "Why are you sleeping on your desk, Alan?" I enquired. Alan replied, "When I tried to get into bed last night, the bed was going round too fast and I couldn't get on it."

The only pub in Yarnfield was called The Labour In Vain. Why? On its gable wall was a huge mural of an African gentleman sitting in an iron bath being scrubbed enthusiastically by two white people. You might guess this is long before diversity training was ever mentioned. You can Google the pub. The last time I looked, the mural was painted over; the current landlady kept the smaller roadside original and placed it in the rear garden. When I was in Yarnfield, the pub manager's name was Ivan; he was from Ballymena. If you were from anywhere in Northern Ireland, you entered The Labour in Vain at your peril. Some brave souls made it out in time for breakfast the next morning.

This is the apocryphal best telephone engineer story ever told regarding BT's training school. Many engineers from Northern Ireland spent months away from their families. Because of the ongoing troubles in Northern Ireland, BT in its generosity, decided engineers from Northern Ireland were entitled to make one free phone call home each evening. To ensure no one hogged the phone they placed it on a wall outside the reception at waist height and made the handset cord 12 inches long. To stand and talk any longer than five minutes risked back injury. It meant a long wait in the cold for a short phone call.

An engineer, on a four-week course, finally decided he better queue and call home for the first time in three weeks. He queued, stooped over and dialled home. A wee boy answered. The engineer said, "Hello son, can I speak to your Mum?" The boy replied, "Sorry Dad, she's up in bed with my uncle."

"What?" Shouted the engineer. "Do me a favour son, run upstairs, kick the bedroom door and shout in you see me coming down the road with my suitcase in my hand. Come back and tell me what happens." The boy did as he was asked and came back to the phone. "Well?" Enquired the engineer. "Well Daddy, I ran up the stairs, kicked the bedroom door and shouted I saw you coming down the road with your suitcase in your hand. You'll never believe what happened. Mummy ran out of the bedroom, tripped, and fell down the stairs. She broke her neck and she's dead. My uncle jumped out the bedroom window, ran across the patio tripped, fell into the swimming pool, drowned and he's dead. The telephone engineer, replied, "Patio? Swimming pool? Is that Belfast 659111? It's the way I tell 'em.

Courses in Stone continued at regular periods over the next 20 years. Often engineers from Northern Ireland tended not to travel home at weekends. Security checks and inevitable delays to flights made efforts to spend a short time at home too tiring and stressful. On one of the rare occasions, I travelled home for the weekend, my flight was called for boarding at Manchester Airport. When I arrived at the gate, all passengers were boarded on coaches and driven to Liverpool John Lennon to catch a flight to Belfast. Manchester Airport was closed due to industrial action by the Airport Fire Service.

Students from Northern Ireland occasionally hired cars for the weekend and travelled around the Pottery towns of Burslem, Hanley, Longton and Stoke on Trent. I enjoyed visiting Kings Lynn and Norwich; I escaped unscathed from driving in the wrong direction along a one-way street in Nottingham. The worst mistake I made was to drive two Scotsmen I met on a course to visit their friends in Ilford, East London. Alan McKinnon and his pal "Tim" were stereotypical "Mad" Scots with permanent chips on their shoulders dating back to the Battle of Culloden. Alan lived in Drumchapel, Glasgow but insisted on calling it Drumchurch. "Tim" was an ardent Celtic supporter. Despite this, they were united in their dislike of Sassenachs or anything English.

Their friend's flat was on the Cranbrook Road. Inside, was straight out of the TV programme hosted by Stacey Solomon, Sort Your Life Out. It was a dump. Rubbish was everywhere; dishes piled in the sink hadn't been washed for weeks. It was stomach-churning to try and find somewhere to sit, never mind sleep. I was relieved when everyone decided to go to the local pub called the Cranbrook Arms. That was Friday night taken care of and my stupor meant I slept well on the filthy living room floor. We cheered on one of our hosts playing in a local derby football match on Saturday before heading to the Lord Napier for refreshments.

I can't remember eating anything that weekend. It was purely a liquid diet. A brave musician took to the piano and tried to play The Entertainer by Scott Joplin from The Sting. As in the famous Morecambe and Wise sketch with André Previn, he played the right notes but not necessarily in the right order. The audience was effusive in its displeasure. Our intrepid musician played on while ducking his head to avoid being brained by numerous glass ashtrays thrown at him. His performance was worthy of The Golden Buzzer on Britain's Got Talent. It was a great relief to make it back to Stone on Sunday evening and catch up on lost sleep before the start of another week in the classroom.

On other occasions, I travelled with friends to London for "cultural events." My first ever trip to London was with Bob Devenny, John Kerry, and

Alan McKinstry. We stayed in Bayswater and bought tickets to see the original cast, including David Essex and Julie Covington, in Jesus Christ Superstar at the Palace Theatre in the West End. On a later trip, Gerry Gilmore and I bought cheap seats in "The Gods" at the King Edward's Theatre to see Marti Webb play Eva Perón in Evita. That trip was memorable for another reason. We met the late Tommy Cooper and his wife when they sat beside us in London Euston while we were waiting on our train to Stafford. "Just like that!"

My trip to the West End to see Oh! Calcutta! with Alan McKinstry is also memorable but for a different reason. We stopped off at a bar close to the theatre for some refreshments. Alan had taken a liking to Crème De Menthe and imbibed a few before we walked to the Royalty Theatre, just down the road. Out of bright sunlight and into the dark entrance of the theatre, Alan didn't give his eyes time to adjust to his new surroundings; he failed to notice the entrance stairs went down instead of up. Ooooops! With his hands still in the pockets of his duffle coat, he tumbled down the stairs where an attendant nonchalantly waited to show us to our seats. "This way gentlemen, please mind the step." A bit late pal.

Until now, I didn't realise there was a link between my friend Alan and my favourite Russian composer Sergei Rachmaninoff. Sergei might have been teetotal, but he found a glass of Crème de Menthe steadied his nerves before playing the technically demanding piano score in the 24th variation of his Rhapsody on a Theme of Paganini. He even nicknamed the piano piece the "Crème de Menthe Variation." Alan didn't play the piano. He just liked Crème de Menthe.

Where else but Stone would a spoon fight end up with riot police being called? Our course on Register Translators was coming to an end and it was magnanimously agreed by everyone on the course to hold an end-of-course party three days before the course finished. This gave everyone time to recuperate and sober up before travelling home. We didn't want our families to think we were just there to enjoy ourselves. Ivan, the bar manager, let us leave The Labour in Vain at closing time to continue our festivities in the Students' Common Room at Howard Hall. Someone sang and played guitar accompanied by a Welsh lad on a trumpet. Then I was witness to the famous Spoon Fight. It takes four people to hold a Spoon Fight. All but one knows what is going to happen. Two contenders and their "seconds" take up positions. Both contenders kneel and face one another. Each holds a spoon by the handle in their mouth. Each "second" stands behind one of the contenders to ensure "fair play" and everyone abides by the rules. "CONTENDERS READY."

The contenders are invited to take turns. They must hit one another on the head as hard as possible, using the spoon clenched in their teeth. The one uninitiated person in the group is invited to go first; he gives it his best effort. He smacks his opponent as hard as possible with the spoon between his teeth. The "victim" cries out and pretends he is hurt. He even rubs his head to ease the pain. Now it's his turn to hit his opponent, who dutifully bows his head and waits for the spoon to hit him on the head. Unknown to him, his opponent's second is holding a soup ladle behind his back and the second whacks him over the head with it. OUCH! And he thinks, "How can a smack from a spoon hurt so much?" I recommend this as a great team-building exercise.

Amidst all the uproar and laughter, the night security guard appeared and informed us we were keeping other students awake due to the racket we were making. We told him that was impossible as the nearest student accommodation was five minutes away. We suspected all we were guilty of was keeping him awake. Walking out the door, he threatened to call the police if we didn't quieten down. And so, the party continued; I was the next victim. Brian, a manager from Reading said he could lift three of us with one arm and invited me and two others to lie on the floor. My two "friends" clung tightly to me by wrapping their arms and legs around mine. Brian gripped my trouser belt with one hand and asked me if I was ready for the lift. "Go for it," I said. He flexed his arm; just as I thought he was going to pull us up, he reached down, undid my belt, pulled my trousers down and poured a pint of beer over me.

I enjoyed the joke with everyone else but I needed to dry off. I sat on a radiator in my Y fronts and played the guitar accompanied by "Taff" on the trumpet. We sang the twelve-bar blues version of I've Been a Wild Rover. Tony Allen, a newly married lad from Dorking shouted that he was going to the public phones to call his wife. He was no sooner out the door when he came straight back in again and declared, "You're not going to believe this, the riot police have just arrived." The next thing, the doors to the common room were kicked open and in stormed six policemen in full riot gear with shields, accompanied by the night security guard. What a riot! By now I was giving off steam as the heat from the radiator dried my underwear. The police took one look at us, dropped their shields, and lowered their truncheons in disbelief at the sight before them. The officer in charge shook his head and said to the security guard, "This has nothing to do with us. This is between you and BT." And off he went with his troop of riot busters.

The next morning there was a court of enquiry. We were called separately into the hostel manager's office to account for what happened the previous evening. I was hoarse from singing but explained everything had been in good spirits; the party demonstrated how much everyone enjoyed the course and one another's company. No disciplinary action was taken against anyone. We found out later that damage had been caused in another part of the school the same evening by some high-spirited apprentices from London. When the damage was discovered, the partygoers in Howard Hall became the chief suspects. We were guilty until proven innocent. 40 years later, Tony Allen still sends me a Christmas card. Another colleague, Martin Hanvey, enjoyed his time in Stone so much that he decided to stay. He retrained and was successful in his application as an Instructor. Martin and his wife Heather still live in Yarnfield.

I have many happy memories of my time in Stone; I have some embarrassing ones as well. On a four-week System X course, I penned a song called The Ballad of System X set to the old Tex Tyler tune "The Deck of Cards." I sang it in the Labour in Vain and became famous overnight. I've been asked for the words many times since, but they're lost to antiquity. While on this course, I was training for the 1983 Belfast Marathon. I ran eight to ten miles each evening. I had only one set of running gear and no sense of smell. After four weeks I travelled home through Manchester Airport and had to present my suitcase for a security search. When the officer unzipped my bag and opened the cover his head flew back as if someone punched him under the chin. "Good grief," he shouted. "What do you have in there?" He kept his head back and only explored the contents with his hands. I explained it was my running gear. "Who's going to wash it for you?" He asked. "My wife," I replied. "She must still love you," he said. After closing the case he set it on a machine that wrapped a secure tape around baggage to prevent it from being accidentally opened in transit. He wrapped three around mine and wished me and all other passengers on the plane a safe trip.

There have been many changes to the school since my time there. Duncan Hall was demolished to make way for new housing. Many locals lost their jobs when BT's training was decentralised, and the school was taken into private ownership. At one time Yarnfield boasted the greatest number of ASBOs per head of population than anywhere else in the UK. Hopefully, life in Yarnfield has improved for locals in recent years. Yarnfield Park is now advertised as a leading training and conference centre in the heart of the UK. You can also do bed & breakfast for £100 per night for two adults. If you go, be on your guard some joker doesn't put a pigeon under your duvet. There has been previous.

Another Prodigal

I don't profess to be a great reader. I like to read but, can't do so for too long before my eyes grow tired, and I lose concentration. I admire people who can read a book in one or two sittings; I've even more admiration for those who can read and remember what they read a week or two later. That is a gift I don't possess!

I hope you've sensed God's Holy Spirit at work in my life throughout the chapters of this book. I didn't come to faith in Christ through reading a book or the Bible. God, in His mercy, knew my limitations in that respect. Instead, He revealed himself through continuous revelations of His power and love. I can't give a specific date when I came to faith in Christ. My faith journey has been more like a kicking and screaming tantrum where a loving Father has patiently implored his recalcitrant child to trust in his love for him.

Perhaps, in a forgotten prayer, I committed myself to Christ whilst in the 29th Boys' Brigade. In 1992, I finished a night shift in Telephone House and, on the way home, came under conviction to give my life to Jesus. I didn't go to bed. I loaded Cagney, our Shetland Sheepdog into the car, and drove to the car park at the foot of Slemish Mountain. In my St. Patrick's moment, I climbed Slemish. Halfway up, Cagney sat down, our little dog was exhausted. I lifted her, placed her around my shoulders and continued climbing until I reached the summit.

On that windswept hilltop, I asked Christ into my life. There was no thunder or bolt of lightning. It didn't feel as if anything had changed. I bought a bowl from a local pottery to convince myself I'd taken a step of faith and help me remember that special day. I called it, "My Promise Bowl." It is still in one piece. My newfound faith didn't survive very long. The Bible doesn't say, "If the storms come," it says, "When the storms come." The storms of life rolled in on me in the form of moving house which exhausted me. Then the Child Support Agency nearly ruined everything I had worked for. I explained this period in "In-Laws and Bad Laws." I never took time to grow in my faith. It withered on the vine.

By 1996, I was a disaster waiting to happen. I would argue with Rhonda when she objected to me going out after work for "a few pints with my friends." It was never only "a few pints." It was always how many pints I could drink before closing time. My social life was taking priority over everyone and everything else. I realised the devil was pulling my strings; I felt challenged to test the limits of what I considered "acceptable behaviour." More than once, I drank and drove. I don't want to sound complacent or flippant but statistically, I was safer driving drunk than driving sober. The only accident I ever caused, happened when I was sober. At work, I took no notice of warnings from my line manager, regarding wasting company time and meeting my appraisement targets. One August Monday morning in June, my line manager suspended me from work for misconduct. What a "wake up "call!

When we moved to Irwin Drive, Rhonda began attending Bloomfield Presbyterian Church. I had no interest in going along with her until Rebekah joined the Rainbows. Reluctantly, I attended the occasional Sunday morning service. I returned several times to hear Peter Hodgett play piano during "The Collection." Peter was the church organist and, a gifted musician; he had trained with Barry Douglas, the classical Concert Pianist. My love of piano music was the net that drew me into the church where, one Sunday, I heard Graham

Connor, give a sermon on the Parable of the Prodigal Son. My conscience said, "That's me."

Everyone is a Prodigal. We walk away from God in our disbelief or, we journey home to God, the moment we come to faith in Christ. I telephoned Graham that afternoon and asked if I could speak to him. Graham invited me to the Manse where I explained to him, although I felt under conviction, my life was in turmoil. I was honest with Graham about my suspension from work and admitted my fear of the consequences if I lost my job. Graham listened patiently; he didn't condemn or judge me for my actions; he prayed for me and invited me to telephone him when I needed someone to speak to.

For seven weeks I fretted about losing the job I loved and taken for granted. We wouldn't be able to afford the mortgage on our house and would have to remove Rebekah from Bloomfield Preparatory School which she loved. I lost three stones in weight during this time. I called it, "my strain drain." I don't know how I would have survived those weeks without the love and support of Rhonda. I wasn't eating, I wasn't sleeping, I wasn't talking, I was morose; I must have been a nightmare to live with. Rhonda managed to drag me to church one Sunday evening, dishevelled and unshaven. I asked myself, "What I was doing there?" I can't remember anything else about the service except the final hymn, What a friend we have in Jesus.

What a friend we have in Jesus,

All our sins and griefs to bear!

What a privilege to carry

Everything to God in prayer!

Oh, what peace we often forfeit,

Oh, what needless pain we bear,

All because we do not carry

Everything to God in prayer!

Have we trials and temptations?

Is there trouble anywhere?

We should never be discouraged,

Take it to the Lord in prayer.

Can we find a friend so faithful,

Who will all our sorrows share?

Jesus knows our every weakness;

Take it to the Lord in prayer.

Are we weak and heavy-laden,

Cumbered with a load of care?

Precious Saviour, still our refuge,

Take it to the Lord in prayer.

Do your friends despise, forsake you?

Take it to the Lord in prayer!

In His arms He'll take and shield you,

You will find a solace there.

I felt something burst inside me. The dam holding all my resentment, pent-up frustration and anger finally cracked. A sense of peace and comfort enveloped me. I felt everything was going to be OK.

I cried with relief. God had reached down into my situation. Instead of staring at the bottom of the pit I dug for myself, I looked up for the first time in two months……and could see light. I find comfort in knowing that the Apostle Peter's journey was also marked by faithfulness and moments of weakness. His struggles highlight commitment to Christ needs ongoing growth and self-awareness. Despite denying Christ three times, God used Peter to build His kingdom on earth.

"And I tell you that you are Peter, and on this rock, I will build my church, and the gates of Hades will not overcome it." Matthew 16:18.

Deny and betrayal have similar meanings. In effect, Peter betrayed Jesus three times. Every sin we commit is a betrayal of Christ. I must betray Christ thousands of times daily; I will continue to do this until He calls me home. In the meantime, the Holy Spirit continues His work of purifying me, making me more Christlike each day.

After seven weeks, I was called for an interview with my Executive Officer Winston Wetherall and Line Manager Peter Cunningham. I name them because I thank them for allowing me to return to work. They concluded my erratic behaviour was out of character and didn't reflect my commitment to British Telecom over the previous 26 years. I thanked God for His deliverance.

My spiritual metamorphosis began.

I realised the truth of Proverbs 31: 10-12. Rhonda never gave up on me.

"A wife of noble character who can find? She is worth far more than rubies. Her husband has full confidence in her and lacks nothing of value. She brings him good, not harm, all the days of his life."

I started attending church regularly with Rhonda and Rebekah. It's natural to feel like outsiders in a big church but that was never the fault of church members. We accepted an invitation to go on a "Church Weekend" to the Share Centre in County Fermanagh. Any misgivings we shared about belonging to Bloomfield Church were swept away when Alfie and Sadie Shilliday "adopted" us into their greater family. By the end of the weekend, I knew we had found our temporal spiritual home.

Just, like Dad and Uncle Stevie before, men like Alfie Shilliday, Robin McCullough, Norman Wright, Davy McAllister, Bobby Boyd, Douglas Cowan and John Maxwell were role models to me. They were quiet, indefatigable men of faith. God gave me a new group of friends that didn't drink in The

Garrick. I enjoyed singing in the church choir until it was disbanded in favour of Worship Teams. I became a Pastoral Care volunteer and helped older members with house repairs and gardening chores. Eventually, I volunteered in the summer Holiday Bible Clubs, organised by Bloomfield's youth leaders. Rhonda became a Rainbow Guide leader and we helped in Sunday School.

One evening in October 2000, Graham Connor called to visit us. "I have some news for you Stephen," he said. "You've been elected as an Elder." I was speechless. When I gathered my thoughts, I said, "Graham, you know better than anyone I can't accept this position as an Elder." Graham explained that he had been a Christian most of his adult life. This meant when he was dealing with pastoral issues and people said, "Graham, you don't know what you're talking about," they were probably right. Graham added, "In your case Stephen, you'll be able to empathise with people and speak from your experiences." I couldn't argue with his logic. Graham knew I had rewritten the rule book.

I was ordained as a Ruling Elder in Bloomfield Presbyterian Church on 21st January 2001. Twenty days after I began work at Northern Telecom.

Northern Telecom

Northern Telecom and companies like it are a good reason to study hard while you can, to obtain the best qualifications you can, so you don't have to work for them; companies that treat employees with total contempt.

My career in British Telecom came to an end in 2000. The job I enjoyed for over 30 years was changing out of recognition. I was feeling unsettled and finding it challenging to keep up with different work patterns and practices. When Doug Riley was chief executive, BT Northern Ireland was rated the best Telecom company in the world and the first in Britain to obtain ISO 9000. ISO 9000 is a set of internationally, recognised standards for quality assurance and management. Published by the International Organization for Standardisation, it aims to encourage the production of goods and services that meet a globally acceptable level of quality. Doug's mantra was "The customer comes first." Doug Riley was an engineer and understood the technical challenges and customer relations involved in running a Telecommunications company.

Doug's reputation was so good he was poached by BT, HQ in London. His replacement, Hanif Lalani, was an accountant who understood the cost of everything and the value of nothing. At his first management meeting in Riverside Tower, he took a £20 note from his wallet, held it above his head and pronounced, "This is my God." To save £5000 per year he ordered BTNI's Network Operations Unit, which provided 24-hour emergency cover and exchange alarm monitoring, transferred to Cambridge. Cambridge engineers didn't know Northern Ireland's geography, neither its customers or engineers and, they couldn't understand its regional accents. Within a year of his takeover, BTNI was a basket case. Reduced to a telecom "Also ran," no different from its competitors in terms of service. Several other engineers and I no longer felt proud to work for BT and decided it was time for a change.

I talked my plans through with Rhonda. We both appreciated the huge step this would be and the possible impacts on our standard of living. We prayed together I was making the correct decision and asked God to open new doors of opportunity if that was His will. I began searching for vacancies in other Telecommunications companies and, in November 2000, was invited to attend an interview for Northern Telecom at The Quality Inn Hotel in Carrickfergus.

In the meantime, Hanif Lalani went on to make a reputation for himself. As expected for someone who worshipped money, not a good one. Lalani was awarded an OBE in 2002 for his services to business in Northern Ireland. In 2007, the Institute of Asian Professionals named him in its Muslim Power 100 list for his work as finance director of BT. Lalani's OBE was removed by Her Late Majesty the Queen in September 2020 in connection with insider trading fraud committed in 2007. France's stock market regulator imposed a €1.5m fine on Lalani in 2012 following claims of insider trading linked to BT's investment in French IT service provider Net2S. Five members of Lalani's extended family were also fined a total of €4.6m. It makes you proud to be British.

It was a wet, morning when I arrived at The Quality Inn Hotel to find the spacious vestibule chock-a-block with other interviewees milling around who, like me, were wondering what was happening. "Attention everyone, please make your way into the dining room," shouted someone. When I entered the dining room, it was laid out like an examination hall with separate tables and chairs for around 100 people. We were invited to find ourselves a table and chair. A spokesperson at the front announced their position in Northern Telecom. In front of us was a paper containing 100 questions on Logic gates which we were given 40 minutes to complete. You may not know what a Logic gate is. If you're wearing a Smartwatch, you have at least a million strapped to your wrist. For these questions, we had to calculate which combination of And, Or, Nand, and Nor gates would light specific colours in a traffic light sequence.

I realised the short time to answer so many questions was deliberately to put examinees under pressure. I decided to concentrate on completing 20 correctly within the time limit. When time was called, I doubted I had succeeded in my ambition; I packed up my belongings, put on my anorak and headed for the exit. I was about to enter the revolving exit door when someone shouted, "Oi, where do you think you're going?" I turned around and explained to my challenger I flunked the logic examination and there was no point in staying. "No, that's not how this process works," he explained. "There are three parts to the interview process, the Logic examination, an interview and a medical. The results of the three sections are combined before a decision is made whether you pass or not. Please take a seat and wait to be called for an interview." The vestibule crowded again as everyone exited the dining room. Nature called and I went to the loo. When I returned, there wasn't a single person in the lobby. While I was wondering where everyone had disappeared, another Northern Telecom representative appeared, and asked me, "Are you Mr McDonald?" "Yes," I replied. "We've been looking for you," he said. I explained I had only gone to the loo and enquired where everyone had gone. He explained that all the hotel rooms were booked to allow interviews to be held simultaneously. He invited me to follow him to the bedroom where my interview would take place.

I followed him through the door to find a table set at the foot of the bed. Behind it sat three interviewers and I was directed to sit opposite them. "Before I sit down, can I take off my coat please?" "Certainly, make yourself comfortable." The coat rack behind the bedroom door was shown to me. I removed my anorak, put it on a hook and walked towards the interviewee's chair. Halfway there I couldn't move. I seized. No matter how hard I tried I couldn't take another step towards my goal. Panic set in. What's happening? Am I having a stroke? I looked directly at the three interviewers. They wore surprised expressions on their faces and were staring at my groin. I looked there as well. The cord of my anorak was trapped in my trouser flies, stretched back to my coat on the rack. With relief, I took one step back to relieve the tension and said, "Excuse me," to my captivated audience, unzipped my flies, which allowed the cord to snap back to its proper position on my anorak. I nonchalantly zipped myself back up and sat, ready for my interview, trying desperately to pretend nothing untoward had occurred.

I can vaguely remember each interviewer taking turns to ask me various questions on electronic theory. I might even have given some correct replies. I found it difficult to offer intelligent answers when a wee monkey was sitting in my head banging on a pair of cymbals. I'm thinking of Homer Simpson. "How can I get out of here?" I said to myself. "Please, let this be over." When it was over, I was directed back to the lobby to sit and wait for my medical. I took a seat and sat in a daze. I didn't know whether to laugh or cry. "Are you Mr McDonald?" I turned to face a young woman who introduced herself as Dr McKeown. When I confirmed who I was, she invited me to follow her upstairs where she would carry out my medical examination. As I followed her through the bedroom door, I noticed the apparatus on the table in the middle of the room. It was a large black Spirometer. A Spirometer is a diagnostic device that measures the volume of air someone can inhale and exhale. It can also record the time they take to exhale after a deep breath. I was diagnosed with Chronic Obstructive Pulmonary Disease over thirty years ago; I still have a deep dread of these machines and their effect on me.

The monkey was still banging cymbals in my head and, I didn't think before I said, "That bed is going to come in handy." "I beg your pardon," replied Dr McKeown. The penny dropped. "No! No! No! Sorry, I meant if you ask me to use the Spirometer, I will probably need to lie down." I explained my COPD background and reservations about using the machine, but the doctor insisted she needed three readings to complete her evaluation. I made it through the first test but passed out halfway through the second attempt to measure my lung capacity. I came around with the doctor slapping my face and asking me how I got to The Quality Inn Hotel that day. When I told her I came by car, she said she couldn't allow me to drive home. I explained I had no alternative but to drive home; she kept me under observation for two hours before announcing I was fit to leave.

I arrived home around four in the afternoon and Rhonda asked how my interview went. Sometimes, there aren't words to describe what sort of day you've had. In this case, I had words but didn't have the will to put them in the right order. I answered with a facial expression that didn't encourage further debate.

A week later, I received a contract from Northern Telecom with a start date of 2nd January 2001.

On the 2nd of January 2001, I reported for duty at Northern Telecom on Doagh Road, Newtownabbey. Along with other "new starts" I was shown into a modern auditorium and given a pep talk by a senior manager on how fortunate we were to be chosen to work for a great multinational company, called Nortel. After speeches and form filling, we were invited to ask any questions. Someone spoke up and inquired about, "Job security." A manager replied, "Nortel can offer you secure employment for the next ten years." "That'll do nicely," I thought to myself. That, added to my 30-odd years in BT, meant my pension would be based on 40 years of employment. At the end of our induction, we were ushered through a different door into a different world. This was The Wizard of Oz moment when Toto pulled back the curtain to reveal the Wizard was a fraud. Everything to do with Nortel was smoke and mirrors. Everything was pure lies.

From a modern auditorium, we stepped into the old Standard Telephone and Cable factory which made Strowger telephone exchange equipment since 1962. I was directed to work on what was known as TNX1. I was to help repair Slide-in units used in internet communications. My new mentor was called Sid Brown, a rather dour gentleman on the wrong side of middle age, very suspicious of newcomers who were possibly going to take his job. I looked down the room and noticed equipment being loaded into large grates. I asked Sid what was happening. "Did they not tell you this place has been sold?" "What!" I exclaimed. "Management told us we had ten years of secure employment." Sid smiled and replied, "Ten years? You'll be lucky if you get ten months. We've been sold to Solectron in Wales." I couldn't see God's plan in this and regretted my decision to leave BT.

With job insecurity concerning me, there was a lot on my mind when I was ordained as a Ruling Elder in Bloomfield Presbyterian Church on 21st January 2001. The church's Elders held a welcome event for new members to the church one Sunday afternoon in August. This is when I met Alan Dickey for the first time. I didn't realise God had a plan for Alan and myself.

As it happened, Sid wasn't far off in his estimate. My contract was terminated after nine months by a call from my Team Leader during a night shift. It was a great relief.

I endured nine months of "working hell" with some truly obnoxious people. For the first time in my career, I hated going to work. Every morning, I crossed the Lagan Bridge to drive along the M5, my stomach turned to water with dread of another day in Nortel. I prayed, "Lord, why did you do this to me?"

I did work with some decent people who, like me, had given up work in other companies to come and work in Nortel because they thought it offered better job security. One was George Hamilton, a fellow Christian. We connected with a few Christians in other departments and shared tea breaks and lunch times for mutual support.

Two weeks after I started, a photo of the female manager who lied to us at our induction, appeared on the front page of the Belfast Telegraph accepting a trophy. The headline read, "Global technology giant Nortel Networks has won the top accolade in The Belfast Telegraph Northern Ireland Business Awards 2001." Ironically, part of the citation read, "The technology company, which employs around 2,000 in the province, also won the 'Excellence in exporting achievement' accolade. Did the Telegraph's judges know Nortel was exporting its business to Solectron in Wales and about to make its 2000 employees redundant? That was the moment I became a cynic. If the "little people" didn't matter in the '70s and '80s, they appeared to matter even less in the late nineties and early noughties. Being mindful the Post Office Horizon Scandal began in 1999 and the guilty still haven't been punished 25 years later.

I discovered the odd personal disagreement between staff at Nortel was settled by fisticuffs in the car park. I didn't want to risk a fight, so I tried a different approach. One woman, whom Sid advised me to avoid, oversaw a test bed I knew would help identify a fault I was trying to repair on a Slide-in unit. Counting on her softer nature, I exited the M5 one Monday morning and called into the filling station in Whiteabbey. No other customers were in the shop. Nearing the checkout, I noticed a pair of feet protruding under the counter.

The attendant was lying semi-conscious on the floor. I suspected he was diabetic and I helped help him drink the remainder of a cup of sweet tea he'd left on the counter. He recovered quickly, stood up and thanked me. "Now, what can I do for you?" He asked. I asked him for a box of chocolates. "Who are these for?" He enquired. I replied, "A two-legged Rottweiler." He laughed when I explained what I intended to do and gift-wrapped the chocolates.

At work, I tentatively approached the lady in question and asked her expert help in fault-finding the unit I placed on her bench. I offered the gift-wrapped box of chocolates as a token of my appreciation. On Tuesday, I was beside Sid when the "Rottweiler" appeared beside us; she placed my Slide-in unit on our workbench and said, "Hello Stephen, my computer identified the fault, it's working now. Just ask anytime you need help." Sid looked at me open-mouthed, speechless.

Our Team leaders in Nortel's Warranty department were foul-mouthed and abusive. One of them, Joe Dorrian, was one of the people who interviewed me. I can't remember the other one's name but he was a part-time shepherd. He owned a small holding in the Glens of Antrim. If I had been one of his sheep, I'd have gone missing and ensured he never found me.

Nortel corporately lied to entice trained engineers from other companies to maintain production levels. Now we were sworn at because we weren't reaching targets. Looking back, I should have walked out after telling Joe what I thought of him. However, I knew what to expect. I was going to need a reference from him. And so, it proved. On August 31st, 2001, I left Nortel with my reference and P45. Good riddance! The site is now home to Spirit AeroSystems. When Nortel closed, I noticed some former unsavoury colleagues working in B & Q. What a change! "Good morning, sir, how can I help you today?" Solectron closed in 2007 making 150 people redundant.

For the first time in my working career, I was redundant. I was sitting in our back garden contemplating what I should do to find work when I heard our telephone ring. Rhonda was calling from work at the Department of Social Development Press Office in Churchill House. She said, "Stephen, turn on the television."

It was September 11th. 2001.

Campbell College

Rhonda has a gift that I will never possess. The ability to read the Belfast Telegraph from cover to cover. It must be genetic because her Dad, Raymond, did the same every evening after his day's work. Later in September 2001, Rhonda's diligence revealed Strathearn Girls' School and Campbell College had vacancies for technicians. Strathearn's vacancy was in the Chemistry department and Campbell College's was in the Design and Technology department. I applied for both, hoping to be accepted for Strathearn and work in the Chemistry department. Even after 30 years, Chemistry still had an attraction for me.

My interview at Strathearn went well with no wardrobe malfunctions. Unfortunately, I didn't excel at the practical exercise I was invited to perform. I was asked to make up solutions of elements based on their atomic weights. It was too long since I had practised chemistry. I flunked my test and didn't get the job. I was disappointed and very annoyed with myself. Within a few days, I was sitting in an office at Campbell College being interviewed by the Bursar, John Monteith and the head of the Design and Technology Department,

Paul Cartwright. Everything appeared to go well, and I was told they would let me know in due course.

While waiting at home for news, I was visited by a couple of friends. The first was the Reverend Mervyn Gibson from Westbourne Church. He asked what I was doing with my time. I explained I was waiting to find out if my job application was successful. He gave me good advice. "Be prepared for where the Lord will send you next." He advised me to contact the Baptist Bible College on Sandtown Road and enquire about vacancies for the coming term. I took Mervyn's advice and enrolled on a Basic Christianity Course, on Tuesday evenings over the next two years. One of my lecturers made a big impression on me. I might have dropped out of the course only for Jim Murdoch.

His lectures on Paul's Letters were fascinating and insightful; it appeared Jim knew St Paul as a friend. More incredible still, Jim was in constant pain due to a spinal injury, caused by a car accident in the south of Ireland, while he worked there as a Baptist missionary. My other visitor was the Reverend Howard Lewis. Howard, the Associate Minister at Bloomfield Presbyterian Church at the time, invited me to the Women's Education Centre in Finvoy Street, East Belfast. He had been invited to talk on the 23rd Psalm and asked me if I would like to give my testimony at the event. I accepted Howard's invitation. This was the first time I shared my testimony with anyone. Little did I know, the impact this would have on my life in the years ahead. Because, across the street, behind a high fence, stood two Portacabins, one on top of the other. Outside was a sign that read, "Walkway Community Centre." What goes on in there? I wondered. It looked foreboding.

I was in Belvoir Park on Friday 28th September when I received a call telling me my application to Campbell College was successful. The caller asked me to report to the Design and Technology Department the following Monday 1st. October 2001.

I was met by the Head of Department, Paul Cartwright. He brought me into his office for a pep talk about my new career as a Technician in the Design and Technology Department of Campbell College. Like me, this was his first term at Campbell College. He moved from England to take up the position, left vacant by the previous HOD Derrick Boyd when he retired. The second teacher in the department moved to Sullivan Grammar because he didn't get the vacant post. Paul brought me into a classroom to meet his replacement teacher. Guess who? Alan Dickey. I met Alan only once at church and didn't realise he was a teacher. Paul noticed the expressions on our faces and asked, "Do you two know each other?" We explained we belonged to the same church. Paul informed us he belonged to Ballynahinch Baptist church.

The third teaching position was filled by a young teacher named Chris Turner. His father was a Methodist minister and Chris was a neighbour until he moved to another school. His position was filled by a lady named Bernadette Mone. "Dette," as she preferred to be called, spent most of her time in the department on Maternity Leave. Her husband, Brendan worked for Thales Missiles. Brendan was responsible for demonstrating the capabilities of the Starstreak Missile System to potential buyers around the world. Dette was a pleasure to work with but I knew her substitute, Peter Campbell, better because of the time he spent "Subbing" in the department. The last teacher to join the department before I left was John "Thumbs Up" Taylor, the former Vice Principal of Cabin Hill Prep School.

Alan Midgley was another Christian staff member, in charge of the school's uniform and tuck shop. One afternoon, he explained he and three Christian teachers prayed all the vacancies, in the T and D department, would be filled by Christians.

T and D was now fully staffed by Christians. Their prayers had been answered.

The school was founded in 1894 by a bequest from Henry James Campbell who made his fortune in the linen trade. The main building is a huge Victorian edifice. The Central Hall is straight out of Hogwarts; one of many locations across Belfast and Ulster where the Ulster Covenant was signed by those opposed to Home Rule on 28th September 1912. The T and D department is a separate purpose-built building, a short walk from the back entrance to the school.

It consisted of a prep store in the rear, containing shelving, storage areas and a Table Saw where "Resistant Materials" were stored before being cut and shaped to the dimensions required for different year groups' projects. It took time to familiarise myself with new surroundings and become acquainted with technicians and teachers from other departments. The technician in the Chemistry Department was George Walls, a retired Line Manager from BT. It took time to get used to hard physical graft. From 8 am to 5 pm, there was never a spare moment. The pressure to prepare for lessons was relentless.

Right from the moment I began work in Campbell, Paul Cartwright made it very clear his one purpose was to enhance his career prospects; his goal was to emulate his father and become a School Principal. "I'm not here to make friends," was the first thing he said. Well, he succeeded in that ambition. I found Paul arrogant and a bully; not only to me but to other staff members and pupils.

In October 2004 I received an appointment from Royal Victoria Hospital for an operation to remove nasal polyps. This would be the fifth time I had this procedure carried out. Paul asked me to cancel the operation and I refused. I told him I had been waiting three years for this surgery and there was no way I was cancelling to suit him and the department. After the surgery, I was given a four-week sick line but went back to work after two weeks. The first day back, Paul called me into his office and told me the department ran better in my absence; I was to "desist" from being friendly with other teaching staff.

That was the gratitude I received for working unpaid until 10 pm some evenings and using my car to transport and collect materials for the department. How's that for man management? One of my greatest regrets was not collecting my coat and walking out, telling Paul I was taking the remainder of my sick line. On another day, after a particularly heated exchange between us, he said, "You think you got your position here because of

342

31 years in BT. Well, you didn't. You got your position here because of your nine months in Nortel."

Boom! God answered my prayers about leaving BT by sending me to a job I hated to prepare me for work at Campbell College. I knew then I wouldn't react in kind to Paul's provocations. I sensed he was deliberately goading me to swear so he could say, "And you call yourself an Elder." The other teachers were a pleasure to work for and, although it was never said out loud, I don't believe anyone had any great respect for Paul Cartwright. The social etiquette at Campbell suited Paul. There was a distinct pecking order accorded to the staff. From the Headmaster, down through House Masters, teachers and the administrative staff. Some of the latter took on airs and graces because of their perceived superior position amongst the echelons of the great and good at Campbell College.

Degrees from Cambridge and Oxford allowed their owners privileged positions on top of the pecking order. Degrees from the University of East Anglia and the University of Southampton mightn't even guarantee their owners access to the Staff Common Room. "Common" in this use is oxymoronic. The Headmaster's secretary, Yvonne, earned herself the nickname "Tin Knickers" which she took pride in. Tin Knickers ran interference for

Ivan Pollock until he retired. Amy Mills oversaw the school's office and ruled it as her private fiefdom. The Bursar, John Monteith and his secretary Jane, made Ebenezer Scrooge and Bob Cratchit look like philanthropists.

Ada was the school receptionist, and she didn't enjoy great health. She was a spinster and lived a very secluded life. Her only "friends" were a few people in Campbell College. I spoke to her one day, shortly after I started and she told me she was robbed the day before. Ada was very slow on her feet; when getting out of her car, she placed her handbag on the roof so she could use both hands to steady herself. In that instant, someone snatched her bag and ran away. She was still upset and quite emotional. I told Rhonda Ada's story when I went home.

The next day Rhonda bought a new handbag, put £20 in it and instructed me to give it to Ada. I did so and Ada cried someone cared enough to replace her lost handbag. From that moment, we became friends. I learned a lot about the workings of Campbell and its staff from Ada who knew all the latest gossip circulating the school. Ada's health was deteriorating, and she would call me some evenings and ask me to pray for her. One evening, she asked me to bring her to the Lord. She died a short time later at home; it is good to know she is in God's presence. Credit to Campbell's Music Department who performed a moving memorial service to celebrate Ada's life and her service to the school.

It was always a pleasure when I visited Lorraine McCutcheon in her wee, pokey office tucked away on the top floor of the school. Lorraine archived pupils' work and exam results. There should have been a health warning pinned to her. "DANGER, ENTER AT YOUR OWN RISK." When you entered her office, Lorraine was barely visible through a cloud of cigarette smoke. She dressed like a 70s hippie, could make a rollie with one hand and chain smoking had given her a deep baritone voice. Lorraine became a firm friend of Alan and I. We enjoyed her wit and devil-may-care attitude. Lorraine's quiet demeanour was the opposite of Napalm Sam's. You can guess how Sam Quigg, a Physics teacher, earned his nickname.

Paul burnished his reputation by arranging the first Northern Ireland-wide Technology Conference in Campbell College's Central Hall. James Dyson massaged his ego further by agreeing to be the Keynote speaker. Every school in Northern Ireland with Technology and Design departments, was invited to send representatives to this auspicious event. This involved a lot of planning, sending invitations, tracking who agreed to attend, printing name badges and preparing sight and sound equipment. It all took long hours and hard work. Unpaid of course!

A fortnight before the event was due in November 2002, Paul received a message that James Dyson had cancelled his plan to attend. Dyson was travelling to New York to unveil his latest vacuum cleaner. His secretary passed on Dyson's apologies and, by way of compensation, sent a crate of Dyson's book, "Against the Odds," to hand to guests at the conference. That pricked Paul's ego. The books arrived and were promptly placed in the department's roof space. I'm sure they're still there if you would like a copy. Now there was a panic to find a new Keynote speaker.

Fortunately, Dette came to the rescue when she suggested her husband, Brendan would be available on the date to give a talk about the technology involved in the Starstreak Missile System. So, Brendan was recruited to rescue the conference. Unfortunately for Paul, Brendan gave him a prepared introduction to himself and his work at Thales. Paul should have read it through beforehand but didn't bother. There were more important things to do. The word "nacelle" was in the speech and Paul, the head of Technology and Design, didn't recognise the word and couldn't pronounce it. He discredited himself in front of 600 pupils and their teachers. He was so pompous he didn't realise he'd made a fool of himself.

A nacelle is the metal housing of an aircraft engine. Any six-year-old boy who ever built an Airfix model plane would've been well acquainted with the word. Well, so much for a university education. However, Brendan rescued the day with a fascinating lecture on the How, Where, and Why of the Starstreak Missile System. He showed films of test firings he made around the world and stated that, without exception, Starstreak never missed a target. The missile had a 100% "Kill" record. Awesome! The audience was engrossed. I doubt some bloke talking about a vacuum cleaner would have made the same impact.

Riding high on the positive feedback from the Technology and Design conference, Paul decided to organise a trip for Sixth-Form Technology pupils to Disneyland Paris. Ostensibly, it was a "behind the scenes" visit to learn how the park's technology made everything work. I was invited along with Paul and Alan to make up the adult-to-pupil safeguarding ratio. We booked into the Cheyenne Hotel on 24th January 2003 where I shared a room with Alan Dickey.

The next morning, after breakfast, we all headed to the main entrance to the theme park. It was lashing rain and directly in front of us, wearing yellow ponchos and linking their arms were 20 mean-looking stewards guarding the entrance gates. "Welcome to Disneyland," I said. "Keep your voice down," said Alan. After displaying our passes, we were allowed into the Magic Kingdom. I have never been in a more soulless, joyless and God-forsaken place in all my life. Our first ride was called, It's a Small World. Please never, ever put yourself or your loved ones through this. My day went downhill from there.

There was no behind-the-scenes visit. We were marched into a dark, dank auditorium and given a Disneyland Customer Service lecture. Paul nudged me back to consciousness three times. I was snoring. Later I ran out of Annette's Diner when staff jumped onto tables and started singing You've Got a Friend in Me. I couldn't take any more faux happiness and found somewhere quiet to call Rhonda. "Hello sweetheart, are you OK? Please talk to me about anything. I think I'm going insane." And we talked for 45 minutes. This turned out to be the most expensive phone call I've ever made. When I received my mobile bill the following month, my 45-minute call home from Disneyland, Paris had cost £55. It was worth every penny.

Alan was enjoying himself too. After checking the boys were in their rooms for the night, we retired to our room. Lying on my bed I asked Alan, "Why is the ceiling fan on in the middle of the winter?" "It's to prevent you hanging yourself from the ceiling rose," replied Alan. I have a photograph of Alan outside Snow White's cottage. You can see in his eyes the moment he decided to give up teaching. I'm still scarred from my last night in Disneyland where I celebrated my 50th birthday in Au Chalet de la Marionette. It was Paul's idea to let the restaurant staff know it was my birthday. A birthday cake duly arrived along with Pinocchio and Geppetto. They sat on either side of me. I got the last laugh when Paul had to pay for the cake.

I haven't mentioned the pupils at Campbell. In general, they were pleasant and respectful. Campbell College has a good reputation for teaching and pastoral care. Boys from different backgrounds and abilities are encouraged to develop their skills and take pride in their school and its reputation. There is a strong emphasis on sports, mainly rugby and cricket. The school has a rifle range, where I enjoyed target practice sometimes, and a strong Officer Training Corps.

One lad who joined the OTC when I worked at Campbell is now a Lieutenant Colonel in the Royal Scottish Regiment. Another young man received the lowest mark possible in his Eleven Plus. His Mum paid his way to Campbell College; she told me her son's "light came on" when he was 14. He received top marks in his A levels and was first in his year. He works for a cyber security firm based in Dublin and paid for another Eleven Plus "Failure" to go to Campbell College.

As you would expect, there was an equal measure of introverts and extroverts. Some lads were creative, others couldn't follow simple instructions to shape a piece of MDF. John Walker was teaching a Year 9 group of boys how to use a coping saw to cut a 25cm X 25cm piece of MDF into the shape of a star. LEDs would then be inserted, and the finished work would decorate pupils' Christmas trees. John brought one of the boy's efforts into my office to show me. The boy had cut away so much of the MDF there wasn't enough space to fit the LEDs.

John was shaking his head at how useless this pupil was with tools. He said, "What can you do with handless boys?" I replied, "Don't worry John, the lad will probably be a lawyer." Ten minutes later John returned in fits of laughter. "You were right Stephen, his Dad is a Barrister, and he wants to be one as well." John earned his nickname by sawing off his left thumb on a bandsaw some years previously. Boys will be boys; when John ordered his classes to do anything, everyone would invariably give him the "Thumbs up" sign with both thumbs, then put one thumb down and say, "Sorry Mr Walker."

On one wall of my office were pinned the charts for each year group which showed the times for each class and what materials were required for each session. Some were quite repetitive, and teachers used abbreviations where appropriate. On one of John's charts, for a Year 10 Wednesday class, he had noted "C Mon." As in "Same as Monday's." I couldn't resist the temptation. On the day, I placed a jar containing a little PVA glue labelled "C Mon" on John's desk. I told him, "It was all I could manage at short notice." I can still see John's face. Paul rushed into the classroom to investigate the reason for his hysterical laughter, shook his head and walked out again. Laughter is the best medicine. To Paul's annoyance, I couldn't help myself.

I became friends with a Sixth-Form pupil called Happy Yip. How could I not like someone with the name Happy? Happy was from Hong Kong and a boarder at Campbell. Our friendship developed over his Year 13 and Year 14 terms in 2003 and 2004. Happy had a happy disposition and great enthusiasm for his Technology projects which I found infectious. It was a pleasure to help and advise on how to make his design ideas a reality.

Before school closed for the Easter break in 2004, I asked the Boarding Master, John McKinney, permission to invite Happy home for dinner some evening over the holidays. John was delighted to agree. We arranged a suitable evening and Happy came for dinner together with Alan Dickey and Martin McNeely. "Marty" was a neighbour then and attended Union College studying for the ministry. Previously, he was a press officer for the UUP and maybe, that helped account for his rather gung-ho approach to evangelism.

As expected, when he met Happy, he went straight in with both feet and enquired what sort of God Happy worshipped. Happy replied in his quiet Chinese accent, "Sure I'm a Christian." I was quite surprised as well as Marty and Alan. Happy had never discussed religion during our time in school together. He invited Rhonda and me to hear his testimony and witness his baptism at Windsor Baptist Church on Good Friday 2004. Happy and around ten other Chinese converts were baptised that afternoon. All the musicians and choir members were Chinese. It was a cacophony of noise.

The Control of Substances Hazardous to Health Regulations (COSHH) were introduced in October 2002. I was instructed to fit and mount a compliant storage locker in the prep store where all the department's hazardous materials were kept under lock and key when not being used. The prep room was open to a workroom where Alan Dickey was teaching a class of Year 8s. I began my task by drilling and fitting the mounting brackets to the wall. I lifted and placed the locker on the brackets, lay on the floor and drilled upwards through the brackets into the cabinet to affix the locking bolts.

However, the drill bit didn't penetrate the locker. Instead, it pushed the locker off the mounting brackets. I looked up to see the locker begin to topple towards me. I remember saying to myself, "This is going to hurt." When the locker landed on me, the internal shelves folded up. This meant I was completely enclosed by the locker with only my feet sticking out. "Sir! Sir!" I heard a pupil shout to Alan, "The locker has fallen on Mr McDonald." I listened to the sound of hurried footsteps and waited to be rescued. Instead, all I heard were peals of laughter from Alan and the boys when they saw my comedy show in the prep room. After being extricated, I walked through the Year 8 workroom back to my office. One of the lads attracted my attention. "Sir! Sir!" "Yes?" I replied. "Do you know they've made a film about you?" "Have they?" I asked. "Yes, it's called Full Metal Jacket."

I didn't particularly like it when people described pupils as Campbell's Soup because they were "Rich and thick." However, some boys did try to live up to that reputation. One lad was swimming breadths in the school's swimming pool when he stopped to shout at the PE instructor. "Sir, what width is this pool?" "Five metres," replied the teacher. "Hold my watch, sir, it's only waterproof to three metres." A pupil was absent from school so many times, Ivan Pollock, the Headmaster, telephoned to enquire about the reason for his absence. When the telephone was answered, Ivan said, "This is Ivan Pollock, the Principal of Campbell College, to whom am I speaking?" Came the reply, "It's my Father, sir."

Always eager to add to his CV, Paul organised another Year 13 and Year 14 trip to London. The plan was to visit the Technology and Design Museum, on the South Bank of the Thames. It has since moved to Kensington. Paul, Alan and I, together with 28 pupils, booked into the Lady Astor Hostel in Westminster. One sniff of the air was enough for a high. We visited the Victoria and Albert Museum and rode the London Eye while on our trip. On our first evening in London, we travelled to the Trocadero Centre in Leicester Square, to play Ten Pin Bowling. None of our university-educated staff, or A-level students, could set up the score displays. So, we called for assistance. We couldn't understand what the assistants were saying and, vice versa. Alan Dickey said something rather profound to me that I have never forgotten. "Stephen, do you realise we are at the centre of the English-speaking world and no one can understand a word we're saying?" Too true.

We left around 11 pm to walk to Piccadilly Tube Station; one of the boys said, "Sir, I've left my wallet in the Trocadero Centre." I suggested it would be pointless returning but reluctantly agreed to accompany him back to the centre. To our amazement, the wallet and all its contents had been handed into the lost property department. The next day, we visited a factory in Streatham on the site where the London Olympic Village would soon be built to see computer-aided design and cutting in operation. During our visit, they were making National Lottery displays for retail outlets. Afterwards, we boarded a bus to travel back to the city centre. I was the last one of our groups to board and said to the driver, "31 to the City centre please." The ticket machine made a beautiful noise.

bzzz,bzzz,bzzz,bzzz,bzzz,bzzz,bzzz,bzzz,bzzz,bzzz,bzzz,bzzz,bzzz,bzzz,bzzz,bzzz,bzzz,bzzz,bzzz,bzzz,bzzz,bzzz,bzzz,bzzz,bzzz,bzzz,bzzz,bzzz,bzzz,bzzz,bzzz.

That evening, we saw Chitty Chitty Bang Bang at the Royal Palladium. Suffice it to say, Alan and I couldn't get out quick enough. On our last day, Paul didn't travel back with the group. He planned to stay and travel from London to visit family. Alan and I were left to ensure 28 boys returned home safely. We showered, packed our bags, and headed to Heathrow. Paul showered after we left and discovered someone had taken his bath towel. He was obliged to dry himself with a bed sheet. The towel thief turned out to be me.

I can't write about Campbell College without describing the most embarrassing moment that occurred while I was there. It involved the Vice-Principal, David Funston. I was walking to the Resource Office in the main school to do some photocopying. I entered through the rear entrance and walked up the long corridor to the T junction, where it forked left and right. Left, led to the Central Hall, right to the Resource Office. Suddenly, David whooshed in beside me, gowns flapping, straight out of Tom Brown's School Days.

"Hello Stephen, how are you?" He said, "I've just bought a house on Earlswood Road and finding it difficult to remove varnish from the bannisters. Would you have a spare plane blade I could use to scrape off the varnish?" I replied, "No problem. I'll find one and make sure it is oiled and sharpened.

I'll have one of the pupils deliver it to your office." All well and good, we parted our ways, and a sharpened plane blade was duly delivered to David's office.

Two weeks later, I was making the same journey to the Resource Office and whoosh, David appeared by my side again. "Good afternoon, Stephen, are you well?" "Yes Sir, I am," I replied. "Were you able to remove the varnish on the bannisters with the plane blade?" I enquired. "No, Stephen, I didn't make much progress. The varnish is proving very stubborn to remove." What I meant to say next was, "What you need is a blow torch." But I didn't. If you understand what I did say, that's proof of how fallen we are; that wee monkey started banging cymbals in my head again.

We had just arrived at the T junction at the end of the corridor. David went left and I went right. I ran into the Resource Office, rushed past all the administration staff, closed myself in the photocopying room, grouched in a corner and shook with laughter. I couldn't tell any of the ladies in the office the advice I rendered to the Vice-Principal, but I couldn't help wondering who he might have shared it with. As a result of my convulsions, I was late returning to the department and, of course, Paul wanted to know the reason. His face was a picture when I shared my conversation with David. I never met David again in the remainder of my time at Campbell. Maybe he was afraid I would offer him further advice. I'm sure I left a lasting impression on him.

Despite Paul, I enjoyed my time at Campbell College. The greatest pressure was during A Level Assessments. All the A-level students designed and made projects containing electronics. Unfortunately, many of them didn't work. This is where my Nortel experience came into play. Using an oscilloscope and test probe, I faulted each circuit and advised pupils what was needed to remedy the problem. Sometimes, it was expedient to repair circuits myself.

Boys couldn't solder very well and dry joints were often the problem. Sometimes microchips weren't programmed properly or there was a faulty component. Time and again, Paul would interrupt my work to ask, "Have you got that fixed yet?" A Level grades in Technology and Design depended on the boys' projects working. The overall results also reflected the standard of teaching in the department. As you can imagine, this added to the stress of my job.

I began having serious headaches which gradually worsened over time. Sometimes, I was physically ill when I returned home. I visited my GP and initial tests were carried out to investigate if I might have a brain tumour. Rhonda commented, "That job is killing you. You need out." Once more, thanks to her diligence in reading the Belfast Telegraph, she pointed out an advertisement for positions in the Identity and Passport Service. Then, it was an agency; now it's known as HM Passport Office and under ministerial control. I applied and was invited to an interview in May 2006. I heard nothing further and forgot all about it.

I could never hear my office landline ring unless in the room beside it. There was too much noise with three classrooms full of students operating tools and machinery. One Friday afternoon in October 2006, I popped into my office to pick up some material when the telephone rang. "Hello, is that Stephen McDonald?" Enquired the female caller. "Yes," I replied. "This is the IPS, you didn't enter your father's place of birth on your application form." "Belfast," I said. My caller replied, "Thank you, goodbye."

That was it. I thought to myself, the IPS must be vetting me. The following Monday morning Paul called me into his office to inquire if I was thinking of leaving Campbell. "Why?" I asked. "I received a call over the weekend from the IPS asking me for a character reference;" I confirmed my intentions and waited for developments.

I received word to report to the IPS, High Street, Belfast at the beginning of November 2006. I gave my notice, and, on my last day, I was called to the Bursar's Office. Jane, Bob Cratchit's descendant, handed me my payslip and advised me they deducted a week's pay because I was leaving before working up my October half-term break. In hindsight, I wish I'd torn up that cheque and thrown the pieces on her desk.

I wonder if the Bursar's office still follows the policy of not paying accounts, until the last possible date. Every September, when school resumed, accounts I set up with suppliers over the year were closed due to non-payment. This meant I needed to set all the accounts up again. Proof again, in my experience, people obsessed with money lack common decency and consideration for others.

The only thing Campbell College ever gave me free of charge, forbye migraine headaches, was two pieces of wood. Both were rough six-inch by two-inch lengths of timber. One piece was seven feet long, the other five feet long. They lay in the storeroom throughout my time as a technician. Paul agreed I could take the timbers as a leaving present because he didn't plan to use them. "Generosity" was his middle name. In our spare time, over the last few days of my time in Campbell, Alan and I shaped the pieces into the full-sized cross that is displayed at Easter services in Bloomfield Presbyterian Church. This was the last practical work I ever did, in the Technology and Design department.

Paul must have been planning his departure as well without telling anyone. In 2007, he informed Alan, Peter and John he was moving to Liverpool to take up the position of Head of Faculty at a public school. After Paul's move to Liverpool, Peter called Paul to tell him he was organising a Sixth-Form trip to the Design Museum in London; did he have any advice to offer from his trip a few years earlier? To Peter's surprise, Paul was arranging the same trip for the Sixth-Form pupils from Liverpool, and they arranged for both sets of pupils to meet and stay in the same hostel in London. At dinner, the teachers from both schools were sharing the same table.

Peter asked Paul, "Well what's it like being Head of Faculty?" Paul's face turned bright red. Before he could answer, one of the teachers from Liverpool said, "He's not Head of Faculty." Pride comes before a fall and Paul fell hard. He revealed his true character when he came to Peter later and informed him, "During our stay, it has become obvious that the boys from Campbell College aren't of the same calibre as the students from my school. The two groups will be kept separate from now on." One of the Liverpool teachers came to

Peter the next day and said, "What a total and utter prat." While all your boys were in their rooms last night, that idiot was up half the night keeping our girls and boys out of one another's rooms." I don't know what Paul is doing now but, whatever it is, I can assure you all his geese will be swans.

There were more changes after I left Campbell. John "Thumbs Up" Taylor retired. Peter Campbell moved to Head of Department in Antrim Grammar. Alan Dickey was promoted to Head of Department in 2007 and didn't enjoy it. Alan left Campbell College in June 2008. By August 2008, Alan and his family lived in Hebron School, high in the Nilgiri Hills in Tamal Nadu, India. Alan taught Technology and Design there for three years. He adapted to a whole different approach to Health and Safety.

Rhonda and Rebekah travelled to India and stayed with the Dickey family as a once-in-a-lifetime experience. I didn't go as I was afraid the air at 7,000 feet would be too thin and exacerbate my COPD. Alan and his family returned to Belfast in October 2011. Alan joined Union College in September 2012 to begin training for the ordained ministry. On 4th January 2018, Rhonda, Rebekah and I attended his Service of Installation at Stewartstown Presbyterian Church. He might be some distance away, but we remain close friends.

Fallen Arches

In 2004, at a meeting of church Elders, our minister Graham Connor suggested the introduction of Action Teams headed by a nominated Elder. He jokingly said if his idea worked it would make him redundant. Instead of Graham having responsibility for every ministry in the church, work would be devolved to a Mission, a Youth Team, a Seniors' Team etc. I was given responsibility for the Community Team. One of the first outreaches I re-established, was with the Arches Care Home, just across the road from Bloomfield church. There had been a previous church ministry to the home which ended in 2000. We were welcomed back by staff and residents; our services continue to this day on the first Saturday of each month.

The two ministries I am deeply committed to are associated with one another in Scripture.

Corinthians 1: 27 – 29 is my commission to bring God's word to the Arches, to the humblest and sometimes the "Most despised," people in our society.

"Brothers and sisters, think of what you were when you were called. Not many of you were wise by human standards; not many were influential; not many were of noble birth. But God chose the foolish things of the world to shame the wise; God chose the weak things of the world to shame the strong. God chose the lowly things of this world and the despised things—and the things that are not—to nullify the things that are, so that no one may boast before him."

Directly followed by Corinthians 2: 1-5 which is my commission to work in Walkway. I quote it in "Stocktaking."

This is a question I challenge people with, "If everyone, without exception, is made in God's image, what does God reveal about Himself when we meet people with different challenging needs?" The best answer I have heard so far is, "God doesn't see disability."

During Holy Week 2010, I spent some time visiting a resident in the Arches named Marjorie Salters. Marjorie had been baptised in Bloomfield the previous year. Despite her additional needs, Marjorie was an ardent reader. She enjoyed reading her Bible together with any Christian books and commentaries. Marjorie welcomed regular visits from me and other volunteers from the church.

When I was leaving, I bumped into a member of staff I hadn't met before. He was finishing his shift. I introduced myself and he told me his name was Patrick Ozegbe. I mentioned I was about to go to a prayer evening in church and asked him if he would like to come along. He agreed and we walked to church together. Patrick joined in our prayers that evening. When he spoke, I sensed, he was a man of deep faith. He gave me his mobile number and asked me to tell him when our next prayer meeting would be held.

A few weeks later, when I saw Marjorie again, I asked her why she was crying. She told me Patrick had been arrested. Julie, one of the Arches managers, confided in me that UK Borders Agency called at the Arches and arrested Patrick. He was sentenced to six months in Maghaberry Jail for entering Britain on false papers. Julie explained that the Arches checked his documents and believed they were all in order. Everyone was shocked. Patrick had been a hard worker and popular with the residents and staff. I wasn't sure what to make of the news. Would a Christian deliberately break the law? I put the matter to the back of my mind. There was nothing I or anyone could do.

Later that year, Majorie informed me that Patrick had been released from prison. Despite Marjorie's physical and mental challenges, she was deeply concerned about her friend Patrick and asked me if I could find out his whereabouts and how he was keeping. I assured her I would do my best to check on Patrick. I didn't tell Marjorie I felt ill at ease about this as I realised, I didn't know what I was getting involved in. I talked my doubts and reservations out with Rhonda so we could decide together what to do. We decided we couldn't know whether to get involved unless we heard Patrick's side of events. Patrick answered his mobile and we planned to meet the following Saturday morning.

On Saturday morning, I was feeling apprehensive about meeting Patrick. Rhonda suggested we read some scripture and pray that God would show us what to do. We read Proverbs 19 v 17. "He who is kind to the poor lends to the Lord, and he will reward him for what he has done." I picked Patrick up from his Home Office provided accommodation off Castlereagh Street and drove to a café on the Lisburn Road. I told Patrick we could talk over breakfast. He explained he had been persecuted in his homeland of Nigeria because he was a Christian. To escape, he applied for a passport and, the necessary visas to work in the UK. Corruption is endemic in Nigeria, and he bribed officials to process his application. Unfortunately for Patrick, he bribed the wrong people and received false papers.

Patrick believed his papers were legitimate and travelled to Northern Ireland where he found work as a Care Assistant. He was PAYE, had set up a bank account and enrolled in further education. His whole life came crashing down when he was sent to prison. I listened to Patrick's story with my cynical head on. I thought, are you telling me the truth? Are you taking advantage of my trust? Why should I believe you? Eventually, it was time to go, and we walked to my car parked on Lisburn Road. When Patrick climbed into the car, he said, "Stephen, thank you for your kindness towards me." I thanked him for his kind words. Patrick carried on saying, "Proverbs 19 v 17 says, "He who is kind to the poor lends to the Lord, and he will reward him for what he has done.""

I was stunned into silence. I knew immediately God had spoken to me. "Patrick is my adopted son, look after him." Patrick saw the astonished look on my face and asked me what was wrong. I explained to him what just happened. We were both overwhelmed by the knowledge God brought us together to work out his plans in our lives. At that moment, a deep bond of friendship and trust was created between Patrick and me. When I arrived home, I told Rhonda everything that happened that morning and we thanked God for His answered prayers.

On that day, our journey with Patrick, through many trials and tribulations, began. Patrick's asylum application failed. The Home Office withdrew his support package, and he became homeless in November 2010 when he was compelled to vacate his accommodation. Rhonda and I were deeply concerned for his well-being. So much so that, on a wet Saturday afternoon in late November, Rhonda said, "Go find Patrick and bring him here to live with us." I found Patrick queuing for a bed at the homeless hostel in Sandy Row. I pulled up beside him, and shouted, "Patrick, get in the car, you're coming to us." And so, Patrick Ozegbe, a destitute asylum seeker, came to be part of our lives and family at 26 Irwin Drive.

Patrick lived with Rhonda, Rebekah & I for 18 months. During that time, he broke every appliance we possessed. These included our kettle, toaster, and even the television cabinet. Nothing was safe. Some people, through no fault of their own, are handless. I would never ask Patrick to help me paint again either. He didn't adhere to the principle of "keep it between the lines." I spent longer repainting what Patrick over-enthusiastically painted before me. He insisted on doing the ironing. How many people must have walked by our living room window and noticed a Nigerian standing over an ironing board with a steam iron in his hand? Our neighbours must have thought we were like a family from "The Help." "Have the McDonalds got servants?" Marley was walked at odd times throughout the night whenever Patrick was fasting and praying. 2.00 am, 4.00 am, Marley didn't mind. Patrick enjoyed cooking African dishes for us which looked different but tasted delicious. All in all, we managed to co-exist extremely well.

In May 2012, Patrick decided to move to London where he would have better access to legal firms that could help him pursue his asylum claim. I became an advocate for Patrick and wrote testimonies to solicitors who handled Patrick's case as it progressed through each stage of the asylum process. The next year Rebekah completed her degree in Youth and Community Work with Practical Theology obtaining First Class Honours; her graduation ceremony was held in London at the Emmanuel Centre on Marsham Street, directly facing the Home Office. Patrick came to meet us and enjoy our celebrations.

Patrick's case dragged on; it all appeared never-ending. Eventually, in March 2016, I was invited to appear before Judge Maxwell at Hatton Cross Tribunal Centre, near Heathrow, to present my support for Patrick. Despite all going well at the hearing, we were informed Patrick's claim had failed again nine weeks later. Patrick was indefatigable. He believed God brought him to live and work in the UK. I wasn't so sure and argued with him God was telling him to return to Nigeria. I suggested he was like Jonah because he appeared to ignore God's will.

We continued supporting Patrick monthly as best we could. He moved from London to Chatham to save on expenses and was supported by a local church and charities. In 2019 Patrick met Adebayo Ademiluyi who had been granted Leave To Remain in the UK under the EU Settlement Scheme. Adebayo became known to us by her pet name Charlotteen. Patrick and Charlotteen's wedding arrangements were cancelled when the COVID-19 pandemic caused chaos in people's lives in January 2020, followed by subsequent lockdowns. Life went on regardless and Charlotteen became pregnant.

On the 19th January 2021, Patrick called me to announce he had become a father. Charlotteen had given birth to a beautiful boy. They had decided to call him Stephen after me. I was struck speechless. Their newborn son was called Stephen

Ozegbe. I shared our good news that evening when our church's monthly Kirk Session meeting was held on Zoom. Everyone was delighted with our news. The British Nationality Act 1982 states that, because Stephen's mother had been granted Indefinite Leave to Remain before he was born, Stephen was born with full rights as a British Citizen. Because Patrick was now father to a British Citizen, he was subsequently granted permission to stay in the UK under the Immigration Rules for Family Members as a Partner on the 10-year route to settlement.

Patrick, Charlotteen, and Stephen are doing well and recently moved to Rochester. Patrick now works for Changing Lives Building Dreams, an organisation that offers bespoke services and 24-hour support to individuals with challenging and complex needs. Patrick and his family visited in March 2023. It was a time of great fun and blessings. By then, Aliona Fedorenko and her son Gleb had lived with us for nearly a year under the UK Homes For Ukraine Scheme. Our home was the League of Nations for two wonderful days.

Rhonda and I continue to pray we are doing God's will.

Deuteronomy 10:18

"He defends the cause of the fatherless and the widow, and loves the foreigner residing among you, giving them food and clothing."

There is nothing more fulfilling.

If God Builds It

Hungary was known as a Satellite state of the Soviet Union and a member of the Warsaw Pact during the Cold War. The Cold War emerged in the aftermath of World War II when the United States and the Soviet Union found themselves in a tense geopolitical struggle which lasted until 1991.

The Hungarian Revolution occurred in 1956. It was a popular country-wide uprising against the Hungarian People's Republic because of its subordination to the Soviet Union. The Uprising lasted for 12 days before being brutally put down when Soviet tanks and troops invaded the country on November 4th, 1956. Thousands of people were killed and a quarter of a million Hungarians fled their country. Hungary remained a Communist country until a peaceful transition to democracy in 1989 when the Soviet Union's grip on the country weakened and the Eastern Bloc disintegrated. The last Russian troops left in 1991.

The former socialist state would never formally admit that there were abandoned children in the country. A group of Christians from the Budafok

Baptist Church began the Menedek Ministry in 1978 to care for homeless young people and children by fostering them with Christian families to give them a home and an education. Menedek means refuge or shelter. The word is taken from Nahum 1 v 7. "The Lord is good, a refuge in times of trouble. He cares for those who trust in him."

In 1985, Menedek bought an abandoned 200-year-old Mansion in a small village called Bodrog, 100 miles south of Budapest. Work began in the Mansion to provide accommodation for the foster families. In 1989, the first couple and their children to move into their new flat was Kornél and Anna Heizer. They were followed afterwards, by three more families with their children and children fostered from state care. There was a total of 30 children growing up in these homes. Immediately, after the arrival of the families, a kindergarten was founded. By 1992 plans for the Bodrog Education Centre began to take shape. In 1994, a primary school was established followed in 1995 by a music school.

The school was at full capacity after two years and the opportunity presented itself to lease the schoolhouse in the village from the local municipality. The school had been derelict for over

20 years and fallen into disrepair, but it helped, by teaching the lower forms in the village school, to establish trust and connections with local villagers. As capacity in the schools became limited due to the increasing number of students and additional syllabuses, work resumed on the Bodrog Education Centre on the grounds of the Mansion House to address the issues.

In the summer of 1991, a member of Bloomfield, Eddie Spence, a Christian singer and songwriter, was invited to sing at various planned evangelistic events in Hungary by David Trimble, (not the politician) a fellow recent graduate from Belfast Bible College. David and his family were serving in Hungary supporting local Baptist churches. Eddie invited his friend and Presbyterian minister Graham Connor to accompany him on the two-week mission.

They travelled by car, an old diesel Peugeot 306. They had arranged to collect several hundred Hungarian Bibles in the European headquarters of the Bible Society in Stuttgart. However, on arrival in the late afternoon, they were told there was no order from the Belfast Office. However, after frustrating conversations and, impromptu prayers, the Bible Society agreed to have their order ready the next morning.

The next day, Graham and Eddie piled as many boxes of Bibles as possible into the boot and back seat of the car, so much so that the rear axle was wedged down on the wheels and the front looked like it was about to take off, despite the added ballast of two large men in the front of the car. More frustration met them when they tried to enter Austria. They spoke no German and the Austrian authorities spoke no English; they were refused entry. As Graham and Eddie prayed, a huge German lorry driver, who had some English, explained to them both, that on entering Austria, they had to declare how much diesel was in their fuel tank. The border guards' refusal had nothing to do with the Bibles. They were already over a day late and had spent several hours at the border, and worse was to come.

The pair arrived at the Hungarian border, the so-called Iron Curtain. It was a border post in the middle of nowhere, with only Graham, Eddie and the armed guards present. The guards looked at the little car filled with boxes and refused to let them cross the border. With no common language, Graham and Eddie assumed the guards thought they were some smugglers trying to make a living from importing illegal goods. They had had enough of bureaucracy. Graham told Eddie, "If the Lord doesn't help us, I'm dumping these Bibles at the checkpoint." Immediately, Graham heard a voice behind him, a woman who spoke impeccable English saying, "What seems to be your problem?" Graham explained their dilemma to her. They had no plans to sell the Bibles, they were gifts to the churches they were visiting and of no monetary value to anyone. The woman spoke briefly to the guards and the guards immediately waved them through. Graham turned to thank the lady, but she had disappeared. There, in the middle of emptiness, and with nowhere to hide, she had disappeared. To quote Graham, "If ever we entertained an angel unawares it was at that border post, as the Bibles became a mighty tool used by God for the conversion of some and the discipleship of many."

Graham and Eddie spent the next two weeks preaching and singing at church services, cinemas, other public buildings and in the open air. Some of the services were conducted alongside an international team of young people working in Hungary that summer, alongside David Trimble and other pastors. It was a time of reaping, as many professed their faith in Jesus Christ. Bibles were offered to new and old converts; local pastors agreed to follow up with one-to-one discipleship programmes. On the day, the Soviet forces officially left Hungary in 1991, Graham and Eddie held open-air meetings on Margaret Island in the middle of the Danube where it flows through Budapest. They could see this older man in tears as the meeting went on. When invited to trust Christ, he came forward and offered his life to Jesus. They spent time with him afterwards and gave him a Bible which he clutched to his chest. "Why has no one told me about Jesus before," he cried in tears.

On many occasions, the pair worked with local translators, during the meetings and services. One young teenage girl, Piling Ottilia, kept in contact with David, Graham and Eddie after they returned to Belfast. Ottilia (Oti) told them that she prayed one day she would go to Belfast Bible College and serve Christ throughout her life. The Trimbles invited Graham and Eddie back to Hungary the following year. By this time, the congregation in Bloomfield was noticing the work in Hungary. After much prayer and Kirk Session approval, the pair gathered a team from the congregation to go to Hungary for two weeks in the summer of 1993 to work with David Trimble and some local Baptist churches in Northwest Hungary and around Lake Balaton.

The team consisted of Graham Connor, John Coulter, Anne Darragh, Michael and Naomi Long, Susan McDermott, Alf and Sadie Shilliday, Eddie Spence, and Ben Smith. They conducted open-air

378

meetings and, church services, visited local schools and met up with local Christians. The Trimble family had settled in that area of Hungary and worked with the team, assisted by Oti as their translator. On that trip, Oti's future husband Selmeczi László (Laci) met up with them and helped the team. Subsequently, Bloomfield supported Oti as a student at Belfast Bible College. She stayed at the Manse at weekends and became a valued member of the fellowship at Bloomfield. On her return and subsequent marriage to (Laci), the Lord led her and Laci, along with five other young couples to join Menedek and move to Bodrog to begin their ministry in June 1995.

In November 1995, they came to Bloomfield and gave an update on their work in Bodrog. In 2003 and 2004, Oti and Laci returned to N Ireland to study Christian counselling at BBC. Graham invited them to Bloomfield to talk about Menedek and its ministry in Bodrog. They finished their presentation by asking if any members of our fellowship were prepared to travel to Bodrog and help with the work.

The first group, consisting of 15 volunteers from Bloomfield, travelled to Bodrog to help with the building work in the summer of 2005. This trip was during the school holidays, and the group was tasked with painting the old primary school in the village and demolishing old outside toilets beside the Mansion House. This was a period of "getting to know one another better," building trust between Bloomfield and our Hungarian hosts. We learned that other churches had sent teams over the years but only two returned after one trip.

Three men with indomitable spirits and strong faith organised and managed the work. Janos, Anti and Gyuszi. Volunteers were divided into teams and given tasks under the supervision of one of them. Every morning, no work began before a Bible reading and prayers. I found painting in 35°C heat exhausting which meant I didn't have too much trouble falling asleep despite the unearthly snoring of my dormitory companions.

One hot morning, several teachers and their pupils turned up at the school to view our progress and thank us for our efforts. There followed an impromptu football game in the playground; afterwards, it was time for cold juice and snack bars. The youngsters queued politely for their cartons of cold drinks and each one was handed a Balaton Bumm wafer bar (with peanuts). There were no dietary forms or questions. No disclaimers, no parental consent, take it or leave it. So, the youngsters enthusiastically grabbed all the nut bars. The only people affected by the nuts were the team from Belfast. There were no casualties. The football match continued after the break and the home team won.

When work moved to the old toilets, there was concern about removing the roofing as the tiles were made from asbestos. The risk of asbestos dust was minimalised when the weather broke; the downpour lasted for two days. No dust was created when the saturated tiles were removed one at a time before we took sledgehammers to the walls.

On Saturday morning, David Hutchinson, "The Hutch," to his friends, and I walked from the Mansion to the village fête to enjoy the atmosphere and meet some of our Hungarian friends. David began filming on his video camera; after a few moments, the battery died. I volunteered to walk back to the Mansion and collect a spare battery. Just as I was leaving the Mansion with the spare battery, a powerful motorbike came screaming to a halt at the front door. The rider, removed their helmet, shook their hair out and said, "Hello, I'm Anita, what is your name?" That was the first time I met Anita Ficsór. Anita was a primary school teacher and taught violin in the music school. I accepted her invitation to ride pillion with her back to the fête.

David Hutchinson and Andrew Shott visited Oti and Laci in the late autumn of 2005. This visit helped establish a genuine bond of trust with our Hungarian friends when David and Andrew assured them that Bloomfield Church was committed to seeing the work through to completion.

The serious work of digging the foundations and trenches for the utilities of the new Bodrog Educational Centre began in 2006. Myself and other volunteers spent a week digging a five feet deep trench for the electricity supply cables. However, with the constant craic and banter, it never became a drudge. At the end of each working day, we looked forward to a hearty meal, followed by table tennis or volleyball at the rear of the Mansion. For some reason, the mosquitoes bothered everyone else but me.

In 2006 and 2007, as well as the building works, teams from Bloomfield helped at summer English Clubs. Karen Reid, Nicola Elwood and Jennifer Waring used all their talent and experience working with young people at home to great effect. Karen taught in Grosvenor and had been leading Anchor Boys for four years. Nicola worked in insurance and was an officer in the 24th Boys' Brigade company. Jennifer worked for the Northern Ireland Sports Council at that time. The language barrier didn't appear to have any impact whatsoever. Although, there are probably some Hungarians, who still greet friends with, "Whataspoutye?" Andrew Shott, now Bloomfield's Clerk of Session, assisted Karen, Nicola, and Jenny in setting up the English Club support teams. Andrew worked for the Ulster Bank. We joked there wasn't a proper day's work in him. Adding some truth to our banter, Andrew insisted on wearing gloves to keep his hands clean.

Somehow, someone in a local Hungarian TV Station heard about the people from Northern Ireland helping locals in Bodrog build facilities for a ministry that supported abandoned children. One afternoon, a crew from Ajka TV rolled into town and pulled up at the Mansion. Because Andrew was the cleanest amongst us, he became our joint spokesperson with Karen Reid. The TV reporter interviewed Andrew and Karen, about our involvement with the project in Bodrog. When the crew were packing up to leave, the reporter informed us our segment would be broadcast the next evening at 6.00 pm.

At 6.00 pm the next evening, we gathered around a TV in the Mansion and eagerly awaited our moment of fame. I'll translate from the Hungarian. "And now, it is over to our correspondent in Bodrog." Our news item began with our reporter setting the scene before her interview started with, "Good afternoon, Pastor Shott." However, in Hungarian Shott sounded more like Sh?tt. We couldn't help ourselves and dissolved into laughter. I don't think we heard the rest of the broadcast. Even today, Andrew calls me Lofty because I wore heavy boots, canvas knee-length shorts and a jungle hat to protect me from the sun. Lofty Boy was a character in the TV comedy, It Ain't Half Hot Mum, played by Don Estelle. The semblance was remarkable. I'll have to refrain from addressing him as Pastor Sh?tt.

Later, in 2006, we learned that Anita had been seriously injured in a motorcycle accident and was in hospital at Szekszárd. The surgeons had reconstructed Anita's badly damaged leg, but it required constant exercise to rebuild muscle and ligaments. The physios had rigged up a Heath Robinson-type machine that constantly flexed her leg to aid her recovery. The best medicine she received was a surprise visit from Graham Simpson who travelled to Szekszárd to visit her. Graham asked a doctor if he could borrow a white coat and face mask. He disguised himself and entered Anita's room where the contraption was clacking away atop her bed. Imagine Anita's stunned expression when she heard, "Whataspoutye Anita?" Graham lifted his face mask and repeated the famous line from the then-popular TV programme Allo, Allo "It is I."

Most years, two to four teams travelled to Hungary to help maintain the momentum of the building work and support the Bible and English clubs. Many of the volunteers made repeated visits and our relationships with our Hungarian friends grew year by year. Some of our volunteers made very generous personal gifts of money to support the project. John Corry contacted his friend Colin McShane, a manager in Belfast B & Q, and asked if the company could supply paint for the project. When John visited B & Q there were two pallets loaded with tins of paint ready for collection free of charge. Ken Groves worked for Profast and arranged for his company to collect and deliver the pallets to Bodrog at Profast's expense. A few visitors from Bloomfield were more pragmatic. They asked to see proof of where Bloomfield's donations were being spent only to discover they couldn't understand Hungarian bookkeeping. A touch of Hanif Lalani I'm afraid. A similar check occurred in Walkway years ago so I can empathise with how our Hungarian friends felt hurt by this lack of trust. Proof that Bloomfield is a church full of gifts but not full of wisdom on how to use them.

Thankfully, there was no lasting damage to the relationship between our churches. Other personal relationships grew resulting in marriages. Gary and Anita, Ancsa and Richard who came with Exodus, Nathan and Eszti; Dezsős's daughter Kata married Philip. I visited Bodrog five times over the years. Rhonda and Rebekah accompanied me on two occasions. Despite the language barrier, there was always great fun, laughter, and music, the universal language. Many of the young Hungarians were talented musicians.

I joined several of them one evening after a table tennis match; I thought I would share a little "Irish culture" with them. I picked up a guitar and played I've Been a Wild Rover. Somehow, the Irishness was lost in translation because the Hungarians thought I had sung a worship song. They picked up their instruments and an impromptu praise service ensued. It was an evening of real blessing. My fellow singer, David Bailie, our church's caretaker, cried for joy. That was a miracle of grace considering the trauma David had experienced recently in his previous work as a Prison Officer.

The Hungarian families we came to know and love were extravagant in their generosity and hospitality. Kornél was now the mayor of Bodrog and made motorbike leathers for a living. He and his wife Anna had nine children. Four of their own and five adopted. When they invited our team of volunteers to dinner, it literally was a full house.

We were hosted by other families who had fostered and adopted children on evenings we didn't cook for ourselves. Thank you to Oti and Laci, Panka néni and Gyuszi bácsi, Kornél and Anna Heizer, Anti and Gabi Fodor, János and Márti Dan, Dezső and Ági Madarász, Tibi and Márti for sharing your lives, your faith and Christ's compassion for the poor and needy through your witness.

Laci taught history and geography and one evening, in his classroom I asked him to explain why the village bell rang every day at midday. In Northern Ireland, "Defenders of the Faith" commemorate William of Orange's victory over King James II once a year on 12th of July. Every day, Hungarians commemorate their victory over the Ottoman Army on 4th July 1456. "They sure don't like them, Turks." I'm led to believe the feeling is still mutual.

In the 15th century, the expansion of the Ottoman Empire began to worry Western powers. Hungary faced the threat of Ottoman invasion. Pope Callixtus III, elected in 1455, recognised the danger. He realised that if the Ottomans marched through Hungary undefeated, Vienna and Rome would come under the rule of the Caliphs of Islam. Desperate for support, the pope issued a Papal Bull in 1456, ordering churches to chime their bells daily, praying for a Hungarian victory. On July 4th,

1456, the fateful siege began in Nándorfehérvár (Belgrade). Just three weeks later, on July 22nd, Hungarian and Serbian soldiers, led by János Hunyadi, Mihály Szilágyi, and János Kapisztrán, defeated the Ottoman army.

Pause for a moment here and take some other history into account.

In 732 AD, a Muslim army led by Abdul Rahman invaded Gaul (France) by crossing the Pyrenees from Spain. However, they were decisively defeated by the Frankish Christian leader Charles Martel at the Battle of Tours. This victory halted further Muslim advances into Europe and played a crucial role in preventing the Islamization of Western Europe. I wonder if any Russell Group University teaches that part of European history today. Thank you to Charles "The Hammer" Martel followed later by Hungarian and Serbian Christian armies we don't have to pray to Mecca five times a day. The victories over Islam allowed for the Renaissance, the Reformation and The Enlightenment. All of these are worth researching.

From all this, a question arises that all Christians should ask themselves. If Europe and the European Union owe their very existence to Christianity, why is there no mention of God at all in the constitution of the EU? Denis Staunton in the Irish Times reported, "The proposed EU constitution will contain no reference to God or Christianity but will refer in its preamble to "The cultural, religious and humanist inheritance of Europe." So, if God's role in its existence isn't recognised, who governs the EU?" Draw your conclusion. I've drawn mine.

Keir Starmer and his Labour Government were voted into power by only 30% of the electorate and are about to renegotiate Brexit. Brexit was voted for by over 50%. It was the largest democratic mandate ever in Britain. As I mentioned before. "The little people don't matter." The liberal elite know what is best for Britain.

Back to Bodrog:

The building of the Bodrog Educational Centre culminated with the completion of the church roof. I had spent hours on the roof in blazing heat helping to slot tiles into place on the roof above the sanctuary. Each volunteer wrote a Bible verse on the underside of every tile as a poignant reminder they had taken part in the Lord's work in Bodrog. Out loud, I said, "My bum is numb," from sitting on the roofing laths; I was overheard by Panka néni's husband Gyuszi bácsi, who climbed off the roof and cycled into the village.

When he returned, he was carrying a large square of thick foam which he handed me to sit on. On it was written, "fáj a fenekem." Much to the amusement of our Hungarian friends, when I asked our translator what Gyuszi bácsi had written she replied, "My bum is sore." It is the only Hungarian phrase I can still remember. Janos, a bear of a man with a heart for Christ, carved a perfect wooden cross using few tools other than a chainsaw and secured it on the pinnacle of the completed tile roof. Pastor Zsolt and his wife Anita joined everyone in our excitement and joy when we gathered to watch Janos complete his work. The centre was officially opened on 23rd May 2010.

Over the years of supporting the ministry in Bodrog, it is estimated that around 120 to 130 volunteers from Bloomfield Presbyterian Church travelled to Bodrog. Each one who took part in the building work and programmes will have fond memories of their time in Hungary and the friendships they made. Three volunteers stand out for their dedication and long-term commitment to the work. The three tenacious men are David Hutchinson, Graham Simpson, and Alfie Welsh.

"The Hutch" worked for British Telecom and, used his annual leave to give his heart and soul to this work he felt God had called him to do. He travelled back and forth from Bodrog so often, I joked he should apply for Hungarian citizenship. I travelled with him on occasion. David had a competitive nature. This trait surfaced in everything he did. He ensured he was first on the plane to secure a seat by the emergency exit. More legroom without paying for it. First off the plane, first to the luggage carousel and so on. He was so competitive at table tennis that his Hungarian opponents would hide his bespoke bat. I confess I took a little pleasure when I beat him in the final of the shooting competition at the summer fête in Bodrog. I still have my medal which I wore when we welcomed Panka néni and her daughter on their visit to Bloomfield in June 2023. Guess what she presented me with. A square of foam labelled, "fáj a fenekem," she had carried the whole way from Bodrog to Belfast. I'm glad my numb bum made a lasting impression in Hungary.

Graham was committed to our work and witness in Bodrog over the ten years and made frequent journeys with the volunteer teams. Graham became the conduit for our connection with Bodrog and, was in constant contact with Oti and Laci, organising and planning what needed doing next. Without Graham's patience, determination and, organising skills, work wouldn't have been completed as quickly. Graham encouraged potential volunteers by quoting from The Message, Philippians Ch1.

"I am so pleased that you have continued on in this with us, believing and proclaiming God's message, from the day you heard it to the present. There has never been the slightest doubt in my mind that the God who started this great work in you would keep at it and bring it to a flourishing finish on the very day Christ Jesus appears."

Graham's wife Jill brought her musical skills and a great "Let's do" attitude. Jill became our resident entertainment officer. She had the same gift as Geordie Wilson, whom I mentioned in my chapter on Telephone House. She is a skilled Spoonerizer. We had just finished dinner with Dezső and Ági in their home when there was a huge thunderstorm. RUMBLE, RUMBLE, FLASH, FLASH. Jill shouted, "Did you see that sh?te lightning?" No Jill, I was too busy laughing. Another guest, Beryl McKee, remarked, "Thank goodness it wasn't fork lightning."

There's no better way to end this chapter than by describing Alfie Welsh's Bodrog experience. Alfie was 69 years old when he first travelled to Bodrog in November 2008 on his understanding that, "Don't think for one minute you're going to make a Christian out of me." No one made Alfie a Christian on that trip. Nor on his second visit in

June 2009. Alfie travelled on his own the third time he visited Bodrog in August 2009 and God made him a Christian as he knelt in Oti and Laci's kitchen. Alfie fell in love with Bodrog and its people who loved him in return. In 2010, he used his pension lump sum to buy a house in the village and, allowed anyone to use it when he wasn't there. Alfie made his public confession of faith in Bodrog where he was baptised by Pastor Zsolt, in September 2011. Alfie's final trip to Bodrog was in September 2017 to attend Dezső's daughter Dorkas's wedding to Balázs Békefi. From 2008 to 2017, Alfie travelled to Bodrog 28 times. Hihetetlen!

Years and health have taken their toll; Alfie donated his house to the church in Bodrog where he is still lovingly referred to as Alfie bácsi. Everyone's, "Uncle Alfie." Since the building work finished in 2015, Alfie has done more than anyone to keep our connections with Bodrog open. He's a dab hand on social media and keeps in touch with all our Hungarian friends and families. He can even speak some Hungarian. Watch out for Alfie if you're walking through C S Lewis Square. Look out for a tall, bald, elderly gentleman walking a small dog. If you ask him about Bodrog, you better have brought a packed lunch.

Áldjon meg téged az ÚR, és őrizzen meg téged! Ragyogtassa rád orcáját az ÚR, és könyörüljön rajtad! Fordítsa feléd orcáját az ÚR, és adjon neked békességet!

4Móz 6:24-26

May the Lord bless you and keep you; the Lord make his face shine upon you and be gracious to you; the Lord turn his face towards you and give you peace.

Numbers 6:24-26

While checking dates and names for this chapter, Anita informed me there was a Thanksgiving Service in Bodrog planned for the weekend of 14th of September 2024 to mark the 30th anniversary of the opening of the new school which she hoped to attend. I made tentative enquiries if Rhonda and I could attend the event. Two days later we received a personal invitation to join the celebrations with our friends in Bodrog. We have booked our flights and will be sitting beside Anita and her husband Gary on the flight to Budapest on 12th September. On 4th June Anita forwarded a message from leaders in Bodrog inviting everyone from BPC who helped in the work over the years to attend the celebrations. They have offered accommodation to anyone who comes along. The invitation has been passed to all concerned.

On 30th May Oti sent me some additional information about her initial contact with Graham and Eddie. Oti mentioned in her email, when Graham and Eddie left to return home, Desi Maxwell joined the European Christian Ministry group. I had to send her this message in reply.

"Dearest Oti, thank you so much for taking all the time to answer my questions and correct my Hungarian spellings. I have made all the corrections and trust I have done justice to God's faithful servants in Bodrog. I am keeping all the information you have shared with me for future reference. I was fascinated to read about your encounter with Desi Maxwell. I have to tell you what happened when I met him in 2012. I was running a Men's Group at home. We named it BOSS. (Band Of SinnerS). Among the group were a drug addict, two alcoholics, two chancers, a Nigerian and a trainee Presbyterian minister. God certainly had his work cut out amongst us. I learned that Desi Maxwell was giving a talk on the Old Testament at Rosemary Presbyterian Church on the other side of Belfast. The men agreed to my suggestion to go to Rosemary Church to listen to Desi. When we arrived on Monday evening, we discovered Desi's lecture wasn't in the main church but at the Rosemary Church Halls on the other side of the road. We were welcomed by the Clerk of

Session, who asked us where we were from and if we had any connection with the church. I informed him we were all from East Belfast but believed my mother and father had been married in the church in 1945. He asked if we were coming back the following Monday and when we said yes, he said he would check the church records and let me know what he found.

The following Monday, the gentleman met me and said he had some news. My mother and father had been married in Rosemary Presbyterian Church in Belfast. The church had been hit by a bomb during the Belfast Blitz and had been transferred "By Licence" to the new church being built on North Circular Road. However, on 30th June 1945, the church building hadn't been completed and my parents were married in the Rosemary Church Halls. I could have fallen over when the Clerk of Session said, "Stephen, you are standing where your parents were married." I showed him the attached photograph and he said, "Follow me." We walked down a short corridor and he showed me into the room where this photograph was taken all those years ago. The only difference was there were no flowers in the vase. I still have goosebumps when I share this story of God's providence with people. Another story to add to my book.

PS: The trainee minister was Alan Dickey. He is now the Minister at Stewartstown Presbyterian Church. The drug addict came to faith. The two alcoholics have stopped drinking and the two chancers disappeared. The Nigerian was Patrick Ozegbe now legally working in the UK who named his son after me. On top of all that, Desi's lectures were wonderful but I haven't seen him since."

With love and appreciation

Stephen

The Gnome Office

The Identity and Passport Service was established on 1st April 2006, following the passing of the Identity Cards Act 2006, which merged the UK Passport Service with the Home Office's Identity Cards program to form a new executive agency. The Identity and Passport Service was then renamed HM Passport Office on 13th May 2013, to distance the agency from the calamitous attempt by the previous Labour Government to introduce Identity Cards. The service was performing so badly that the HMPO's executive agency status was removed on 1st October 2014. It became a division within the Home Office under direct ministerial control. I hope I helped in rebuilding the reputation of the service. All it took was common sense and a little empathy.

I began my career as a Passport Examiner at the IPS offices in High Street, Belfast on 6th of November 2006. I entered a work environment different from anything I experienced in the previous 37 years of working life. The next four weeks were spent learning the British Nationality Act 1981, the British Nationality Act 1948, and the Immigration

Act 1971 under the guidance of two trained instructors. This knowledge, along with applying Government rules and policies, allowed Examiners to decide if applicants' documents proved they were British Citizens and entitled to British Passports.

The first ever mention of a passport being used is in the Bible. King Artaxerxes granted Nehemiah a letter to travel. In this letter, Nehemiah was granted safe passage to Jerusalem and timber to construct beams for the gates of the fortress near the Temple, the city walls, and his residence. Nehemiah wouldn't qualify for a British Passport unless he Naturalised. If Nehemiah's name had appeared on a Naturalisation Certificate, I would have sent it to the Fraud Investigation Unit.

When the instructors were satisfied with all the recruits' progress, we were each assigned to a Passport Examiner on one of six Examining Teams, labelled A to F, to begin our "Live Desk Training." I was placed under the supervision of Malachy on Team F. For three weeks he supervised me handling real applications and pointing out my errors. Every decision had to be case-noted. Sometimes, more documents had to be requested. Photos failed the online quality checks and possible fraud issues had to be investigated. It was interesting and stressful work. Production targets had to be achieved. 120 renewal applications or 32 first-time applications per day to be Passed For Issue meant little time for daydreaming.

When an Examiner decided to issue a passport, they pressed the "PFI" key on their keyboard. One of two things happened. Either, it went straight to De La Rue, a company based in Basingstoke for printing, or a Security Check was requested. In this event, the entire application, documents, photos, certificates, and everything in the file, was sent to the Quality Control Team. There, experienced Examiners went through every detail of an application to ensure the Examiner had followed every rule and regulation in processing the application to issue. Errors were recorded and sent back to the Examiner for correction.

Concentration was essential and very tiring. One mistake meant an error on an Examiner's accuracy record. Team F's accuracy target was 99.4%. This meant, that considering the volume of applications eight Team members were processing, I could only make two mistakes per month. Anymore, would have been noted on my performance appraisal. When my three-week desk training period was over Malachy was satisfied, I had demonstrated I was competent to examine on my own. I was assigned to Team F as an Examining Passport Officer Grade 3. 2007 was off to an interesting start.

In practice, an Examiner was always accountable for any mistakes they made. If the Quality Control Team missed any errors, the applicant found them when they checked their new British Passport. A name might have been misspelt, or a wrong date of birth entered. Invariably, the customer sent the "Sub Spoil" passport back to have any mistakes corrected. Some mistakes had different consequences for the customer and the Examiner. Some were amusing; others were life-threatening. Let me explain.

One of the first applications I processed as a new Examiner was for a gentleman named Wilfred Dickey. Wilfred was the father of my good friend and ex-Campbell College colleague, Alan Dickey. Wilfred had applied for a new British Passport to replace his "Old Blue." By right, because I knew the applicant, I was obliged by policy to refer the application to another Examiner. However, my pride and ego dictated otherwise; I went through all the necessary checks and controls.

Surname, Forename, Date of birth, Place of birth, Home address, check photo quality and Countersignature etc. All good. PFI'd. It went straight to De La Rue. There were no security checks. I called Alan that evening and boasted I had issued his father a new British Passport and he would receive it by post within 10 working days. "That's great," said Alan. "He's travelling to America with my sister Heather next month." Ten working days later Alan rang to say his father had received his new passport. I was chuffed until Alan asked me, "How do you spell Randalstown?" Wilfred didn't send his passport back to have the error corrected. He travelled on it for the next ten years and no one spotted the mistake in his place of birth. I had spelt it with two "L" s. I was still an Examiner when he submitted his passport for renewal ten years later. This time, I referred it to another Examiner with a note to correct the spelling of the POB. Happy travels Wilfred.

I sincerely believe God intervened in the worst mistake I ever made as an Examiner. I was relatively new with limited experience in complicated casework. One such application was for a child. It involved issues around who held parental responsibility and which of the separated parents was entitled to the child's passport. I failed in my due diligence and proceeded to PFI the application. This time SECURITY CHECK. The application and all the relevant court orders and certificates were sent to the Quality Control Team.

Two days later, the Head Executive Officer Keith Lorimer, asked me to his office. On his desk was the child's application form. Keith explained I had mistakenly granted parental responsibility to the child's father who was attempting to take his daughter to Afghanistan. The father was in London waiting for the delivery of his daughter's passport. If that application hadn't gone to Security Check, that child would have been condemned to life as a second-class citizen in a failed state. I felt sick and numb when I realised my carelessness nearly condemned a young girl to a living hell.

I offered to resign on the spot. When Keith saw my reaction, he said he was satisfied I had learned from my mistake; he placed me under the supervision of an Executive Officer, David Martin for two weeks, until I was experienced enough in more complicated applications to examine on my own once again. David was the first "gay" person I ever worked with. Like all gay people I've known, he was always immaculately dressed; his hair and eyebrows were waxed and his teeth were unnaturally white. I enjoyed his self-deprecating sense of humour. I liked working with him and respected his hard work and support. David and his "husband" Matthew waited five years for permission to adopt a young boy. They named the child Aston. What a great name! Aston Martin. Unfortunately, David and Matthew split up two years later with joint custody of Aston. I met him in Belfast recently; he has a new partner and they have set up home together. I wished him well for the future.

I took that lesson to heart and concentrated on being as good an Examiner as possible. My efforts were rewarded when Joanne Hylands, my line manager nominated me for an award. I won the New Employee of the Year Award in 2008. Rhonda accompanied me to London to collect my trophy at a ceremony in the Tower Bridge Hotel. Imagine being called "New" anything at the age of 55. Eventually, I became a Desk Trainer and enjoyed teaching recruits how to examine passport applications.

I acquired a good reputation for thoroughness. Due to a lack of Desk Trainers, I volunteered to train Examiners in other Passport Offices. I trained staff in Peterborough, Newport, and Glasgow in addition to Belfast. The worst place I ever stayed was the Celtic Manor Hotel in Newport. Hugh Hefner would have felt right at home. The most challenging training I did was in Peterborough. It was difficult to explain anything to someone wearing a full black Hijab. I wasn't comfortable speaking to someone when I could only see their eyes. Muslim staff had a separate washroom and prayer room. Equity, Diversity and Inclusion has a huge presence in the Home Office. Its malign influence is the reason I named it the Gnome Office.

I enjoyed training so much that I applied for promotion to Executive Officer on the Training Staff Team. I was successful in my initial paper application and was invited to HMPO Headquarters in Durham. I had to deliver a pre-prepared ten-minute PowerPoint presentation on Home Office examining processes. Afterwards, I had an interview with two Line Managers. I had worked hard on my preparation; everything went well. My presentation went according to plan and I was competent throughout my interview until the last question. "Stephen, how would you analyse complicated data from different sources?" My mind went blank. I couldn't think. I just waffled. The more I waffled, the more anxious I became. That monkey with his cymbals turned up again. My interview ended in a "car crash." I had recently completed an OCN Level 3 on Microsoft Excel. All I had to mention were Excel Spreadsheets and Pivot Tables. A Pivot Table is a powerful tool to calculate, and analyse data that lets you see comparisons, patterns, and trends in data.

To everyone's surprise, my colleague in Team F, Richard "The Duke" Hazard got the post. My Line Manager, Emma Maguire, informed me Durham had reported I made a good impression on my visit and, "hit the crossbar." I was put on a Reserve List. If the successful candidate pulled out, I would be their replacement. I was very disappointed but tried hard not to show it. I was magnanimous and congratulated Richard on his promotion. Richard moved upstairs to the Training Team. I stayed where I was and trained Richard's replacement. A young man called Danny Lavery. I mentioned to Danny I used to drink in The Garrick Bar with another Danny Lavery who worked in the Government Bookshop on Arthur Street. "That's my father," he replied. We were off to a good start.

Within a short period, huge policy changes occurred in the Passport Office and a new computer system was rolled out. New rules and procedures regarding applicants from EU member states were implemented. At an "Inspiring Changes" meeting, hosted by managers from London to brief Examiners on upcoming changes, their strapline was, "If you can't go the distance, get off the bus." All necessary staff retraining fell on the shoulders of our in-house Training Team. Richard and two colleagues had to be retrained themselves. They spent weeks studying in Liverpool before they had to deliver training courses for the staff in Belfast. Thank God He blanked my mind that day in Durham. I couldn't have worked under the pressure our Trainers experienced. By staying where I was, I worked for 13 years to 2018. If I had been successful in that interview, I'm certain I would have "jumped off the bus" in 2010. God always knows best.

Wilson Bovenizer and I were the two oldest Examiners in the Belfast Branch of HMPO, apart from Kathleen. Kathleen's age was indeterminate; no one dared ask her how old she was. Kathleen was often stopped in Belfast and asked for her autograph. She was the spitting image in looks and size of Olivia Nash, "Ma" in the TV comedy Give My Head Peace. Most Examiners tried to ensure applicants received their passports. I'm convinced Kathleen did her best to prevent them from getting passports. She was ruthless; she applied rules and policies to the letter. She lacked any empathy whatsoever. I often heard her say to frustrated applicants on the telephone "Well, you shouldn't have booked your holiday until you had your passport." Imagine hearing those comforting words when your holiday plans are in ruins.

Kathleen was a contradiction in terms. She boasted two degrees. One in History, and the other in Psychology. I never asked her from which universities. Kathleen travelled frequently to Washington or as she called it, "DC;" some of her family lived there. I'm glad I was sitting down when she told me, that on her last trip to DC, she visited DC Zoo and found a Giant Panda in residence. "I watched Kung Fu Panda and thought Pandas were only cartoon characters," she said to my amazement and disbelief.

I met a former colleague a while ago and was saddened to learn Kathleen passed away a short time after she retired in 2022.

I mentioned training Danny Lavery. Danny's previous job was as a Runner in Game of Thrones. Danny was a charismatic character, popular with younger staff and those who watched the TV series. A young female Examiner asked, "Danny, what did you do on Game of Thrones?" Like his Dad, Danny had a droll sense of humour. He replied, "I had to look after the dragons and ensure they were fed properly." She was fascinated and asked, "What was their favourite food?" It beggared belief that someone, employed by the Home Office with the responsibility of deciding if a person could hold a British Passport, believed dragons were real.

Another young Examiner gave me cause to wonder at the younger generation's lack of general knowledge and common sense. Colleen was a single mother in her early thirties; we worked well together and were happy to help one another work through different issues raised by some applications. We had just returned to work after the Christmas break in 2009; during our conversation, Colleen asked if I had watched The Vicar of Dibley over Christmas. I told her no, I hadn't. "Oh," she said. "I forgot you're a Christian."

I explained to Colleen, "The reason I didn't watch the Vicar of Dibley has nothing to do with being a Christian, I simply don't find it funny." I added, "By the way I'll not hold my breath waiting on the BBC making a comedy programme about Mohammed." A moment later, Colleen asked, "Stephen who is Mohammed?" Before I could answer Colleen said, "Oh, I remember who Mohammed is now. Isn't he the man who owns Harrods?" Mohammed Al-Fayed did own Harrods then; he was never successful in his application for a British Passport. Maybe, his application was failed by Kathleen. However, there were other "Mohammeds" who were more successful.

The most complicated application I ever dealt with concerned a Muslim gentleman named Mohammed and his descendants. He was born in Bradford before 1st of January 1983. This made him British by birth. He was married to a British Citizen; they had five sons born in Britain who claimed British Citizenship through their parents. Mohammed had two other wives living in Iraq. Polygamy is illegal in Britain but not in Iraq. With these two wives, Mohammed had another twelve children, ten boys and two girls. The children born in Iraq were eligible for British Citizenship by descent through their father. Mohammed and his entire family lived in a council-provided property in East London. No one can deny Britain's demography is changing rapidly.

The worst part of working for HMPO was the woke culture. From the moment I began in the Passport Service, it pervaded everywhere. I witnessed paranoia at Nortel, brought about by job insecurity but Home Office paranoia was brought about by deliberate attempts to control people's thoughts and make them feel guilty if they disagreed with woke policies. I never worked anywhere before where people glanced over their shoulders to check who was within earshot of their conversations.

Posters and displays were put up at the appropriate time of the year to celebrate Pride, Travellers, Black History Month, Diwali, and Ramadan. I don't remember posters inviting staff to celebrate Christianity. Why does the Home Office commend a month to celebrate Black History and only two minutes to remember those who died for Britain in two World Wars? What did it cost and how much production time was wasted due to staff spending time on Unconscious Bias courses? I did ask but never received an answer. I always confessed I was consciously biased to do unto others as I would have them do unto me. If that Biblical truth had been taught, it would have saved the government millions, and more applicants would have received their passports on time.

Equality, Diversity, and Inclusion (EDI) is all about promoting a particular view of history and culture. I regard it as a cog in the wheel of Cultural Marxism, designed specially to unravel our Western faith, culture, and civilisation. In the workplace, people might no longer refer to Chinks and Paddies but the good is far outweighed by the bad. I liken it all to a Castor bean. When I was young, children were given doses of Castor Oil because "It's good for you." However, before the Castor bean is processed, it contains enough Ricin to kill two adults. "Who cares if you wear a rainbow lanyard or what your preferred pronoun is, stop your pathetic virtue signalling and give me my passport."

I'll finish here with my trip to Globe House in London. After winning the Employee of the Year Award, I was sent to London to take part in a celebration of the diverse range of people who worked for the Passport Service. I didn't know what I was letting myself in for. I was thirty years older than anyone else and felt ill at ease amongst blokes wearing skirts, lipstick, and mascara. It looked like a meeting of the Danny La Rue Appreciation Society. One was crying because a customer at the counter had passed some deprecating remark about his makeup. We were advised by a Stonewall representative, that there was an accelerated promotion programme for LGBT employees within the Home Office. Thank goodness I didn't wear my twin set and pearls to my interview in Durham.

One other Examiner stood out. Nikolas Konstantinos. Nikolas was a former Greek Orthodox priest, straight out of central casting for Zorba the Greek. He was intelligent and an interesting person to speak to. While serving in Kefalonia, he wrote a book on St. Paul during a drought. One day the Bishop arrived and asked Nikolas to accompany him on a walk. The Bishop asked," Nikolas, have you been praying for rain?" "Of course, your Right Reverend." The Bishop enquired, "Then where is your umbrella?"

Just as there are bad laws, there are bad policies on how to apply them. A case, in point, arose after the Passport Office introduced a One Name Policy.

In effect, it meant names on any applicant's foreign passports had to match their British Passport. For example, someone with dual citizenship from Pakistan must match the names on their Pakistani Passport with those on their British application. When applied, this might reveal Christian names to Pakistani authorities. Stone me! Or them if they were persecuted for being Christian. Some pestiferous members of the Home Office Blob hadn't thought that through. Just as their previous mistakes led to Windrush which was a British political scandal concerning British Citizens from the West Indies who were wrongly detained, denied legal rights, and deported from the UK.

The one person who spotted this dangerous scenario was a lowly PO3, Mr Nikolas Konstantinos. The same rank as myself. Paid a pittance in comparison to "the experts." He flagged his concerns to his Senior Executive Officer. Within a week, Nikolas was promoted to Head Executive Officer. He's now a Level 7 working for the Secretary of State for N Ireland. He didn't have to wear a twin set and pearls as recommended by Stonewall. He earned it all by pure merit. If Hilary Benn's advisors ask the PM how they should instruct him on difficult local matters, Starmer should say, "Take him to the Greek."

I hope you understand why I called this chapter The Gnome Office.

"In folklore, gnomes are mischievous beings. They play pranks on humans, hide belongings, and rearrange things."

Other, professional journalists, frequently refer to the Civil Service as "The Blob."

I couldn't put it better myself.

Footnote:

In 1896, at the height of the British Empire, 500 Civil Servants helped to govern all of India. Then, India had a population of approximately 500 million.

Today, there are 518,000 Civil Servants in the UK, controlling a population of 68 million from the cradle to the grave. Nice work if you can get it. You'll be able to work from home.

Alternatively, why not join the Quangocracy? A quango is a quasi-autonomous non-governmental organisation funded by taxpayers but not controlled by central government. There are

318,000 people employed by quangos which cost
UK taxpayers £224 billion every year, 21% of total
government expenditure.

One Giant Step.

In Bodrog, we built facilities for families to help provide homes, an education and a Christian upbringing for their children. Alcohol and drug addiction weren't an issue, neither were debt and social deprivation and the children were being raised in stable two-parent homes with male and female role models. Not all these relationships ended happily, but at least the children were given a fighting chance to build lives for themselves. This isn't the general situation in East Belfast where families have fragmented due to divorce, poverty, debt, the negative influence of paramilitaries, unemployment, poor health and lifestyle choices. These, and other pressures that families face, put a huge burden on our Welfare and Health systems. Today, those issues are even more pronounced and, exacerbated by a lack of political leadership, an emasculated Police Service of Northern Ireland and the rapidly changing demographics of our community.

The Government recognises parts of East Belfast as some of the most socially deprived areas in Northern Ireland due to challenges related to income, employment, education, health, and access to services.

When I and other volunteers from Bloomfield Presbyterian Church began travelling to Hungary in 2005 to help with community work, I wondered why we were prepared to travel 1500 miles to share our work and witness when there was a community, in even more need of help, on our church's doorstep. I recalled how our neighbours in Ardgowan Street helped Rhonda and I set up home together and welcomed us into our new neighbourhood. Decent, working-class people who shared a concern for others by generously sharing what little they possessed. This was the genesis of my commitment to community work at home.

However, "our contemporary working class" is a far cry from my childhood and Ardgowan Street experiences. In a relatively short time, social media has become the preferred method of communication with more negative than positive influences on community cohesion. Truth is always a slow runner-up to lies. God and Jesus are mentioned only as swear words, young mothers are mainly single parents and young men are nowhere to be seen except during the preparations for the Twelfth celebrations. The terms "marriage" and "family" have no meaning whatsoever, in contrast to their meaning for older generations.

The breakdown of families and marriage has had another impact on working-class communities that no one likes to mention or discuss. Many teenagers don't realise they are related to other teenagers whom they are having sexual relations with, resulting in children born with additional needs. All this, together with drug abuse, paramilitary influence and low education standards adds up to a fractured community with all sorts of physical and mental health issues.

There's probably a PhD in Social Anthropology waiting to be written on how the Liberal Establishment has betrayed the Working class over the last 40 years. It has fooled people into believing that abandoning their social and religious heritage, would offer them more choices and improve the quality of their lives. For example, it's now not proper to smack a child to correct bad behaviour but it's OK to label them with ADHD and prescribe them Dexedrine.

Surely, it would take a miracle to repair a community which is no longer a "Community." Who could follow St Paul's example in 1st Corinthians 9?

"To those not having the law I became like one not having the law to win those not having the law. To the weak I became weak, to win the weak. I have become all things to all people so that by all possible means I might save some. I do all this for the sake of the Gospel, that I may share in its blessings."

So, God weaved His tapestry to bring the best people he knew with the abilities and commitment required to step into this social morass and demonstrate his unconditional love for the people of East Belfast in all their brokenness.

In August 1991 Rachael and Tony Davison lived at 21 Finvoy Street. The back of their home led onto the derelict and overgrown path of the Belfast and Co Down Railway which ceased running to Donaghadee and Newcastle in 1950. This area in East Belfast is still known as The Holywood Arches because it is where two iron bridges carried the original railway line over the Newtownards and Holywood Roads. The bridges weren't dismantled and removed until the mid-1960s.

Tony was a lorry driver and worked 12-hour night shifts, leaving the house at 6.00 pm and returning at 6.00 am. During the summer months, he had difficulty sleeping due to the noise of children playing on the old line, where they were safe from traffic. The youngsters lived in small, terraced houses without gardens, so this was their playground. Tony was frustrated and tired asking why there was nothing in his neighbourhood for the young people to do when other communities were holding Summer Schemes and youth events.

After another morning with little sleep, Tony lifted the phone book and called any number that mentioned "East Belfast Community." He spoke to a lady named Pearl Sagar who came to visit Tony and Rachael. Pearl explained her role in Community Development and suggested ways she could help. Tony and Rachael spoke to neighbours and parents of children who played on the old train line and asked if they would be interested in organising activities for their children. Soon, they held meetings in their 'parlour', set up a committee of volunteers and organised activities for their community.

They formed working relationships with Belfast City Council, the RUC, the East Belfast Development Agency, Belfast Action Teams and other voluntary and statutory groups. The association was formally constituted on 23rd August 1992. Between then and 1995 the Association met in members' homes and hired a local church hall for activities and events. Following negotiations with the Department of Environment and Belfast City Council, they secured a site and a Portacabin for Walkway Community Centre. On November 24th, 1995, Sir Reg Empey performed the opening ceremony.

In 1999, the organisation succeeded in applying to the European Partnership Board, to fund a Community Development Worker to help further the Association's aims and objectives. Space to house the many user groups and projects was becoming scarce. A successful funding application resulted in another Portacabin placed on top of the original. In June 2001 Councillor Sammy Wilson opened the upper extension of the building. The whole structure was surrounded by a high metal fence which boasted a sign that read, "Walkway Community Centre." Because of the increased workload, the association received funding for a Centre Supervisor and an Administrator to help with the upkeep and day-to-day running of the premises.

After returning from another working trip to Bodrog in 2006, my conscience led me to ring the bell at the entrance to the "foreboding" looking Portacabins I had first taken under my notice back in 2001. That was when Howard Lewis invited me to speak at the Women's Education Centre just across the street.

I was "buzzed in" and climbed the metal staircase to the first floor. The centre's office was situated along a narrow corridor adjacent to a small kitchen. A door on the opposite side of the corridor gave access to a games room. Through a Perspex window, I could see a TV with a game console, a large settee, and several chairs. At the far end of the room was a full-size Pool table. I rapped the office door. "Come in," was the response. I entered a little office furnished with a desk, two chairs, cupboards, and a filing cabinet. There wasn't much room left for the chair's occupant sitting behind the desk. Her back was to the only window in the room protected by an outside grill.

First impressions are always deceiving. The lady sitting in the chair looked like Sister Mary Stigmata from The Blues Brothers. Only this Sister looked like she was sucking a bee. Maybe, I got her at a bad time. Maybe, I should leave and come back another day. Maybe, I should have minded my knitting and stayed at home. Before I could speak, she said, "My name is Rachael Davison, I'm the Centre Manager, how can I help you?" This was my moment. I told Rachael who I was. I was an Elder in Bloomfield church given the responsibility for Community work within our parish. Bloomfield church's strap line is, "To know Jesus and share His love." I asked, "How can Bloomfield share Jesus's love with our community?"

It looked like Rachael had given up sucking that bee and swallowed it. I felt rather nervous in the silence that followed and assumed I was about to be escorted out of the building. I wasn't escorted out; rather Rachael put me firmly in my place. She explained other churches had been there before Bloomfield; they had tried to oppose policies and programmes that conflicted with their theologies, mainly around birth control and the Marie Stopes Organization. Eventually, the relationships had broken down. Summing up, Rachael explained I was welcome to stay and volunteer but Walkway Community Association was a secular organisation, and I wasn't allowed to proselytize. My introduction to Walkway couldn't be described as auspicious or encouraging. But....God was still weaving.

From those humble beginnings in 1992, Rachael and her team worked tirelessly to improve the quality of life for those in the local area. At a huge cost in time and effort, they established a busy, fully constituted, community association in the centre of East Belfast. Financial support from Belfast City Council, Education Authority, Urban Villages, Department for Communities, Community Fund for Northern Ireland and others enabled the association to work in the local community on many identified areas of need such as youth work, adult training, community safety and crime prevention, mental health advice, and pre-school support.

How wrong was my first impression of Sister Stigmata? The more I got to know Rachael and her work at Walkway the more my admiration for her and her team grew. I have never met anyone more principled and dedicated to helping others than Rachael Davison. She epitomises the word "indefatigable." I don't know where she sources her energy. She is a human dynamo, determined to improve the quality of people's lives and, make Walkway Community Association the "beating heart" of her community.

While Walkway was evolving as an organisation, so was that part of East Belfast. In 2005 East Belfast Partnership recognised the need for a significant intervention in East Belfast to combat social deprivation and improve the physical environment for residents of the area. With £30 million from the Lottery, Belfast City Council and the Department of Social Development, work began to create a six-mile linear park through East Belfast called the Connswater Community Greenway. It would follow the courses of the Connswater, Knock and Loop rivers reconnecting communities and helping create vibrant, attractive, safe and accessible parkland for leisure, recreation and community events.

There was also discussion around reopening the Comber to Belfast section of the old County Down railway as a light railway or Busway to alleviate traffic congestion on the busy commuter route between the two. Houses in Finvoy Street were vested for possible demolition to make way for the proposed track. At the end of 2010, Peter Robinson launched the Social Investment Fund project in Walkway. This was the genesis of Walkway's new community centre. The project began with a feasibility study between Belfast City Council and the Department of Social Development highlighting the community needs.

Due to a lack of funding, the plans for reopening the old route of the railway were abandoned in 2011 and Walkway was able to rent the vested building at 8 Finvoy Street from the Department of

Social Development for a "peppercorn rent" to use as extra office space and run programmes. A major concern in East Belfast is pupils' low academic achievements. To help counter this, Walkway Management Committee proposed a homework support club should be set up in the new premises. But who would be able to deliver that huge challenge? Step up Mandy Lee, a member of Bloomfield Presbyterian Church and another human dynamo who has taught on the Shankill for many years. Mandy volunteered to establish the Hot Chocolate Homework Support Club to run after school on Tuesday and Thursday afternoons. More volunteers cleaned and redecorated the building. The classroom furnishings were all provided by BPC. The building was named, "Cross Section," to reflect that this building was where the "Church" and "Community" worked together.

Mandy enlisted teachers, retired teachers and helpers from Bloomfield to help her with this. Mandy and her helpers were tenacious in their work over the next number of years, but they felt frustrated that most children attending the club weren't from the local community but had been referred by their primary school teachers. Can anyone understand parents who have a convenient free resource to improve their children's education and can't be bothered to send them "across the street?"

Despite disappointment and setbacks, everything contributed to a great deal of trust and goodwill being established between BPC and Walkway. Although Walkway's lease agreement meant the premises couldn't be used for "religious purposes," Rachael reneged on her previous objections and agreed to allow Mandy and more intrepid volunteers from BPC to set up Walkway Sundays in 2014. It was a Sunday School programme for primary-aged pupils, running between 11.00 am and noon. It consisted of songs, Bible teaching and activities. Rachael described this breach of rules as "running under the radar." It was never brought to Walkway's Management Committee for approval and was never minuted at any meeting and no one ever objected to it. Local children who came along tended to be from ethnic backgrounds. One Sunday morning, I asked a "Chinese" child, in my best slow English, where he was from. In a broad Belfast accent, he replied, "East Belfast." Eventually, attendance dwindled, and the Sunday school closed.

The work in Walkway hadn't gone unnoticed. Rachael was awarded the British Empire Medal in 2014 for her "Services to the Community." No one deserved this recognition more. This also marked the time plans for Walkway's "New Build" began to take shape. Opposition to the plans from some residents proved there are some people you "can't get through to." They don't have the intellectual capacity to assimilate information and determine what is best to enhance their neighbourhood and quality of life. Lies and rumours spread on anti-social media resulted in the decision to go with Plan B and build the new premises on the existing site.

Walkway's achievement in delivering programs for people across all age groups was officially recognised when it was awarded the Queen's Award for Voluntary Services in 2017. After the official presentation of the award in Belfast City Hall, I had the dubious pleasure of accompanying the oldest committee member, Violet Hudson, to the Queen's Garden Party at Buckingham Palace on 1st June. I can't say we met Her Majesty but we waved to her and she smiled.

When we arrived in London, I called Rhonda and the first question she asked was, "Are you smoking?" "Yes, I was." After 30 years of abstinence, Violet had broken my resolve. I had one nerve left and Violet was bouncing on it. It was akin to minding a recalcitrant ten-year-old child who couldn't follow advice. We stayed in The Services Club in Seymour Street which I mentioned in an earlier chapter. Smokers are consigned to their pleasures on a pokey first-floor outdoor platform. I think God had a message for me. That's where we met a Freemason, a Warlock, and a White Witch. I'd only met D-Day and Eighth Army Veterans on my previous visit. Our world is changing fast.

To round off our Ecumenical experience, a Jehovah's Witness approached us as we sat in Hyde Park on Friday morning watching a practice for the next day's Royal Gun Salute by the King's Troop Royal Horse Artillery. The whole troop had pulled up in front of us, complete with a horse ambulance. In the event, a different ambulance was required when one of the troopers fainted and fell from their horse. I would have liked to have engaged with our visitor, but Violet was doing all the talking. The inevitable happened. The Jehovah's Witness decided it wasn't worth the pain of listening to Violet any longer, so she stood up and left to protect her sanity. I was tempted to go with her. At Heathrow, Violet wouldn't join the queue for Security as that meant going without a cigarette until we landed in Belfast. When we finally passed through Security, she lost her Boarding Pass. That was the moment my remaining nerve snapped. TWANG!

In 2018, activity levels went up a notch. Walkway's equipment and resources had to be moved to Cross Section. McKelvey Construction Ltd had been awarded the contract to build the new centre and demolition of the old premises was to begin in October of that year. The Village Church and Bloomfield Presbyterian offered their halls so that as many groups could continue operating as normal. Then, just as the building work began, Covid struck. Everything ground to a practical standstill.

However, Rachael and her team didn't stand still. By coordinating efforts and resources with local churches and statutory bodies, she helped establish a COVID-19 Response Team for East Belfast. Volunteers helped bring food relief and collect prescriptions for vulnerable people in the neighbourhood. The Response Team was extolled as a great success and an example of volunteers working for the good of everyone in the community regardless of race or creed.

As the pandemic dragged on it caused a large increase in the cost of building materials. The new centre was meant to be clad in steel costing £29000. The cost rose to £139000; plans had to be redrawn with cheaper cladding and resubmitted to the City Council for approval. That was more delay. A container ship carrying building materials became wedged in the Suez Canal. More delay. It is fair to state, there could never have been a worse time to be involved in a building project. Credit to the builders who persevered through their difficulties, and everyone involved with Walkway who soldiered on and delivered programmes across all age groups as best they could.

Eventually, the building was completed and officially opened by Robin Newton MBE and Gareth Johnston from The Executive Office on 23rd March 2023. Has all the time and effort over the last 18 years been worth it? How do Christians measure worth in terms of their community work and witness? On my 71st birthday, I was awarded the East Belfast Volunteer of the Year Award at the Stormont Hotel in Belfast. Tara Mills must have been so pleased to meet me when she handed me the trophy. I regard it as an award for all those dedicated people in Walkway, filled with Common Grace, who made me look good. Sadly, very few of them share my faith in Christ.

One of my favourite Bible stories is in Luke 16 called, "The Rich Man and Lazarus." It tells the story of Lazarus, a poor man who dies and is taken to Heaven, the rich man dies and goes to Hell. The rich man isn't named because God didn't know him. He had never confessed his faith in his creator. That's why I haven't shared many names of the people I know and respect in Walkway, compared to those I named in my previous chapter on Bodrog. I did this to emphasise the difference in the spiritual conditions of the two communities. Where should the church send volunteers?

So, was it all worth it spiritually? Take this story into account before you read the final chapters.

In 2006 I had the idea to run an evangelistic event aimed at members of the Orange Order. Strangely, so many members of the order swear to defend the Protestant faith but never darken the door of a church. I asked the rector of St Christopher's Col in Mersey Street if I could attend the upcoming Reformation Day Parade on 28th October which would be attended by approximately 500 members of the Ballymacarret No.6 Loyal Orange Lodge. I asked his permission to hand out invitations to come along to Ballymacarret Orange Hall and listen to an explanation of the Christian faith which they espoused to defend. The Ballymacarret Orange leaders were delighted to host our event in their hall.

Our historian on the first night was Nelson McCausland, a well-known Belfast City Councillor. Alan Dickey, Trevor Lee, Drew Gibson and I supported Nelson with his presentation. Drew was about to take up his new post as Professor of Theology at Union College, Belfast. We all joked he could deal with the difficult questions. Around 50 men turned up on the first evening. Over subsequent evenings, the numbers dwindled until there was one man left. Kirk McDowell. He was awkward and persistent in his stubbornness to believe the Bible was the infallible word of God. Eventually, only Alan and I were left trying to convince Kirk to accept Christ as his Saviour. It proved too difficult and time-consuming. We gave up and walked away.

Marlene Dempster is a member of Walkway's Women's Group. Marlene is a Christian married to John Dempster, the Clerk of Session of Westbourne Community Church. Last year, Marlene and five other people were elected as Church Elders. Because of her relationship with Walkway, Marlene invited Rachael and I to her Service of Ordination in April 2024. The service was held in The Hub, the old primary school that had been renovated on Templemore Avenue, which has been home to Westbourne Community Church since it was closed for renovations five years ago. The main hall was packed to capacity. Rhonda came along with me, and we were both deeply moved by the worship and Ordination of the new Elders as they knelt, and everyone sang the Aaronic Blessing. The service was concluded by one of the new Elders, Michael Briggs on guitar and John Dempster on a Beatbox, singing "The Westbourne Hymn" composed by Eddie Spence. It was beautiful and everyone bopped along.

After the formalities were over, I gave a short message of support on behalf of Bloomfield Presbyterian Church, then headed off to have a cup of tea and a traybake. I bumped through the crowd and found a seat to enjoy my cup of tea and Fifteen. "Hello Stephen," I heard someone say and looked up to see who had spoken to me. It was one of the new Elders. "Do you not recognise me?" He asked. "No, sorry," I replied again. "I'm Kirk, Kirk McDowell, you're the reason I came to faith and was ordained here this evening." It was fortunate I was already sitting down. I would have dropped everything I was holding. Eighteen years later, our labour had borne fruit. A beautiful God moment when He gives you a glimpse of His work. Goosebumps and hair tingling all at once. Wow! When we step out in faith to do His work, we can trust that none of our efforts are wasted.

After I regained my composure, Kirk introduced me to his fiancée. I said, "Do you realise this guy is hard work?" She smiled; she already knew.

Way Out West

Muriel, Rhonda's Mum continued living in Ballyclare working for McNinch's Solicitors after Raymond, my father-in-law, died from Oesophageal Cancer in 1993. Rebekah began school at Bloomfield Preparatory in 1996 and Muriel retired to become Rebekah's full-time nanny. Muriel lived with us during the week in Irwin Drive and spent her weekends recovering at home in Ballyclare. These were formative years for Rebekah during which a deep bond formed between Rebekah and her Nanny Muriel.

In 1999, Muriel joined us on holiday to Glenbeigh in Co Kerry. We hired a cottage near the beach and set off from home on Saturday morning in our nine-year-old Citroen BX for an estimated six-hour drive. The little house proved snug and comfortable, and we settled in for our week-long holiday. The following Tuesday we were driving through Killorglin on our way to Dingle when Rebekah said, "Dad, I smell smoke." The smell grew stronger as we drove down the town's main street. I pulled to the side of the road outside the local Spar to investigate.

Before we left home, I had taken out extra car insurance to cover any breakdowns due to the vintage of our BX. It was called RAC World Cover. Eire wasn't included in UK car insurance policies 25 years ago. It cost me £60. It was the best £60 I ever spent. When I inspected the car, the rear near-side suspension had collapsed, and the wheel was rubbing against the wheel arch. The smell was burning rubber from the tyre.

There were no mobiles then. There were but they were too big to carry around. The shop assistant allowed me to use her telephone to call the RAC helpline. A breakdown truck appeared within an hour, and the mechanic loaded our BX onto the flatbed. "We need to get you another car," he said. Rhonda and I climbed into the cab beside him, and he drove us to Farranfore Airport, a half-hour drive away, where I collected a new Rover 25 from Hertz Car Hire. The mechanic gave us his address and, said he would arrange for our car to be returned to Belfast. Rhonda and I drove back to Killorglin to collect Muriel and Rebekah who we'd left outside the Spar.

It turned out, they were having a great old time. Muriel had rapped on the door of a house and asked if Rebekah could use the toilet. When the owner listened to Muriel explain their predicament, the lady invited them in and made tea and biscuits for the three of them. They had enjoyed chatting the time away until we returned in the hired car.

Halfway through our stay in Glenbeigh, Rebekah suggested we check if our car was still in Co Kerry. If it was, we could load it with all our unwanted baggage to leave room in the smaller car for shopping and gifts to take home. I rang our breakdown hero. "Yes, your car is still here." He gave me directions to his depot. We piled what we no longer needed into the Rover and set off. No Nat-Sav back then and an hour later we were completely lost in deepest Co. Kerry.

I pulled over when I spotted a gentleman standing at the door to his cottage. I said hello and asked him if he could give me directions to the address the mechanic had given me. "Oh dear, oh dear," he said. "If I wanted to go there, I wouldn't start here." I didn't know whether to laugh or cry. It could only happen in Ireland. We eventually found our destination and loaded the BX with our excess belongings. The next day we drove through the Connor Pass on the Dingle Peninsula. It was a relief to be in a car with good brakes.

When we arrived home our car was sitting outside. A £10 rubber bush fixed the suspension. I drove the hired Rover 25 to the Long Stay Car Park at George Best Airport and left the keys at the Hertz Desk as instructed. I received a call from Hertz six months later asking where I had left the car. They found it eventually.

In 2001, we returned to Co Kerry in our Citroen Xsara. We stayed in Sheen Falls Holiday Homes outside the town centre close to Kenmare Bay. One evening Rhonda and I walked to the adjacent Sheen Falls Lodge Hotel, to see how the other half lived. There was a helicopter parked on the front lawn. Inside the luxurious lounge bar, we met Bertie Ahern and his partner. We said hello. We weren't even frisked. Maybe Rhonda and I looked like another dodgy couple.

A bedraggled black and white collie met us each evening in the car park for the holiday homes. It would never come close enough to let us stroke him. We left out water and dinner leftovers which were always eaten by the next morning. One evening, we followed him back into the undergrowth and found his "home." A circle of flattened grass contained old food wrappers he had taken from the bins in the storage area. As the week progressed our friend became bolder and, allowed us to pat him on Thursday morning. There was a thunderstorm that evening, so we allowed him into the house and let him sleep in the hallway. On Friday, he came with us on a drive to Glengarriff. All was quiet until he saw a woman brushing her doorstep. Our canine friend went boogaloo. Of course, we all assumed he had been beaten by someone using a brush. On Saturday morning we were packing up to return home and Rebekah said, "Dad, what are we going to do?" I knew exactly what she meant. There was no objection from anyone. I suggested we contact the stables where Rebekah had gone riding during the week and ask them the name of the local vet to give "Beara" the once over before we brought him home.

Mr Dignam arrived an hour after I called. He met us in the car park. It was a scene straight out of All Creatures Great and Small. I hear the theme tune playing in my head as I write this. He was quite elderly and wore a cloth cap and brown dust coat. A small dog connected to a drip was in the front passenger seat of his Morris 1000 van. He had a soft, gentle manner and we trusted him immediately. We explained how we met Beara and hoped to take him home with us if he gave him a clean bill of health. He reached down, patted Beara on the head and said in his Irish brogue, "Sure now, aren't you one lucky dog." That was it. We were good to go. We panicked a little at the border because there was an outbreak of Foot and Mouth disease at the time. We imagined being stopped and told we couldn't bring Beara into Northern Ireland. There were no checks and Beara became a fully licensed "British dog."

Beara, from the Kingdom of Kerry, set up home with us in Irwin Drive for the next nine years until his death from old age. Two "volunteers" from our BB Company dug a grave in our back garden and we laid him to rest. He had been a great companion and popular with our neighbours. I spoke to our neighbour Brenda and told her Beara had died. Brenda was an ardent animal lover and burst out crying. I said, "Brenda, he's not far away, we buried him in the garden." "I've no room left in my garden," she replied. "I've buried two dogs and three cats." Then she added, "My brother is still in my wardrobe, he's been there for three years." I replied, "Well, that's a change from potpourri."

I never enjoyed driving our Xsara and changed to a brand-new Citroen C5 diesel in 2002. Wow! It was like driving in your sitting room minus the TV. On our next trip to County Kerry, we travelled to Kenmare again. This time, the house we rented was in the Caha mountains, a few miles from the town centre on the Beara Peninsula. We arrived, after an eight-hour drive through October Bank Holiday weekend traffic in the middle of a thunderstorm. It was a minor miracle we found the house and staggered in with our luggage as quickly as possible. Beara was so glad to be back in The Kingdom, he peed up the hallway wall. A quick scrub and no one was the wiser. When we woke the next morning, we were greeted with stunning views across Kenmare Bay to Carrauntoohil, seen through the floor-to-ceiling windows. The house had been built by a Dutch man named Harm who we met when the heating stopped working. Claire joined us for two days. She had travelled to visit her friend in Tralee, and we collected her from there.

When I returned to Campbell College, a pupil came to my office one afternoon to tell me I had a flat tyre. I thanked him and headed to the car park to change the tyre. However, I couldn't find the locking nuts. Hursts hadn't checked they were in the car when I collected it from their showroom. They sent a pick-up to load the car and take it to the Citroen Garage on Boucher Road. Why didn't they send a mechanic with the requisite nuts and tools?? Answers on a postcard, please. I still break into a cold sweat thinking about what might have happened if we had experienced a flat tyre in the Caha mountains, miles from anywhere, with no mobiles or locking nuts. We would have been the nuts.

Muriel came on our trip to Paris in 2003, the only time I used my N. Ireland O-Level in French. After we returned to our hotel one afternoon, I thought I would impress Rebekah and ask the receptionist for our room key in French. "Pourrais-je avoir la clé de notre chambre s'il vous plaît?" I said with my best French affect. The receptionist replied, "Monsieur McDonald, it would be better if you spoke English." We enjoyed sightseeing and dinner on the world-famous Avenue des Champs-Élysées. There is a photograph of the four of us sitting in the restaurant, somewhere in our house. Rebekah used the chocolate cream on her dessert to draw a moustache under her nose and uttered the famous French phrase, "Haw, he-haw, he-haw." The French gentleman at the next table found this amusing and welcomed us to Paris in impeccable English. The biggest disappointment of the trip was the Virtual Reality Theatre in the Cité des Sciences et de l'Industrie. It didn't hold a candle to Turbo Tours at the Dunluce Centre in Portrush.

A choir from Bodrog came to Bloomfield in 2010. I collected them in the church mini-bus and drove them to the Dunluce Centre on a wet Wednesday afternoon to experience the thrill of a virtual roller coaster ride. It was closed.

"Granny Mac" was on her own since Dad died in February 2006. She accepted our invitation to join us on our trip to Lahinch in County Clare during Rebekah's October half-term break. We laughed our way to Clare via every public convenience en route and back again. I remember that holiday best for a lady driver in Ennis who nearly drove over me twice. Traffic was queued in the main street. Every time I tried to cross behind her car it lurched backwards, and I had to step back. I walked around the car and said through the open driver's window, "Madam, I'll be safer walking in front of you."

Our mothers-in-laws were great company for one another and we had no reservations about bringing them with us again to Clifden in 2008. We stayed in a beautiful house in the heart of the town which was on the market for nearly €1 million. We enjoyed driving the Sky Road and visiting the site, just outside Clifden, where Alcock and Brown landed after the first transatlantic flight from Newfoundland in 1919. Clifden is where Marconi set up the world's first commercial transatlantic telegraphy service.

I found out who my friends were in 2010 when Rhonda and Rebekah travelled to India to stay with Alan Dickey and his family at Hebron School, 7,000 feet up in the Nilgiri Hills. I confess I was afraid to go. I'm not a great traveller and worried the altitude would affect my COPD. I didn't want to end up as a burden to anyone. How Rhonda and Rebekah were able to make the journey to India was a work of deliverance.

Rhonda and Rebekah had applied for Indian visas and posted their British Passports to the Indian consulate in London. However, when they returned, only Rhonda's passport carried an Indian Visa. Rebekah had declared on her application she also held an Irish passport. Her British passport returned with instructions that any Indian Visa should be added to her Irish passport. This was 29th December 2009 and both were due to depart from Belfast International Airport on 11th January. "Sick with worry" hardly describes how we felt. I was due to go to a men's dinner at Wolfes in

Dundonald with a group of friends from church on Wednesday evening but I was in no form to socialise. However, Tony Davison, Rachael's husband depended on me for transport and, I felt obliged to go after all. In the restaurant, Malcolm McClure asked me why I wasn't in great form and I explained the situation regarding Rebekah's visa and the plan I had to drive us to the Indian Consulate in Dublin the following morning. Without anyone knowing, Malcolm went home to collect a portable TomTom Satnav. He programmed the Consulate's address in Lower Leeson Street, into the device, handed it to me and said, "I think you'll need this." Truer words were never spoken.

Rebekah and I set off for Dublin at 6.00 am the next morning. It was a bitterly cold and bleak start to the day. To add to our misery the demister wasn't working in the car and I placed a hot water bottle on the dash to thaw and demist the windscreen. We arrived in Dublin around 8.00 am and had breakfast while waiting for the General Post Office in O'Connell Street to open at 9.00 am. I collected the €120 cash required for the visa and returned to the car. We followed the TomTom directions and arrived at the Indian Consulate where we queued, and Rebekah handed over her visa application to a rather dour counter assistant. One of the "don't think for one moment I'm here to help you" brigade. Sure enough, she abruptly informed Rebekah she had applied for the wrong type of visa if she was planning to work as a volunteer at Hebron School. Furthermore, the fee for the correct visa was €180. "Goodbye."

We sat in the car and Rebekah cried her eyes out. She was inconsolable. Then we had to call Rhonda and tell her the bad news. Something stirred me to start the car and drive back to the GPO. When I turned the corner into O'Connell Street, a car pulled out of a disabled bay, allowing me to park right outside the Post Office. We queued again and I collected another €60 before returning to the car. This time the TomTom kept "recalculating route" so we drove off hoping the Sat Nav would rectify itself. It did eventually and we found the Consulate. I couldn't find a parking space, so I told Rebekah to run in and fill out a new application form as quickly as possible while I found somewhere to park.

When I ran into the Consulate Rebekah was still filling out her application and Miss "Dour" was announcing, "Visa applications close in five minutes." "Hurry, Rebekah," I implored. Rebekah signed the application form with a flourish, lifted it and handed her Irish passport with the form and fee to the cashier, just as she reached up and closed the blind on her position. Phew! We needed strong coffee. It was a relief to call Rhonda from the nearby café and tell her we thought everything might be OK. We would know at 4.00 pm when we returned to collect Rebekah's Irish passport. At 4 pm no one could find Rebekah's passport. We were both despairing about what to do when someone appeared behind the counter with a "misplaced box of passports." There was Rebekah's passport and when we opened it, there was her Indian visa. Hallelujah.

That day's excitement wasn't over. It was dark and raining when we began our journey home. We didn't bother with the TomTom. I was glad to be leaving Dublin and drove north out of the city. At one point, our road crossed over the DART railway line. I turned left and noticed two headlights coming towards us. "Dad, that's a train," shouted Rebekah. I steered right onto the proper road again. "Do you want me to drive?" Asked Rebekah. "Yes." I was tired mentally and physically. When we approached Newry, we drove into a snow blizzard. "Do you want me to drive?" I asked Rebekah. "Yes, please."

Due to a miracle of provision, Rhonda and Rebekah set off on their Indian adventure as planned on 11th January 2010. During their first week away, Muriel was ill, and I travelled to and from the Ulster Hospital to check on her progress. I kept what little I knew from Rhonda and Rebekah as I didn't want to worry them so far from home. This was the beginning of Muriel's decline in health. On top of this, I was under pressure at work training recruits; I was glad to accept the hospitality of friends and family. Eventually, in 2014 due to her ill health, we found a place for Muriel in Corkey House, a care home run by the Presbyterian Church in Ireland where Muriel fell asleep and collected her crown on 21st October 2014.

Rhonda and Rebekah teamed up with a bottle of Yellow Tail Merlot and convinced me to travel to America in May 2015. We all enjoyed it immensely. New York was friendly and vibrant. Our hotel was off Times Square and a short distance from Broadway where we saw Les Misérables and Rebekah announced, "I get it!" when the police captured Valjean with the stolen silverware and took him back to the Bishop's house. Bishop Myriel pretends that he had given the silverware to Valjean and presses him to take two silver candlesticks as well, as if he had forgotten to take them. It is a beautiful description of Grace in action. I felt distinctly uneasy when we visited Ground Zero. This Hallowed Ground is a major tourist attraction. We only went so far inside before I had to leave. Like Auschwitz, some places deserve our greatest solemn respect. Not idiots and hen parties posing for selfies.

Attending Rolling Thunder in Washington DC restored my faith in human dignity when an estimated 850,000 riders and spectators attended the 28th Ride To The Wall. The event was originally organised to draw attention to the issue of prisoners of war and those missing in action from the Vietnam War but has since grown to honour all veterans and raise awareness of their sacrifices. Washington DC is a fascinating city deserving of a chapter on its own. Maybe, I'll do that another time.

In November 2015 we took Granny Mac to "Bernie's," a beautiful bungalow outside Clifden with access to a private beach. It was great to let Marley off the lead and let him run about to his heart's content. Marley just stole balls I threw and dropped them wherever he pleased. He never learned to bring them back. On this visit to Clifden, my dear Mum bought me yet another brown coat.

In Easter 2016, we enjoyed a holiday in Amsterdam and discovered why many Dutch people speak with American accents. They learn English by watching American TV programmes. A photo of me in a coffee shop shows me morphing into my father. We were shocked when Rhonda received news that her routine Mammogram result was positive later that year. There followed a series of 20 radiotherapy treatments between August and October at the Cancer Centre in Belfast City Hospital. To help Rhonda recuperate from the effects of her treatment, the three of us returned to "Bernie's" again in November 2016 for a week's rest and recovery. The €1 million house where we had holidayed in Clifden in 2008 was now on the market for €350,000. The Celtic Tiger had died and been made into a hearth rug.

The "Glory Boys" came to decorate our living room in January 2018. We took the opportunity to vacate the house and take our last trip with Granny Mac to Clifden in County Galway. It is a bleak but stunningly beautiful part of Ireland. The house was comfortable with all the amenities and a great base for touring the Wild Atlantic Way. Gary rang me one evening to tell me I hadn't supplied enough wallpaper. One wall was blank. Our living room is bigger than I thought. Ah well! A part of our adventure was to help Rebekah collect photos along the Wild Atlantic Way. There are numerous Discovery Points, marked by signs with the WAW logo. Her enthusiasm led us to some of the remotest parts of Co Galway, including Patrick Pearse's Cottage and Visitor Centre at Ros Muc in the heart of the Connemara Gaeltacht.

On a cold January morning, I was the only visitor and received the personal attention of one of the guides who invited me to join him on the walk from the centre up to Pearse's cottage. On the walk, we introduced ourselves and I explained my background, my faith, my love of Ireland, its culture, language, and music. I took the opportunity to ask my guide, "When did Ireland become a sovereign nation?" He replied, "In 1949." I asked, "When did Ireland cease to be a sovereign nation." My guide stopped, pointed to the badge on his uniform and stated, "While I'm wearing this Government uniform, I am not allowed to express any political viewpoints." I pointed out, we were the only people present and no one else was within earshot. He told me Ireland ceased being a sovereign nation in 1973 when it joined the EU.

The Shinners repeat the lie that Ireland is a Sovereign nation. How can Ireland be known as a Sovereign Nation when it can't make its own laws; it can't set its own budget; it can't print its own money or secure its own borders? After the sacrifices of Pearse, Connelly, Plunkett and their comrades in arms, the Irish Free State became a Republic and sovereign nation in 1949. Ireland held the keys and deeds to its own house. Then, by permission of the citizens of Ireland, the deeds and keys were handed to Brussels in 1973 on the promise of €1.5 billion per year ever after. I wonder what the Founding Fathers of the Irish nation would have made of their Irish descendants maintaining their hard-won sovereignty for only 24 years.

Here's a scenario I play in my head sometimes. I invite Mary Lou McDonald and Michelle O'Neil to the Nomadic in the Titanic Quarter for breakfast one morning. When they ask me the purpose of the meeting, I tell them, after breakfast, we're sailing out into the mid-Atlantic to reunite the Nomadic with its mother ship the Titanic. When they say that's impossible, I explain that's what they have been trying to do for years, reunite Northern Ireland to a mother country that doesn't exist anymore. Ireland is the name of a province of Europe where some people speak Gaelic.

The old wreck of Ireland floated to the service in 2008 and the Irish had a chance to salvage it. Instead, it was torpedoed by the First Referendum on the Treaty of Lisbon held on 12th June 2008 which was rejected by the Irish electorate by a margin of 53.4% to 46.6%. Oops! That was a dud. Quick! Reload. The wording was tweaked and the Second Referendum on the Treaty of Lisbon was held on 2nd October 2009. This scored a direct hit and sank the wreck when it was approved by 67.1% to 32.9% of the electorate. So, who sold Ireland down the river? It wasn't the Brits, it wasn't the Hun, and it wasn't the Prods. At least Bertie Ahern joined the rest of the plenipotentiaries for the signing ceremony in Lisbon. Gordon Brown turned up late at the Jerónimos Monastery and entered by the back door to avoid publicity. He didn't want the "little people" to know he was signing away more of their British sovereignty.

How come there are still people prepared to maim and kill to try and achieve an impossible goal?

Imagine if the Shinners told the truth that Ireland was betrayed by the Irish themselves. By their parents and grandparents for billions of pieces of silver. If Pearse was alive today, who would he shake hands with, Mary Lou McDonald or Stephen McDonald? The former is afraid to admit that Ireland was betrayed by the very people her party represents. The latter is a citizen of a country that re-established itself as a sovereign nation. A Labour Government is about to betray that to the EU.

I live in the only ward in Belfast that voted for Brexit. Most people in Northern Ireland, Protestants and Catholics, voted to remain in the EU. If Sinn Fein admitted a United Ireland was impossible but the North and South of Ireland could be a joint province in Europe, the Prods would have nothing to fear and all the Remainers might vote for them.

Stocktaking

On our holiday to Clifden in January 2018, I felt exhausted after our day trips and didn't have a great appetite. I went to bed early some evenings and used the time to consider whether I wanted to continue working after I reached 65 later that month. I had a good supervisor in the Passport Office, and quite enjoyed my work, so I asked permission to work on after 26th January. My timekeeping, absence records and appraisals, were instrumental in the management's decision to allow me to work past my due-retirement date.

Over the following weeks, I continued to feel tired and lethargic with no great appetite at times. Eventually, I gave in to Rhonda's demands to visit the doctor. Three days later, I was enjoying coffee with my friend and fellow Elder, Geoff Gordon, in The Lamppost Café on Newtownards Road, when I received a call from my doctor asking me to come immediately to the surgery. My doctor said one of my blood readings was, "Off the scale." What should have read around 20 was reading over 1,000 and she was referring me for a liver biopsy.

I continued working the next month until the day of the appointment for my biopsy at the RVH. After a local anaesthetic, a specialist stabbed me in the side with a special instrument to take a sample of my liver for analysis. Afterwards, I went back to work feeling none the worse. Around noon, Emma, my supervisor said, "Stephen, you need to go home." "Why?" I asked. "You look very unwell," she replied. I didn't realise I had turned a strange yellow colour. I drove to the surgery where the doctor was shocked by my appearance and advised me to go home and pack a bag. She would call the hospital and arrange an emergency admission. I went home and packed a bag but there was no phone call from the hospital.

Rhonda insisted we didn't wait any longer and we went to the E & D at the RVH. I didn't make it home that evening. I became a guest in Ward 6A of the Acute Medical Wing, I even had a private room. Over the next few days, I was diagnosed with Auto Immune Hepatitis. This meant my immune system was attacking my liver. There are three consultants I owe my life to. Neil McDougall, Roger McCrorry, and Ian Cadden. Ironically, I had been in a private healthcare scheme for over 30 years until an atheist challenged my beliefs by asking, "Do you believe God plus Benetton Health will provide all your needs?" In response to that challenge, I had resigned from Benetton ten years previously and now I found myself in the best liver unit in Britain under the care of one of the best liver specialists in Britain and his Team. Philippians 4:19 took on a special significance for me.

"And my God will meet all your needs according to his glorious riches in Christ Jesus."

The worst part of my treatment was huge doses of steroids that were part of my daily drug regime. 50mg of Prednisolone each day fried my brain. I couldn't sleep even though my eyes were burning out of my head. Day turned to night and night back to day without any breaks. It was mind-altering and debilitating. I was down to my last nerve when I agreed to move into the general liver ward to allow a female patient to have my room. I'm not proud my last nerve snapped when the patient opposite was the type who must speak loudly on their phone so everyone within the room is privy to their conversation.

On and on he went endlessly. I snapped and shouted, "What type of phone is that?" "A Nokia," he replied. I shouted again and drew the attention of other patients in the ward, "I don't mean the make, I mean has it got square or round edges?" He sounded confused and asked why I wanted to know. I shouted, "I'm very ill and haven't slept for five days. Your phone better have round edges because if you don't quieten down, I'm going over there and I'll jam it up your jacksie." To everyone's relief, my threat appeared to work. I found out from other patients during my follow-up treatment, our young tormentor had died. I regret being rude to him.

Everything happens for a reason. The patient in the next bed told me he'd never drank alcohol all his life and yet he needed a liver transplant to survive. Before he could have the operation, he needed to lose three stones in weight in addition to the drug treatment he was on. His phone rang and I couldn't help hearing him mention Rodney McCurley during his conversation. Later, I excused myself and asked him if the Rodney McCurley he mentioned was the Rodney McCurley I knew from BT. Indeed, he was. Rodney was also my friend's Masonic Lodge Master. I tried to witness to my neighbour in the ward. He told me he had no soul. I asked him why he thought that. I explained to him, "The god of this age has blinded the minds of unbelievers so that they cannot see the light of the gospel of the glory of Christ." 2nd Corinthians 4. When he was discharged, I asked him to give Rodney a note with my telephone number asking him to call me sometime.

Early one evening, the general ward was buzzing with activity. I couldn't concentrate on reading anything; I looked forward to Rhonda's visit later. My mobile rang and I answered. "Hello Stephen, how are you?" It was Rachael calling me. "I wanted you to be the first to know I gave my life to Jesus today." My eyes welled up with tears and I couldn't speak with the lump in my throat. Rachael continued, "Other churches came and went but you and Bloomfield came and stayed. I saw Christ at work through your work and witness." Rachael had just confirmed the power of Paul's words in 1st Corinthians Chapter 2. We don't have to preach God's word to demonstrate His love to people.

"And so it was with me, brothers and sisters. When I came to you, I did not come with eloquence or human wisdom as I proclaimed to you the testimony about God. For I resolved to know nothing while I was with you except Jesus Christ and him crucified. I came to you in weakness with great fear and trembling. My message and my preaching were not with wise and persuasive words, but with a demonstration of the Spirit's power, so that your faith might not rest on human wisdom, but on God's power."

One soul saved to show for 12 years of labour. Was it worth all the effort? If you're a Christian ask Rachael when you meet her in Heaven.

One morning I was sent for an MRI scan. I confess I felt nervous, not about the scanner but about what they might find. My liver wasn't responding to the treatment as well as expected and I suspected the medical team was checking for other issues that were hampering my progress. The porter delivered me in a wheelchair to the waiting room outside the MRI room and left me alone. In that moment, I prayed that no matter what the scan revealed I would rely completely on God. My life was in His hands. Like my father, I had no fear of death.

I was wheeled in, helped onto the MRI table, a thick protection vest was placed over my chest, I was handed a panic button, and the nurse asked me what type of music I preferred. I chose Classical and she put a pair of headphones on my head. OK, good to go. Click. Whirr! I slide automatically into the centre of the scanner. I felt claustrophobic and then, Click! "Are you OK? Relax." The technician said through my headphones. Click! "Just follow my instructions when I ask you to breathe in and hold your breath." Click! "OK, you're doing well, I'm going to play you some music." Click! My headphones were flooded with the strains of Liebesträume by Franz Liszt. This is one of my favourite piano pieces I spent months learning to play very badly years ago. The title is German for Dreams of Love. I felt God's hand touch me in the middle of that huge magnet and heard Him say, "I love you Stephen, my son." I cried. The next 20 minutes in the scanner were the most relaxing I enjoyed during my four weeks in hospital. When I exited the machine, I had tears on my checks because I couldn't wipe them off. The technician asked me if I was OK. I told her what had happened. She smiled and said, "That's simply beautiful." Yes, it was.

After the scan, I was moved into a private room again. It was a great relief to be away from the hustle and bustle of the main ward. Outside of the hospital, I know the chief consultant, Neil MacDougall, as a friend and fellow Elder in Bloomfield. He told me that Auto Immune Hepatitis is extremely rare in men and asked my permission to allow student doctors to examine me for training purposes. I was happy to oblige.

Sometimes, twice a day a group of trainees would turn up under the supervision of Neil or his colleague Ian Cadden to carry out examinations on me to determine if they could diagnose my condition. Neil warned me they would ask me difficult questions. Sure enough, I was asked by a young student if I had had unprotected sex. I pretended to think and replied, "Not since they built the new bus shelters."

The first time Ian Cadden introduced himself to me he asked me where he knew me from. After whittling down our possibilities, we found he knew me from Bloomfield Church. I told Ian I had been a member of BPC for over 20 years and couldn't say I recognised him. He explained, "Stephen, I sit upstairs and you never look up!"

The wide degrees of illness were evident throughout Ward 6. There were screams from patients who were hallucinating due to high toxin levels in their brains and two patients "escaped" during my stay. One I know couldn't cope with nicotine withdrawal. The medical and ancillary staff coped heroically. They displayed great professionalism, aided and abetted by a wry sense of humour. Neil knew I had been asking if I was going home anytime soon. He called in on a Friday morning to tell me he was going to Spain for a week to visit his daughter Suzi. He looked at the book on my bedside table and said, "You should have brought a thicker book, you'll be here when I get back."

Neil and Ian deferred my actual treatment to Roger McCrorry. Another East Belfast man and member of Kirkpatrick Presbyterian Church. Thanks to his God-given skills I'm writing this paragraph to commend him for saving my life. I didn't realise how serious my illness was until a year later when Roger informed me that he feared my treatment wasn't working and my only option would have been a liver transplant. As it happened, my blood statistics began to improve after four weeks, and I was discharged on a Tuesday morning to continue my drug regime at home.

Rhonda was still working and I sat in our half-decorated living room wrapped in two blankets to keep warm. Until then, I had never worried or feared the worst. That changed on Thursday morning when I realised, I wasn't out of the woods. I had a sense of foreboding and the need to put my affairs in order. All this was swirling around in my mind when I noticed a woman walking through our gate and up to the front door. I unwrapped my blankets and opened the door to speak to her. "Hello Stephen, do you not recognise me?" I hadn't any idea who she was. "I'm Lorna, Lorna Boyd and I have something for you." I was dumbfounded. Lorna was the first girl I ever dated as a teenager. Her parents, Martha and Hugh, were lifelong friends of my parents and Uncle Stevie.

Lorna handed me a plastic bag and said, "I was clearing my parents' house when I found your Uncle Stevie's Bible and thought you might like to have it." Lorna could see the expression on my face with tears in my eyes and asked me what was wrong. I said, "Lorna, today of all days, you brought me my Uncle Stevie's Bible." I went on to explain why I was so emotional. "Isn't God good," I said. Lorna began to cry too when she realised how God had used her that day.

When Lorna said goodbye, I closed the door and climbed the stairs. I sat on our bed and opened Stevie's Bible. I couldn't remember the last time I cried. Maybe, 25 years ago, but I let go that day. It was a catharsis of all the pent-up strain and emotion of the previous month. God had wrapped His arms around me and held me to Him. Through my tears, I read where Stevie had written his name and address on the inside cover of his Bible. When

I closed the cover, it read, "Property of Townsend Street Presbyterian Church." True to form, my wonderful "tight" uncle had procured a church Bible and labelled it his own. I was crying one minute and in hysterical laughter the next. That's how close God is in our trials.

In April of that year, Rodney McCurley rang me to tell me he received my message from Ray, my fellow patient in the RVH. We arranged to meet for a coffee and catch up with one another. After an 18-year separation, there was much to talk about when we finally met. Well, Rodney had a lot of talking to do. He told me Ray had died before he could have his liver transplant. Then, I had to listen to how well Rodney and his family were doing. Not once did he ask me anything about my family. He then mentioned his involvement with the Masonic Order and how much money he had helped raise for the new Children's Hospice in Newtownabbey. He wasn't impressed when I explained my deep reservations about the order and that no Christian should be a member. "No one can serve two masters." The only way to argue with a Mason is to state facts. There is their viewpoint. There is your viewpoint. Then there is God's viewpoint. I advised Rodney to read Ezekiel Chapter 8. If he believed his

Masonic vows didn't contradict his Christian faith, that's another example of "The god of this age has blinded the minds of unbelievers." He is now the Masonic Grand Master of Ireland. I have "friends" in very low places, who are lost for eternity.

By October 2018, I was in remission and only returned to work to resign and complete all the necessary paperwork. It felt strange not joining the daily trudge to the office, after 49 years of full-time work. Initially, I missed work, but I soon adjusted to my new way of life. God and people made sure of that.

Rebekah married Tim Barr on 27th June 2019. We had asked Esther Drennan, one of Bloomfield's Prayer Warriors to pray for good weather. There wasn't a cloud in the sky on that perfect day. Micah James Timothy Barr arrived in our world on 9th December 2021, and we have been best friends ever since. He's teaching me how to be cute and I'm teaching him the joys of chocolate and pizza.

On 24th February 2022, Russia invaded Ukraine and the war dominated our news media for weeks. The scenes of destruction and suffering were horrific, and the UK Government launched a scheme to allow UK residents to offer accommodation to Ukrainians fleeing the war.

Rhonda suggested we join and signed us onto the Home Office Homes for Ukraine website. The Home Office never made contact. Instead, Starfish, a Christian organisation telephoned us about a young Ukrainian mother and her son from Kharkiv. They were living in a refugee camp in Romania. After a great deal of emailing, form-filling and Google Translating, Aliona Fedorenko and her son Gleb joined our family on 19th May 2022. We have just celebrated the second anniversary of their arrival with pizza and cake. It is testing sometimes for everyone as we don't live in a mansion and space is at a premium.

We have received more than we have ever given by sharing our faith and home with those Christ brought across our path. God continues to surprise and bless with moments that affirm His love.

I mentioned telling Norman McNeilly I was never at a football match. I went to Solitude in 1987 to watch Cliftonville play Glentoran. However, I don't count this as I missed all three goals because I was in the members' bar. The only football match I have watched in person is Ukraine vs Norway in the Under 19 UEFA Cup at Seaview along with Aliona and Gleb. Alex, her Ukrainian work colleague, bought four tickets and asked me to join them.

Andriy Shevchenko, famous for scoring Ukraine's two winning goals against Sweden in the 2012 Euros, was there to watch his 17-year-old son Kristian. It ended in a scoreless draw. Shevchenko is now Vice-President of the National Olympic Committee of Ukraine and Aliona was delighted when he signed her Ukrainian flag. Andriy and Aliona live in Kharkiv and never met until they came to Belfast. Their enthusiasm and patriotism was contagious. I couldn't understand the loud chants and Aliona wouldn't translate what the Ukrainian supporters were calling Putin.

Through Starfish and Aliona we have met many Ukrainians living in Northern Ireland struggling with everyday life after fleeing the war with Russia. They are a constant reminder never to take our freedoms for granted. We came to know Liubov Kulakevych who worked with Aliona in Beaufort Interiors. Liubov has a sister and four brothers. One brother is a Pastor in Kyiv and another a missionary in Nebro. Liubov had to return to Ukraine for medical reasons; she occasionally returns to visit friends and her UK Sponsors who live in Lisburn. We are always pleased to see her and pray for peace between Russia and Ukraine. Aliona and Gleb are homesick and pray they will be reunited with their family soon. Everything is in God's hands.

I pray we continue to honour God's call in Romans 12:9-13: "Don't just pretend to love others. Really love them. ... When God's people are in need, be ready to help them. Always be eager to practice hospitality."

The Why

I quoted Mark Twain at the beginning of this memoir, "The two most important days of your life are: The day you were born and the day you find out why." I pray you recognised God at work throughout these chapters of my life. A God who loved me so much He let me go my own way; a God so full of grace and mercy that he will welcome me home again when I draw my last breath. A generous Father whose infinite patience allowed me time to find the answer to why I was born.

It took me 43 years, much of it in a "foreign land," to discover why I was born. I was born so that I may glorify God and know Him forever. I trust this testimony of His goodness and providence glorifies His name.

Remember, we are all Prodigals. We either walk away from God in life or accept Christ as our Saviour and journey back to our Heavenly Father for the remainder of our lives.

My memoir's title is based on Henri Nouwen's wonderful book The Return of The Prodigal Son, A Story of Homecoming. I couldn't think of a more appropriate title than, "Another Prodigal, *another homecoming.*" That is how I see myself and why I love Jesus's Parable of The Lost Son in Luke Chapter 15.

Jesus continued: "There was a man who had two sons. The younger one said to his father, 'Father, give me my share of the estate.' So, he divided his property between them.

"Not long after that, the younger son got together all he had, set off for a distant country and there squandered his wealth in wild living. After he had spent everything, there was a severe famine in that whole country, and he began to be in need. So, he went and hired himself out to a citizen of that country, who sent him to his fields to feed pigs. He longed to fill his stomach with the pods that the pigs were eating, but no one gave him anything.

"When he came to his senses, he said, 'How many of my father's hired servants have food to spare, and here I am starving to death! I will set out and go back to my father and say to him: Father, I have sinned against heaven and against you. I am no longer worthy to be called your son; make me like one of your hired servants.' So, he got up and went to his father. But while he was still a long way off, his father saw him and was filled with compassion for him; he ran to his son, threw his arms around him and kissed him."

I wanted to feel God's arms around me, just like the young man in the parable. However, I didn't know how to bring myself closer to Him. I didn't know what God had planned for me but I am grateful for the place He has led me to by revealing Himself throughout life's journey. Now, my purpose is to share His story of love and forgiveness as we all face the realities of our short existence in this world.

Henri Nouwen puts it beautifully, through faith and prayer, "I can kneel before my Heavenly Father, put my ear against his chest and listen, without interruption, to the heartbeat of God."

God is sowing together your life. I pray this book will encourage you to read the Bible, step into faith, give your life to Christ and see your tapestry revealed in all its vibrant detail and colours. Let Jesus take your wheel and steer you through life.

Amen

To Christ be all the glory.

Stephen McDonald

21st July 2024

Printed by Amazon Italia Logistica S.r.l.
Torrazza Piemonte (TO), Italy